BERENGARIA OF NAVARRE

C000182695

Berengaria of Navarre was queen of England (1191–99) and lord of Le Mans (1204–30), but has received little attention in terms of a fully encompassing biography from Navarrese, Anglophone, and French perspectives. This book explores her political career whilst utilising the surviving documentation to demonstrate her personal and familial partnerships and life as a dowager queen.

This biography follows Berengaria's journey from a Navarrese infanta, raised in the northern Iberian kingdom, to her travels across Europe to marriage and the Third Crusade, venturing through Sicily, Cyprus, and on to the Holy Land in 1191. Berengaria's reign and early years as dowager queen are examined in the context of the Anglo-French conflict and domestic disputes, before her decision to negotiate with the king of France, Philip Augustus, and become lord of Le Mans, for which she is far better known in local memory.

The volume flows chronologically discussing her roles as infanta, queen, dowager, and lord, and is an ideal resource for scholars and those interested in the history of gender, queenship, lordship, and Western Europe in the twelfth and thirteenth centuries.

Gabrielle Storey is a historian of medieval queenship, gender, and sexuality, specialising in co-rulership and Western Europe in the twelfth and thirteenth centuries. She has published on the memory and representations of monarchy, and royal sexualities in journals and edited collections, and has co-edited two volumes on monarchy, memory, and sexualities.

Lives of Royal Women

Series Editors:
Elena Woodacre, Ellie.Woodacre@winchester.ac.uk
Louise Wilkinson, LWilkinson@lincoln.ac.uk

This series features academic, yet accessible biographies of royal women - consorts, dowagers, royal mothers and female sovereigns - inclusive of all periods, cultures and geographic regions. These biographies include a deep engagement with the premise of queenship studies and the exercise of the queen's office (or equivalent), in addition to covering the lives of particular women. The series is divided into three sub-strands: Queens of England (blue), Queens and Empresses of Europe (purple), and Royal Women of the World (red).

Joan of Navarre
Infanta, Duchess, Queen, Witch?
Elena Woodacre

Early English Queens 850–1000
Potestas Reginae
Matthew Firth

Berengaria of Navarre
Queen of England, Lord of Le Mans
Gabrielle Storey

BERENGARIA OF NAVARRE

Queen of England, Lord of Le Mans

Gabrielle Storey

Routledge
Taylor & Francis Group

LONDON AND NEW YORK

Designed cover image: Photograph of Berengaria's effigy at
L'Abbaye de L'Épau, Le Mans. Photographs provided by
Caroline Menryol on behalf of © Sarthe Culture.

First published 2024
by Routledge
4 Park Square, Milton Park, Abingdon, Oxon OX14 4RN

and by Routledge
605 Third Avenue, New York, NY 10158

Routledge is an imprint of the Taylor & Francis Group, an informa business

British Library Cataloguing-in-Publication Data
A catalogue record for this book is available from the British Library

ISBN: 978-1-032-12148-2 (hbk)
ISBN: 978-1-032-12147-5 (pbk)
ISBN: 978-1-003-22330-6 (ebk)

DOI: 10.4324/9781003223306

Typeset in Sabon
by codeMantra

Dedicated with love to Da and
Grumps – Michael Parker and
Michael Storey.

Written to, and for, all the women
who have been forgotten, erased,
and misremembered in the history
books – your stories will continue
to be told.

CONTENTS

ILLUSTRATIONS

TABLES

ABBREVIATIONS

AD   Archives Départementales
AGN Archivo General de Navarra, Spain
AN   Archives Nationales, France
BL   British Library, UK
BNF Bibliothèque Nationale de France
TNA The National Archives, UK

ACKNOWLEDGEMENTS

When I started my PhD in 2016, I had no idea at the time how much I would be captivated by a queen, largely forgotten by history in the shadows of her crusading husband and legendary mother-in-law. Though my thesis was a comparative history of four Angevin women, early on I was determined to write a biography of Berengaria to bring together new perspectives and further documentation which had been overlooked or not fully explored in the earlier English and French biographies of Berengaria – a venture well worth its undertaking.

My deepest thanks go first and foremost to Professor Nicholas Vincent for his generosity in sharing his Berengaria file with me from the *Angevin Acta* project, and pointing me towards documentation, including the Templars charters, discussed in chapter five. My deepest gratitude must also go to Professors Ghislain Baury and Vincent Corriol for their support, encouragement, and sharing their own research on Berengaria in advance of their publication of their biography of Berengaria in French, and for their fruitful discussions of her life in Le Mans. Thanks are also owed to Professor Eloísa Ramírez Vaquero who provided with me her early research on royal women and their familial possessions in Navarre, and for her guidance on Berengaria's relationship with Monreal. Professors Martin Aurell and Stephen D. Church have been particularly generous in their granting of material and encouragement for the biography and beyond and they have my enduring gratitude. Ana Maria Seabra de Almeida Rodrigues, Miriam Shadis, Erika Graham-Goering, Cathleen Sarti, Dean

Irwin, Peter Edbury, René Despert, Bénédicte Fillion-Brauget, Kathleen Nolan, Daniel Power, Richard Cassidy, and Herwig Weigl all shared publications that I was otherwise unable to access.

I have received generous support from the *Lives of Royal Women* series editors, Dr Elena Woodacre and Professor Louise J. Wilkinson, for the initial proposal and their shepherding through of the final work, as well as from the editorial and production staff at Routledge, Laura Pilsworth, Georgia Lloyd, and Isabel Voice. Without them this book would not have seen the light of day, and they have my unwavering thanks for their guidance and feedback. I am also grateful to the four anonymous reviewers who examined the original proposal and offered their initial thoughts and suggestions.

This book has undergone several revisions during its conception, and I must also thank several colleagues for their feedback on the earlier drafts: Professor Stephen D. Church, Professor Natasha Hodgson, Dr Richard E. Barton, Dr James Ross, and Dr Elena Woodacre. Particular gratitude also goes to Dr Katy Mortimer and Dr Emily Ward who read through the entire manuscript in its final stage. Any errors that remain are of course my own.

During the course of this project, I've had the privilege to visit several archives and libraries to piece together Berengaria's life, which proved to be no simple feat at times. Therefore, the archivists of the Archives Départementales de la Sarthe, Archives Départementales de la Seine-Maritime, the Archives Nationales, Bibliothèque Sainte-Geneviève, and Bibliothèque Nationale de France, Paris, the Archivo General de Navarra, and Archivo Eclesiásticos de Tudela, Spain, and the National Archives and the British Library, UK are all owed thanks for their assistance in this project, not least for their willingness to digitise manuscripts during the initial COVID-19 lockdowns as I was completing my thesis and beginning this biography in earnest.

Berengaria has been the topic of many conference papers and public talks over the last seven years, and I am grateful for the feedback and congeniality of my colleagues and the public who have offered insights and feedback, as well as to the organisers of such events, particularly Kings and Queens, and the various sessions at International Medieval Congress, Leeds. I would also like to thank the Society for French History, whose initial grant during my PhD allowed me to visit French archives, and the Royal Historical Society and Institute of Historical Research whose grants enabled further visits to Navarre, Paris, and Le Mans during this project. My thanks go to the Conseil Départemental de la Sarthe, particularly Caroline Meneyrol and Aitor Calleja for their permission to reproduce the photographs of Berengaria's tomb, L'Abbaye de L'Épau, and Berengaria's statue in the book.

As most writers and historians will know, writing a book – particularly your first – can be quite the rollercoaster and journey. No book can be completed without the support of good friends who provide encouragement, emotional support, and supplies when required. Estelle Paranque, Nicola Tallis, Emily J. Ward, Emily Stanborough, Katy Mortimer, Katia Wright, Paula del Val Vales, Paul Webster, Anaïs Waag, Louise Gay, Sally Spong, Faye Coleman, Debi Carter, and Kim McCann have all delivered pep talks, good humour, cake, and much needed motivation when writing this biography. Louise has my eternal gratitude for being my Paris companion and relentless corrector of French when needed.

Lastly, my thanks need to go to my loved ones – to my parents, Vanessa and Stephen, who have encouraged me in my love of history from day one and only occasionally complained about the sheer number of books that were scattered around the house. For my brother, Doms, who has proven a welcome distraction from all things history when needed. I also need to share my deepest gratitude to my grandparents, Barbara and Michael Storey, whose love and pride has been there every step of the way. Last, but definitely not least, my partner Tony has offered love, support, humour, and patience in all its forms whilst I have completed this biography: thanks are not enough.

It is to my grandfathers, Michael – fondly known as Da – and Michael, my Grumps, who this book is dedicated to.

NOTE ON NAMES AND LANGUAGE

Reconciling the names of many monarchs and figures who were not English into a book on a queen of England requires some moderation and courtesy: particularly when the eponymous queen's name has already been anglicised in the title, and the kings of England in this period were of Norman, Angevin, and Aquitainian origins. To differentiate between the two Blanches who regularly appear, Berengaria's sister and the countess of Champagne is known as Blanca, whereas the thirteenth-century queen of France is known as Blanche of Castile. For ease, Berenguela refers to the queen of Castile who lived from 1180 to 1246. Blanca's son, known as Theobald, Thibaut, and Teobaldo, count of Champagne and king of Navarre in various works, is referred to as Teobaldo to differentiate him from his father, Thibaut III, count of Champagne. Finally, for the majority of this biography I have referred to the early kings of England as Plantagenets, not the Angevins, which is common in some areas of scholarship. Thus, references to Angevins are for those originating from or residing in the county of Anjou, apart from specific noted references to Henry II, Richard I, and John. All transcriptions and translations, unless otherwise noted, are my own.

WHO'S WHO

The below table is a guide to those not intimately acquainted with the politics of the twelfth and thirteenth centuries, to navigate the Henrys, Blanches, Williams, and other figures who appear in the biography.

Usage for this biography	Elaboration	Dates	Dynasty
Adam of Perseigne	Abbot of Perseigne Abbey, Le Mans	c. 1145–1221	
Adela of Champagne	Queen of the Franks, third wife of Louis VII	c. 1140–1206	Blois
Alfonso VII of León and Castile	King of Castile, son of Queen Urraca, grandfather of Berengaria	1105–1157	Ivrea
Alfonso VIII of Castile	King of Castile, husband to Leonor of England, father of Berenguela of Castile	1155–1214	Ivrea
Alix of France	Countess of Blois, daughter of Eleanor of Aquitaine and Louis VII	1150–1197/8	Capet
Alys	Daughter of Constance of Castile and Louis VII, sister of Philip Augustus	1160–c. 1220	Capet

(Continued)

Usage for this biography	Elaboration	Dates	Dynasty
Amaury (I) of Craon	Lord of Craon, husband to Jeanne des Roches, daughter of William des Roches and Marguerite de Sablé	1170–1226	Craon
Arthur I, duke of Brittany	Duke of Brittany, son of Constance, duchess of Brittany and Geoffrey II, duke of Brittany	1187–c. 1203	Plantagenet
Berengaria of Barcelona	Queen consort of Castile, León, and Galicia, wife of Alfonso VII of Castile, mother of Sancha of Castile	1116–1149	Barcelona
Berengaria of Navarre	Queen of England and lord of Le Mans; subject of this work	c. 1165–1230	Jiménez
Berenguela of Castile	Queen regnant of Castile, queen consort of León, daughter of Leonor of England and Alfonso VIII of Castile, wife of Conrad II, duke of Swabia, and Alfonso IX of León	1179/80–1246	Ivrea
Blanca of Navarre	Countess of Champagne, sister to Berengaria and Sancho VII, wife of Thibaut III of Champagne, mother of Teobaldo IV, count of Champagne and king of Navarre	c. 1177/79–1229	Jiménez
Blanche of Castile	Queen of France, daughter of Leonor of England and Alfonso VIII of Castile, wife of Louis VIII, mother of Louis IX	1188–1252	Ivrea
Celestine III	Pope	c. 1106–1198	
Constance (I)	Queen of Sicily, Holy Roman Empress, daughter of Beatrice of Rethel and Roger II of Sicily, wife of Henry VI, Holy Roman Emperor, mother of Frederick II	1154–1198	Hauteville
Constance of France	Countess of Toulouse, sister of Louis VII, wife to Raymond V, count of Toulouse	c. 1126–c. 1190	Capet

(*Continued*)

Usage for this biography	Elaboration	Dates	Dynasty
Constance of Castile	Queen of the Franks, second wife of Louis VII, daughter of Alfonso VII and Berengaria of Barcelona, mother of Margaret of France and Alys	1136/40–1160	Ivrea
Constance, duchess of Brittany	Duchess of Brittany, wife to Geoffrey II, son of Eleanor of Aquitaine and Henry II of England, mother of Eleanor, Arthur I, Alix, and Catherine of Thouars	c. 1161–c.1201	Penthièvre
Constanza	Middle daughter of Sancho VI and Sancha of Castile	?–c. 1202/7	Jiménez
Dreux des Loches	Fifth of his name of the Mello family, married to Isabelle of Mayenne	d. 1249	Mello
Eleanor of Aquitaine	Queen of the Franks, and England, duchess of Aquitaine, mother to Henry, Geoffrey, Richard, John, Matilda, Leonor, and Joanna	c. 1124–1204	Ramnulfids
Ella d'Alençon	Sister of Robert d'Alençon	?	Montgomery-Bellême
Empress Matilda	Holy Roman Empress and Lady of the English, grandmother of Richard I	c. 1102–1167	Normandy
Eustace of Ely	Bishop of Ely, Lord Chancellor	d. 1215	
Fernando	Son of Sancho VI and Sancha of Castile	d. 1207	Jiménez
Frederick II	Holy Roman Emperor and king of Sicily, Italy, and Jerusalem, son of Constance I and Henry VI	1194–1250	Hohenstaufen
García Jiménez	Sub-king of Pamplona, first known member of the Jiménez dynasty	Late 9th century	Jiménez
García Ramirez	King of Navarre (Pamplona), husband of Margaret of L'Aigle, father of Sancho VI	c. 1112–1150	Jiménez

(*Continued*)

Usage for this biography	Elaboration	Dates	Dynasty
Geoffrey III	Count of Perche, son of Rotrou IV of Perche and Matilda of Champagne, second wife Matilda, daughter of Henry the Lion and Matilda of England	d. 1202	Châteaudun
Geoffrey (II), duke of Brittany	Duke of Brittany through marriage to duchess Constance, son of Eleanor of Aquitaine and Henry II, father of Arthur I and Eleanor	1158–1186	Plantagenet
Gilbert of Rochester	Bishop of Rochester	d. 1214	
Gregory IX	Pope	1145/70–1241	
Hamelin	Bishop of Le Mans	d. 1214	
Henry I, count of Champagne	Count of Champagne, husband to Marie of France, father to Henry II and Thibaut III, counts of Champagne, and Marie and Scholastique	1127–1181	Blois
Henry II	King of England, husband to Eleanor of Aquitaine, father of Henry, Geoffrey, Richard, John, Matilda, Leonor, and Joanna	1133–1189	Plantagenet
Henry III	King of England, son of John and Isabella of Angoulême, nephew of Berengaria of Navarre	1207–1272	Plantagenet
Henry the Lion	Duke of Saxony and Bavaria, husband to Clementia of Zähringen and Matilda of England	1129/31–1195	Welf
Henry the Young King	Son of Eleanor of Aquitaine and Henry II of England	1155–1183	Plantagenet
Henry VI	Holy Roman Emperor, king of Germany and Sicily, husband to Constance of Sicily	1165–1197	Hohenstaufen

(*Continued*)

Usage for this biography	Elaboration	Dates	Dynasty
Herbert, bishop of Salisbury	Bishop of Salisbury, family name Poore	d. 1217	
Honorius III	Pope	1150–1227	
Hubert, bishop of Salisbury	Bishop of Salisbury, family name Walter, chief justiciar, and archbishop of Canterbury	c. 1160–1205	
Hugh IX de Lusignan	Count of La Marche (Aquitaine), betrothed to Isabella of Angoulême, father of Hugh X	1163/68–1219	Lusignan
Hugh X de Lusignan	Count of La Marche, second husband of Isabella of Angoulême	c. 1183–1249	Lusignan
Innocent III	Pope	1161–1216	
Isaac Comnenus	Ruler of Cyprus (1184–91)	c. 1155–1195/96	Komnenos
Isabella of Angoulême	Queen of England, wife of John and Hugh X de Lusignan, countess of Angoulême, mother of Henry III, sister-in-law to Berengaria	c. 1186/88–1246	Taillefer
Joanna of Sicily	Queen of Sicily, countess of Toulouse, daughter of Eleanor of Aquitaine and Henry II, wife of William II and Raymond VI, sister-in-law to Berengaria	1165–1199	Plantagenet
John	King of England, father of Henry III, brother-in-law to Berengaria, son of Eleanor of Aquitaine and Henry II	1166–1216	Plantagenet
John de Gray	Bishop of Norwich, elected but unconfirmed archbishop of Canterbury	d. 1214	
Leonor of England	Queen of Castile, mother of Berenguela and Blanche, sister-in-law to Berengaria, wife to Alfonso VIII	c. 1161–1214	Plantagenet

(*Continued*)

Usage for this biography	Elaboration	Dates	Dynasty
Louis IX	King of France, son of Blanche of Castile and Louis VIII, grand nephew to Berengaria	1214–1270	Capet
Louis VII	King of the Franks, husband to Eleanor of Aquitaine, Constance of Castile, and Adela of Champagne, father of Marie, Alix, and Philip Augustus	1120–1180	Capet
Louis VIII	King of France, husband to Blanche of Castile, father of Louis IX	1187–1226	Capet
Margaret of L'Aigle	Queen of Navarre, wife of García Ramírez, granddaughter of Geoffrey II of Perche, grandmother to Berengaria	d. 1141	L'Aigle
Margaret of France	Wife of Henry the Young King and Béla III of Hungary, daughter of Constance of Castile and Louis VII	1158–1197	Capet
Marie of France	Countess of Champagne, daughter of Eleanor of Aquitaine and Louis VII, mother of Henry II and Thibaut III, counts of Champagne, and Marie and Scholastique	1145–1198	Capet
Matilda of England	Duchess of Saxony and Bavaria, daughter of Eleanor of Aquitaine and Henry II	1156–1189	Plantagenet
Matilda of Saxony	Countess of Perche and Lady of Coucy, wife of Geoffrey III, count of Perche, daughter of Henry the Lion and Matilda of England	1172–1209/10	Plantagenet/ Welf
Mauger of Worcester	Bishop of Worcester	d. 1212	
Maurice	Bishop of Le Mans, opponent and sometimes ally of Berengaria	r. 1215–1231	

(*Continued*)

Usage for this biography	Elaboration	Dates	Dynasty
Nicholas	Bishop of Le Mans	r. 1214–1216	
Peter des Roches	Bishop of Winchester, chief justiciar, relative of William des Roches	d. 1238	
Petronilla	Queen regnant of Aragon	1136–1173	Jiménez
Philip Augustus (II)	King of France, son of Adela of Champagne and Louis VII, husband of Isabella of Hainault, Ingeborg of Denmark, and Agnes of Merania, father of Louis VIII	1165–1223	Capet
Philippa	Countess of Toulouse and duchess of Aquitaine, Eleanor of Aquitaine's grandmother	c. 1073–1118	Rouergue
Ramiro	Possible son of Sancho VI and Sancha of Castile	?	Jiménez
Raymond V	Count of Toulouse, husband of Constance of France, father of Raymond VI	c. 1134–1194	Rouergue
Raymond VI	Count of Toulouse, second husband of Joanna of Sicily, first husband of unnamed Byzantine princess	1156–1222	Rouergue
Reginald	Archbishop of Canterbury-elect	Fl. 13th century	
Richard I	King of England, husband of Berengaria, son of Eleanor of Aquitaine and Henry II	1157–1199	Plantagenet
Robert (I) d'Alençon	Count of Alençon	d. 1217	Montgomery-Bellême
Rotrou	Bishop of Châlons, brother of Geoffrey III	d. 1201	Châteaudun
Sancha of Castile	Queen of Navarre, wife to Sancho VI, mother to Berengaria, Blanca, and Sancho	c. 1139–1179	Ivrea/ Jiménez
Sancho Garcés III	King of Pamplona	c. 992/996–1035	Jiménez

(*Continued*)

Usage for this biography	Elaboration	Dates	Dynasty
Sancho VI	King of Navarre, and father to Berengaria, Blanca, and Sancho VII	1132–1194	Jiménez
Sancho VII	King of Navarre, brother to Berengaria and Blanca, last of the direct male Jiménez line	c. 1157–1234	Jiménez
Stephen Langton	Archbishop of Canterbury	c. 1150–1228	
Tancred	King of Sicily, illegitimate son of Roger III, duke of Apulia and Emma, grandson of Roger II, king of Sicily	1138–1194	Hauteville
Teobaldo IV	Count of Champagne, king of Navarre, son of Blanca and Thibaut III, nephew of Berengaria	1201–1253	Blois-Navarre
Thibaut III	Count of Champagne, husband to Blanca, son of Henry I and Marie of France, brother-in-law to Berengaria	1179–1201	Blois
Thibaut V	Count of Blois, husband to Alix of France	1130–1191	Blois
Thomas Becket	Archbishop of Canterbury	1119/20–1170	
Unnamed Byzantine princess	Daughter of Isaac Komnenos, known as Damsel of Cyprus, companion of Berengaria of Navarre	c. 1177–?	Komnenos
Urraca	Queen regnant of León-Castile	c. 1080–1126	Jiménez
William de Longchamp	Lord Chancellor, chief justiciar, bishop of Ely	d. 1197	
William des Roches	Seneschal of Anjou, Maine, and Touraine	d. 1222	
William II	King of Sicily, husband of Joanna of Sicily, son of Margaret of Navarre and William I of Sicily	1153–1189	Hauteville
William II	Count of Perche and bishop of Châlons, son of Rotrou IV and Matilda	d. 1226	Châteaudun

CHRONOLOGY

	Returns to Plantagenet heartlands overland, plausibly via Pisa, Genoa, and Toulouse
6 April 1199	Richard I dies
21 April 1199	Berengaria witnesses a charter of Eleanor of Aquitaine and King John at Fontevraud Abbey
1 July 1199	Berengaria is at Chartres for the marriage of her sister Blanca and Thibaut III of Champagne, and witnesses their marriage settlement
2 August 1201	John announces an agreement with Berengaria for her dower settlement at Chinon
1201–1204	Berengaria resides at the court of her sister in Champagne
August/ September 1204	Berengaria exchanges her Norman dower lands with Philip Augustus for the city and lordship of Le Mans
1204–1205	First interdict placed on Le Mans by the cathedral chapter of Saint-Julien against Berengaria's collections of revenues
January 1205	Berengaria renounces her rights to Loches in favour of Philip Augustus
1209	Berengaria found in Paris with Blanca for negotiations with the Templars regarding a loan for purchase of properties, paid for by Blanca
July 1212	Berengaria in Paris with Blanca for further negotiations with the Templars on the basis of the 1209 agreement
September 1215	Berengaria agrees a settlement with John regarding her dower, in Le Mans
1217–1218	Second interdict placed on Le Mans by the cathedral chapter of Saint-Julien and the bishop Maurice regarding Berengaria's jurisdiction and collect of rents
	Berengaria resides in Thorée

14 August 1218	Berengaria meets with the chapter to resolve and lift the interdict in the comital residence
6 July 1220	Berengaria is at Canterbury for the translation of Thomas Becket
July 1220	Berengaria is at Westminster for the negotiations of her dower settlement with the regency council
27 March 1222	Maurice closes the cathedral to Berengaria and the canons of Saint Pierre-de-la-Cour
August 1228	Berengaria receives the lands of Espal from Louis IX
1229–30	Berengaria issues multiple charters to establish L'Abbaye de L'Épau and acquire donations for it
15 December 1230	Berengaria is at Melun to confirm the will of her clerk, García
23 December 1230	Berengaria's death
January 1231	L'Épau confirmed by Gregory IX

INTRODUCTION

Why Berengaria?

The history of Berengaria of Navarre (c. 1165–1230), queen of England, *suo jure* duchess of Aquitaine and Normandy, countess of Anjou, Maine, and Touraine, and latterly lord (or lady, by popular note) of Le Mans, is one not known to many. She is historically misrepresented as the only queen consort of England never to set foot in the country, visiting England only in 1220 during her widowhood. Berengaria was the wife of one of England's most famous military kings, Richard I, yet Berengaria is a name that has often been lost in the history books. Even works focusing on queens of the crusades have paid scant attention to her, despite her presence in the Holy Land for the initial years of the Third Crusade. It is as the lady of Le Mans, the city she ruled over in her widowhood, that she is best known, and the city still commemorates her to this day as their patroness and heroine of the city.

It is the intention of this biography to bring to light evidence which has been underexamined in the context of Berengaria. She has received attention largely in relation to published letters and references in the *Enquête de 1245 relative aux droits du Chapitre Saint-Julien du Mans*, a medieval documentary record that comprises several eyewitness and oral accounts relating to the ecclesiastical inquests in Le Mans.[1] This biography also brings to light new material previously neglected in English. Though the evidence for Berengaria's life is by no means extensive, archival digging and deeper scrutiny of the surviving record paints a different picture to the idea of the forgotten, shadow queen that has so

DOI: 10.4324/9781003223306-1

often been associated with her. She features in chronicles from the Iberian peninsula to the Holy Land, is recorded as receiving revenues or requesting recompense in the English financial records, including the Pipe Rolls, issued charters in her own name in France, and was the recipient (and sender, though less of these survive) of several diplomatic letters, predominantly to the papacy.

Although the queens of England are by no means understudied as an entirety, there is plentiful work still to be done. Queenship studies has started to fill the gap during the late twentieth century and the first three decades of the twenty-first century. A collective biographical approach can be found amongst Agnes Strickland's *Lives of The Queens of England* volumes, which gave us short miniatures and biographies of each queen, though these have been recently overtaken by a revised corpus of biographies.[2] In the nineteenth century, Henri Chardon penned the first complete biographical study of Berengaria, which though predominantly concerned with Le Mans – as most works associated with her are – paints an interesting picture with regards to the outline of her ecclesiastical patronage in the region. Other biographical studies followed – by Luis del Campo Jesús in Spanish, Mairin Mitchell and Ann Trindade in English (the latter recently translated to Spanish), and Gérard Levacher, Ghislain Baury, and Vincent Corriol in French. Scholarly articles have tended to focus either on notable elements of her life – such as her marriage and partnership with Richard I, as explored by John Gillingham – or her tomb and effigy, as examined by Kathleen Nolan and Nurith Keenan-Kedar.[3]

A queen without a particularly scandalous life, who was not involved in English rule and politics, explains in part her absence from Anglophone historiography: the disunity of Navarre between Iberia and France also explains in part why Navarrese historiography has been neglected in non-Iberian scholarship, and with it, the fate of many royal Navarrese women in particular. It is through attempts to redress this imbalance, through queenship and gender studies, that Berengaria will receive more due attention in history. Berengaria forms an interesting case study through which to analyse gender and power, and to understand the position of a dowager queen in local, national, and international histories. Her connections with the many rulers of Western Europe including John and Henry III of England, Philip Augustus (II), and Louis IX of France, as well as the popes Honorius III and Gregory IX, are also cause for further study and interest.

More recent developments in royal studies scholarship have highlighted the need to consider monarchs as co-rulers: they could share power as a marital couple, with family members, with favourites, or other nobles as part of a regency council. Using co-rulership as a model through which to study the Angevins forms a core part of my current research, and it is a useful tool to understand Richard and Berengaria's partnership. By understanding how power is shared (or in some cases, not) with a consort, and the flow of power between both partners, one can gain a greater understanding of royal authority, governance, and especially female power in the premodern world. Co-rulership, by way of utilising the foundation of composite (multiple domains under one or a pair of rulers) and corporate (a united pairing) monarchies, provides us with a lens to draw out female power and agency that has not always been documented, formalised, or visible.[4]

The question of how to refer to Berengaria – and indeed other noblewomen exercising power typically ascribed to a male lord – has cropped up several times during my research. When originally envisioning the project, referring to Berengaria by her traditional epithet of lady of Le Mans seemed appropriate, as the research underpinning this biography firmly cements the notion that Berengaria was a lord: *domina*, as I note in chapter six, can be literally translated as female lord. Work discussing gender and lordship continues apace, however it is evident that women could and did exercise power as female lords: not as honorary men, and not as 'exceptional' women.[5] Noblewomen were lords on several occasions, and Berengaria was not short of powerful women in the near vicinity to see as an exemplar and contemporary influence.[6] Power exercised by women is visible across the Middle Ages – even if it takes some more digging to unearth it.

The names of the queens who endure in popular culture are often due to their 'unusual' political activity or associated (and often unfounded) scandal – Eleanor of Aquitaine, Isabeau of Bavaria, Anne Boleyn, and Marie Antoinette are but four queens who have all received plentiful attention from historians and the general public owing to the intrigue and rumour intertwined with their lives and legacies. Berengaria had no such scandal attached to her name and faded further from the historical record and public memory. Though she is by no means invisible, her actions and petitions are often found in ecclesiastical or legal documents, or through the responses sent by male rulers. Berengaria's visibility can be seen most clearly after she moved 'beyond the boundaries of married queenship.'[7]

One of the most fascinating and remarkable aspects of Berengaria's life is that she defies what has, until recently, been seen as the tradition of queens fading further into obscurity in their dowager period. Many studies have shown that, instead, dowager or widowhood can be a point of invigoration whereby some women become more politically active, more notable, and heavily involved in governance. Women can grow into power and become more powerful with age. Recent discussions on the exceptionalism of women grounded the need to do away with the notion that women 'retired' or 'rescinded themselves' from public life, when in reality residing in a religious institution or elsewhere from court life did not mean inactivity, but control and power being exercised outside of the immediate political sphere.[8] Definitions of power and authority can become nebulous, and each historian interprets them slightly differently.[9] Power can be exercised both formally and informally – and indeed for the twelfth and thirteenth centuries, much genuine female power is not always immediately visible, but nevertheless there. Authority, on the other hand, has sometimes been viewed as being reinforced by another factor: sometimes violence, sometimes by another royal – often male, at times by decree. Gender studies and work by feminist medievalists in particular has shown that 'information about women that scholars once proclaimed simply irretrievable has been sought out, recovered, and reported.'[10] This work is a contribution to this growing body of literature which disproves that women's power and agency are unable to be recovered.

One could argue heavily for the need for more visibility of the early Plantagenets, particularly the Angevins, in comparison with their Tudor successors. John is a name known to many, primarily in association with what has been viewed as a disastrous reign, and his brother Richard the Lionheart also, but their wider lives (and wives) are not. The Angevins have received modest attention in popular media: dozens of novels consider the figure of Eleanor of Aquitaine, and some Isabella of Angoulême, but even fewer choose Berengaria as a case study, particularly in English. When it comes to visual media, her earliest depiction in the 1911 silent movie *Il talismano* barely casts her as a figure of importance, and successive depictions have done little to remedy this, basing their representations of Berengaria on highly romanticised ideals.

How can we change perceptions of Berengaria? She has been the recipient of scholarly attention in English by myself and by Ghislain Baury and Vincent Corriol in French, the latter of whom contributed to a graphic novel to coincide with the biography and exhibition launch at L'Abbaye de L'Épau in November 2022, which was warmly received.[11] However, attention remains much concentrated in the form of local memory, or slightly further afield in 'Plantagenet Country,' the regions stretching from across western France and into the Loire Valley. Some local connections have also been made between Berengaria and Tudela, a city in Navarre, her supposed place of birth and the location of a new gisant, unveiled in May 2022 (see Figure 0.1). She also has a place in local memory in Limassol, Cyprus, the site of her marriage and coronation, with Queen Berengaria Street down from the Old Port, as well as local amenities named after her. Biographical studies of many queens of England are in need of composition or revising, and Berengaria was not exceptional in being forgotten (consider Margaret of France and Matilda of Scotland, both relatively unknown figures from the medieval English monarchy as well). She was also not exceptional in how she exercised power, when examined by the revised understanding whereby the exercise of power by women was normal and powerful women were not the exception to the rule.[12] However, Berengaria needs – and deserves – to be brought to a wider, and Anglophone, audience.

Lacking support from the male relatives of her natal and marital families, and with no children, Berengaria had few avenues to turn to in order to access power. Her position as a childless queen was relatively unusual, although several of her queenly successors

FIGURE 0.1 Photograph of the gisant of Berengaria of Navarre, created for the twinning of the cities of Tudela and Le Mans, 28 May 2022. Created and photographed by Aitor Calleja. Photograph reproduced with his permission.

across Europe faced a similar dilemma. How did a queen operate in the political sphere without a royal heir to influence or intercede alongside?[13] Failure to produce an heir was often blamed on the woman in the relationship, although fertility issues, time spent together, and desire to reproduce were undoubtedly affected by both parties. As Berengaria never went on to remarry, we will never know whether she was able to produce a child. Not having a child did not deter her from being politically active however. A minor king could be problematic without a secure transition of power, and a child ruler did not always afford the queen mother a role in government, as seen with Berengaria's sister-in-law, Isabella of Angoulême.

This biography takes a traditional chronological approach, with attention paid to key themes that hold relevance to Berengaria and her exercise of power. The first chapter, which addresses her time as infanta (princess) and early life in Navarre (1165–91), touches on aspects of female inheritance and succession, topics that were particularly pertinent to Berengaria and her younger sister Blanca in relation to their positions as theoretical heiresses to Navarre. The second chapter analyses Berengaria's time as queen consort of England (1191–9) and her experiences on the Third Crusade (1189–92) to consider the themes of regency and co-rulership, critical aspects of rule that Berengaria was often denied during her time as queen consort and dowager queen. Chapter three examines her early years as a dowager queen, between 1199 and 1204, and her decision to insert herself into the Western European political arenas after being neglected both politically and financially during her reign. Although this period is often glossed over due to lack of evidence, contemporary financial records can help uncover more of Berengaria's agency and power, as well as that of other women in the Middle Ages. The fourth chapter is an analysis of the broader themes of queenship that are connected to Berengaria, namely her experiences of power and rulership, as well as being a childless queen. The fifth chapter considers her familial and political relationships with the rulers and royal families across England, France, and the Iberian kingdoms of Navarre and Castile when she was queen dowager. The sixth chapter focuses on the most active and well-resourced period of Berengaria's life, her time as lord of Le Mans from 1204 to 1230. Woven through this chapter are discussions of her relationship with the Church and interactions with the papacy, both of which were crucial to her longstanding campaign and struggle to gain her dower resources and rule in Le Mans.[14] The seventh and concluding chapters consider Berengaria's legacy and memory. Although she is underrepresented in traditional media, like many of the early Plantagenets, this section considers why Berengaria has been so forgotten by and isolated from historiography, and her representations in popular media and culture. It will also address her local legacy in Le Mans, the city she resided in as dowager queen, which had a close affinity for her and of which she was mutually enamoured.

So why Berengaria? As noted, she has received scant attention in Anglophone and French historiography, most recently through an extensive scholarly biography by Ghislain Baury and Vincent Corriol.[15] Yet, despite being a queen of England, there is no updated, scholarly yet accessible work in English that places Berengaria's life within a fuller context, including a detailed analysis of her correspondence with the papacy. The intention of this biography is to bring Berengaria to a wider audience, providing a fresh perspective on the myths and misinformation surrounding her, and integrating important evidence that previous English biographies have not discussed. Underpinning the scholarly discussion is a woman of great tenacity, determination, and stubbornness, whose story deserves to be told outside the sphere of Anglo-French-Navarrese relations. In Berengaria, I hope readers will find the story of what it means to never give up.

Notes

1 Richard Barton, '*Enquête*, Exaction and Excommunication: Experiencing Power in Western France, c.1190–1245,' *Anglo-Norman Studies* 43 (2021): 177–96.

2 See Aidan Norrie, Carolyn Harris, J. L. Laynesmith, Danna Messer, and Elena Woodacre, eds., *English Consorts: Power, Influence, Dynasty* (Cham: Palgrave Macmillan, 2022–3).

3 The biography by Ghislain Baury and Vincent Corriol, alongside the article by Elizabeth Hallam, should otherwise be the main starting point for any study of Berengaria; for full works, see the bibliography.

4 Theresa Earenfight, 'Highly Visible, Often Obscured: The Difficulty of Seeing Queens and Noble Women,' *Medieval Feminist Forum: A Journal of Gender and Sexuality* 44.1 (2008): 86–90.

5 Kimberly LoPrete, 'The gender of lordly women: the case of Adela of Blois,' in *Pawns or Players?*, eds. Christine Meek and Catherine Lawless (Dublin: Four Courts Press, 2003), 90–2.

6 For other examples of lordly women, see Michelle Armstrong-Partida, 'Mothers and Daughters as Lords: The Countesses of Blois and Chartres,' *Medieval Prosopography* 26 (2005): 77–107.

7 Quote adapted from Miriam Shadis, *Berenguela of Castile (1180–1246) and Political Women in the High Middle Ages* (Basingstoke: Palgrave Macmillan, 2010), 96.

8 Beyond Exceptionalism II, Women in Medieval Society, The John Rylands Research Institute and Library, Manchester, 11–13 July 2022.

9 There is extensive reading on women's power and authority, the most recent and relevant of which is Theresa Earenfight, 'A Lifetime of Power: Beyond Binaries of Gender,' in *Medieval Elite Women and the Exercise of Power, 100–1400. Moving Beyond the Exceptionalist Debate*, ed. Heather J. Tanner (Cham: Palgrave Macmillan, 2019), 271–93, alongside the wider volume. I build upon the discussions in my doctoral thesis on power and authority; see Gabrielle Storey, 'Co-Operation, Co-Rulership and Competition: Queenship in the Emerging Angevin Domains, 1135–1230' (PhD Thesis, University of Winchester, 2020), ch. 1. For an alternative view, see Janna Bianchini, *The Queen's Hand. Power and Authority in the Reign of Berenguela of Castile* (Philadelphia: University of Pennsylvania Press, 2012), 5–14.

10 Judith M. Bennett, 'Medievalism and Feminism,' *Speculum* 68.2 (1993): 326.

11 Bruno Rocco, Olivier Renault, Bénédicte Fillion-Braguet, Ghislain Baury, and Vincent Corriol, *Bérengère de Navarre, du trône de l'Angleterre à l'abbaye de l'Épau* (Nantes: Petit a Petit, 2022); Exhibition *Bérengère, à la rencontre d'une Reine*, L'Abbaye de L'Épau, 19/11/2022–13/03/2023.

12 See Tanner, *Moving Beyond the Exceptionalist Debate*.

13 See Kristin Geaman, 'Childless Queens and Child-like Kings: Negotiating Royal Infertility in England, 1382–1471' (PhD Thesis, University of Southern California, 2013); Theresa Earenfight and Kristin Geaman, 'Neither Heir Nor Spare. Childless queens and the practice of monarchy in pre-modern Europe,' in *The Routledge History of Monarchy*, eds. Elena Woodacre, Lucinda H. S. Dean, Chris Jones, Russell E. Martin, and Zita Eva Rohr (London: Routledge, 2019), 518–33.

14 A fuller exploration of dower and its meaning is given in chapters 3 and 5.

15 Ghislain Baury and Vincent Corriol, *Bérengère de Navarre (v. 1160–1230). Histoire et mémoire d'une reine d'Angleterre* (Rennes: Presses Universitaires Rennes, 2022).

INFANTA

Navarre, Adolescence, and Female Power in Iberia

Berengaria, often designated 'of Navarre' by historians and in popular culture, is named as such to identify her with the polity in which she was born and spent the first three decades of her life. Abutting Aquitaine in south-western France and the modern provinces of La Rioja, Basque, and Aragon in north-eastern Spain lies the province of Navarre, encompassing much of what formed its medieval kingdom. The kingdom of Navarre was not only the location of her earliest experiences of rulership, but as her homeland also held importance throughout her life. Based around the city and early kingdom of Pamplona in the early tenth century, it became known as the kingdom of Navarre under the rule of García Ramirez in 1134. The kingdom was predominantly ruled over by the Jiménez dynasty, founded by García Jiménez in the late ninth century, though his origins are debated. Situated between various competing kingdoms in the high Middle Ages, Navarre was a useful ally against neighbouring conflicts and for protection in times of dispute, and it is from this concept that the Anglo-Navarrese alliance at the end of the twelfth century arose. The strategic position of Navarre to the Angevin territories in the Midi was also of central importance to the alliance with the Angevins. This chapter will outline the history and background of Navarre to place Berengaria's origins and her alliance with Richard I (1189–99) in context, alongside with a discussion of Berengaria's early years prior to her betrothal to Richard. It will then move to discuss Navarre in its twelfth-century context at the time of the Anglo-Navarrese pact, before placing Berengaria

DOI: 10.4324/9781003223306-2

within the various frameworks of female succession and rulership in twelfth- and thirteenth-century Western Europe. The final
area of discussion for this chapter considers the negotiations for
Berengaria's marriage.

Navarre and Berengaria's Early Years

The kingdom of Navarre, with its origins in the kingdom of Pamplona, reached its greatest extent under the rule of Sancho Garcés
III between 1004 and 1035. During Sancho's reign, his control
extended north of the Pyrenees and into the south-west of what
is now modern-day France, namely Bayonne and Bordeaux, expanding eastward until just short of Toulouse. This expansion
elevated the Navarrese to a position of one of the prominent
powers in Western Europe, confirmed by the conquest of León in
1034 which saw the temporary union of all Christian Iberia under
one ruler. Despite splitting the kingdoms upon his death, the rule
of Sancho Garcés III saw the transition to Jiménez control across
much of the peninsula whether through blood or marriage. Even
with the loss of territory throughout the later eleventh and early
twelfth century, Navarre held a strategic position which was val-
ued by kings of the surrounding polities, and as such Navarre was
often pursued for alliances as the high Middle Ages progressed.
The Navarrese spoke Basque and/or Navarro-Aragonese; however, the official records were in Latin, and Spanish Romance was
also to develop as a vernacular language from the eleventh century onwards. As an infanta (the Spanish term for princess, or
royal daughter), Berengaria would have been expected to be flu-
ent in Latin and the lingua franca of the court, and it is likely that
she had knowledge of Occitan as well due to Navarre's close connections with the Gascons, residents of the neighbouring duchy of
Gascony, a former Basque province that had been conquered by
the duchy of Aquitaine by 1053.

Berengaria's paternal grandfather, García Ramirez, mentioned
above, was a central figure of the Jiménez dynasty. García had
been elected as king of Navarre (Pamplona) in 1134, bringing
Navarre back to independence, as it had been in a personal union with the Aragonese since 1076. García and his eldest son,

Sancho VI, also known as Sancho the Wise (1150–94), Berengaria's father, restored Navarre to its former glory, making significant developments, particularly with regards to urbanisation.[1] On 20 July 1153 Sancho married the infanta Sancha, daughter of Alfonso VII of León and Castile and Alfonso's first wife, Berengaria of Barcelona. Together, they had six known children, four of whom survived to adulthood: Berengaria, Blanca, Fernando, and Sancho, the future Sancho VII (1194–1234). One daughter, Constanza, sometimes named Teresa erroneously in contemporary sources, and a son, Ramiro, are also named as children of the pair. We know little further of Constanza and Ramiro other than their burial sites and can only assume that they died young. With his children, Sancho VI had an eye to furthering his dynastic ambitions as well as stabilising the frontiers after many years of warfare. The marriage of Blanca, to the count of Champagne, ensured that Navarre had strong allies in the kingdom of France, and the marriage of Berengaria to the king of England enabled an alliance with the duchy of Aquitaine against Sancho's Iberian enemies, and are explored in more detail in chapters two and three. At the time of Berengaria's and Blanca's marriages, the king of England possessed territories in Normandy, Brittany, Aquitaine, Maine, Anjou, Touraine, and Poitou, being duke of the first three and count of the latter territories. Sancho VI's own union with an infanta of Castile, however, had done little to assuage the warfare between Navarre, León-Castile, and Aragon. The marriage of Alfonso VIII, king of Castile, to Leonor of England, in 1170, led to further invasions of Navarre between 1173–6 as Alfonso sought to exert his claims over the region and into Gascony, which had been reportedly granted as part of Leonor's dowry.[2] Although a seven-year truce was agreed in 1177, tensions erupted shortly thereafter, and intermittent warfare continued throughout the latter half of the twelfth century. In the wake of these conflicts in the Iberian peninsula, Navarre may have appeared an unlikely choice for the Plantagenets to ally with, however, as will be explored more in the following chapter, Navarre had strategic importance for Aquitaine and its own neighbouring enemies.

The births of Berengaria and her siblings are noted in several medieval and some early modern chronicles. For the history of

Navarre some of the most notable histories include the work of Garci López de Roncesvalles and the Príncipe de Viana's chronicle, written in the fifteenth century.[3] A sixteenth-century chronicle that is also of use for the history of Navarre is José Moret's *Anales del Reino de Navarra*.[4] These three early modern histories utilised a range of medieval records, including some which have not survived in their original form. The earliest record that mentions Berengaria is the twelfth-century *El Liber Regum*, which includes her in a list of the children of Sancho VI:

> The king lord Sancho of Navarre, his first wife the daughter of the emperor of Castile, and from her their children, the king lord Sancho, the prince lord Fernando and the queen of England, and the countess of Champagne, and the princess Constanza, who died in Daroca.[5]

Another chronicle, produced shortly after Berengaria's death by the Archbishop Rodrigo Jiménez provides a more detailed reference to Berengaria, including a note of her marriage.

> Berengaria, who was wife of Richard, king of England, died without children, and lived for a long time in praiseworthy widowhood, in the city of Le Mans, which was a gift from her marriage.[6]

It is difficult to ascertain Berengaria's date of birth; it has been traditionally listed as between 1165 and 1170, based on Henri Chardon's study.[7] Chardon's estimate was based primarily on an underlying assumption that Berengaria would have been aged around twenty at the time of her marriage to Richard, but with no real justification. Given the variance in marital ages of princesses – some betrothed in their infancy and married between thirteen and fourteen years of age, others were not married until their early twenties dependent on geopolitics and power, Chardon's argument is very tenuous. Given the lack of dating provided by Spanish chroniclers, we can only presume that she was born some point after her brother Sancho, in 1154, and before her sister Blanca, who was born between 1177 and 1179. Berengaria's listing as the first daughter, indicating that she was the eldest, in the chronicles, pushes her birth date closer to the 1160s based on the births of three other siblings between Berengaria and Blanca. Contemporary chronicles record that Berengaria's mother, Sancha, died in August 1179, which some historians have ascribed to dying shortly after childbirth, however no evidence can corroborate this hypothesis with any certainty.[8] Recent work by Ghislain Baury and Vincent Corriol has proposed that her birth date was several years earlier on the assumption that rulers would generally intend to marry off their daughters when they reached the age of legal responsibility, alongside other factors that argue for an earlier birth date. The dating of a female skeleton in L'Épau in 1960, assumed to be Berengaria, was aged between sixty and sixty-five years at her death, which would suggest a birth date at the end of the 1160s if it is her.[9] It is therefore difficult to convincingly argue for Berengaria's birth date with complete accuracy, and thus a birth date of c. 1165 seems the more plausible given her activity in Monreal twenty years later.

Sancho VI did not remarry after his wife's death. The continued harmonious relationships of the three siblings – Berengaria, Blanca, and Sancho – in their later lives may be indicative of formative companionship and shared residences growing up, and certainly Blanca appears to have held an affection for both her siblings in her later life, assisting when both Berengaria and Sancho faced challenges.

Of Berengaria's early life as infanta of Navarre we know little, as is so often the case for medieval children, royal or not. It is likely she spent her time between Tudela, home to the Jiménez dynasty, and Pamplona, which was the capital of Navarre and the original site of the kingdom of Navarre. Berengaria's father, Sancho, was the first monarch to use the title 'king of Navarre,' with *rex Navarrae* appearing in his charters from 1162 onwards.[10] Berengaria may have spent her early years with her family; however, it is also plausible that she was dispatched to a convent or religious institution for her upbringing, as was often the case in royal families, the Jiménez included. The residences she spent her youth in are unknown but may have included castles or royal monasteries in the cities of Tudela, Estella, and Pamplona, which were of importance to the Jiménez dynasty.

Navarre was subject to continually changing borders throughout its history, and its union with the county of Champagne after the throne passed to Teobaldo IV, count of Champagne and son of Blanca of Navarre, Berengaria's sister, in 1234, ushered in a new era of rulership with regards to royal women and their power. From the thirteenth to the sixteenth centuries Navarre was ruled at various points by five queens regnant, an unusually high number of queens regnant for European monarchies in this time frame.[11] Navarre was not the only kingdom in the Iberian peninsula to have a queen regnant: Urraca (1109–26) had famously ruled over León-Castile in the early twelfth century, and Petronilla (1137–64) ruled over Aragon in the decades thereafter, and were both of Berengaria's house, the Jiménez.[12] In the western Iberian kingdom of Portugal, the daughters of Sancho I and Dulce of Aragón, Teresa, Mafalda, and Sancha, were all recorded as queens regardless of their marital status, and participated heavily in co-rulership, holding genuine and real political power.[13] These sister queens heavily utilised religious patronage and ecclesiastical networks to demonstrate their legitimacy and royal authority, and held the status of queen along with the many facets of royal power throughout their lives.[14] Berengaria employed these tactics of religious patronage and networks to showcase her authority as lord of Le Mans, and her continued disputes with local ecclesiastical figures in Le Mans, as discussed in chapter six, demonstrate that she was not willing to be pushed to one side when it came to the exercise of power. Imbued with a powerful sense of royal authority and self, Berengaria's early years and influences came to the fore during her dowager period.

The precedents of Urraca and Petronilla for strong female rulership may have influenced Berengaria in her early years, and her assertiveness during her dowager period may well have been due to growing up in regions where female authority and power were visible and not universally viewed with scepticism as they were in other European countries. Berengaria only had to look northwards to the kingdoms of France and England to view the complexities royal women faced with exercising authority and power, although the exercise of female power anywhere was not without its own struggles in the European continent. Southern European countries appeared to be more tolerant and accepting of female rulership than their northern counterparts.

We know little of the tenure of Sancha of Castile, Berengaria's mother, and her involvement in the rule or regency of Navarre, and thus what example Berengaria may have taken from Sancha directly with regards to women holding power.[15] However, it is entirely plausible that Sancha would have influenced Berengaria's childhood and with it imparted the history of Leónese and Castilian royal women who were involved in the rule of their respective kingdoms. Medieval mothers were often responsible for organising, if not directly influencing, the education of their children, and it is likely that Sancha imparted her wisdom and knowledge regarding the challenges and expectations of female rulership to Berengaria. Sancha's political activity is notably absent from the Navarrese record, with only a few indirect references to her in the documents of her husband and brother.[16] It is plausible Sancha had a role to play in organising the education and marriages of her children. Iberian women from the noble classes and below often played a role in choosing and arranging marriages, and there is further contemporary evidence for the activities of Plantagenet royal women in matrimonial politics.[17] However, how far back this Iberian tradition extended is difficult to ascertain: royal female power and activity was certainly more advanced and accepted in Iberia than in the rest of Western Europe, but whether this exercise of female power extended to matrimonial politics for Sancha is unclear.

Monreal and the Infanta

As Berengaria entered adolescence and then early adulthood, it is plausible that she would have become more politically active. One of the earliest extant records we have for Berengaria outside of the chronicles is her inclusion, by name only, as a participant, in an 1185 charter as part of a wider confirmation of lands held by Navarrese ecclesiastics and nobles, noting her residence next

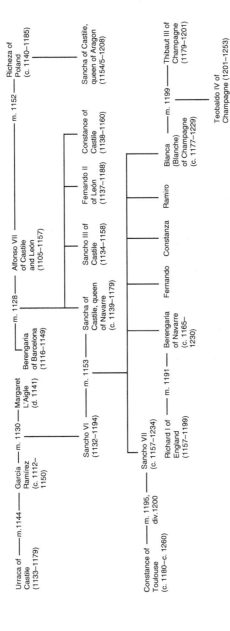

FIGURE 1.1 Family tree of Berengaria of Navarre

to Monreal, a town to the south-west of Pamplona.[18] Why Berengaria was present in this particular area at this time is uncertain; Baury and Corriol note that either Sancho VI or his father renamed the town and had a residence there.[19] This territory establishes the connection between the Jiménez and Monreal, which later develops into a more extensive royal site. Berengaria was now of an age to be married, between twenty and twenty-five years old, with medieval marriages for women taking place from the age of twelve–thirteen years old upwards. Given her age and the plausibility that negotiations for her marriage with Richard began in the late 1180s, the grant may have served as an opportunity to show her landholding, diplomatic skills and status before Sancho began to engage in marital plans for Berengaria. Monreal appears again in a grant in 1188 by Sancho VI, who gave a house in the town to Diego Sánchez de Munoztán, and notes that this will be a noble house with Diego recognised as a member of the nobility.[20] Such ennoblement, known as *infanzíona*, was particularly prudent in this case since, at this time, Monreal was a Frankish bourg, or town, having received a Frankish fuero, or set of law codes, in 1149.[21] Nobles did not typically live in bourgs and to live there was often viewed as a lowering of one's status, and thus Sancho's ennoblement of Diego and his house elevates his status in what is typically viewed as a bourgeois area. There are two possible reasons Berengaria appeared in the Monreal grant of 1185 and, in either case, the transaction provides an insight into her status and action at the time.

Firstly, it is possible that Berengaria was resident in a local monastery near Monreal and was therefore conveniently placed to witness the charter *apud*, meaning at, Monreal. There was a history of royal female donations in the area surrounding Monreal, which would lay the foundations for Berengaria's involvement with the town of Monreal. Two eleventh-century donations by women, Sancha and her granddaughter Toda Jiméz de Elizaberría, consist of the granting of the monastery of Saint Michael and the church of Hija, and the monastery of Atea with the village of Sansoain respectively to the nearby monastery of Leire.[22] The donations of smaller or 'private' churches, with associated lands, rents, and monasteries, to a larger institution have wider precedents across Asturias and Navarre in the tenth and eleventh centuries, with the ultimate resolution of the larger monastery absorbing the smaller churches in the area, as is the case with Leire. Leire, founded in the ninth century, originated with royal connections and continued to do so throughout its history.[23] This historical association between women and religious institutions in the region may have laid the foundations for future donations and involvement by royal women in the twelfth century, and may have tied the Jiménez women to the area.

By the twelfth century, royal women across the Iberian peninsula often had access to ecclesiastical properties which formed the infantazgo, 'a collection of religious institutions held by and passed down to royal daughters and sisters who lived unmarried.'[24] The infantazgo was not limited to certain kingdoms or families, although it is difficult to trace in Navarre during the twelfth and thirteenth centuries, not least due to a dearth of royal women – Berengaria and Blanca were the prominent royal women from their mother's death in 1179 to the accession of Margaret of Bourbon as queen consort of Navarre in 1234 through the third marriage of Teobaldo, Blanca's son.[25] The visibility of the infantazgo in other regions such as Castile and León mean it is possible such a practice was in place in Navarre, and this is an area in need of further attention. The importance of ecclesiastical institutions, undoubtedly impressed on Berengaria from an early age, also contributed to her activities as religious patron as lord of Le Mans in her dowager period.

A second possibility, currently being researched by Eloísa Ramírez Vaquero and Fermín Miranda García, is the granting of revenues to royal women in Navarre in the tenth and eleventh centuries to enable them to maintain their status.[26] This granting of revenues differed from the traditional infantazgos that can be seen elsewhere in the Iberian peninsula across the high Middle Ages, which were typically tied to a religious foundation as well as control of a manorial or residential property. The evidence for infantazgos in Navarre in this period is at present scarce, and since it was a Castilian system, it would not have been automatically replicated in the other Iberian kingdoms. Ramírez Vaquero's recent research on the tenth- and eleventh-century women of

Navarre indicates that Navarrese royal women were more closely tied to certain spaces and networks than previously thought.[27] Though we know frustratingly little about Berengaria and her activities in Monreal – with any further evidence of her activity in Monreal unfortunately lost – developing research on the networks and patronage of royal women in Navarre is indicative that she may have acted as part of a wider system of association between royal women and religious institutions. The other figures mentioned in the Monreal charter do not appear in any further documents related to Berengaria, but some, such as the Pedriz family, do feature in future grants of Sancho VII, therefore indicating that they were part of the male Jiménez networks, and plausibly not Berengaria's.

In his study of '*tenancia*,' or landholding, in Aragon and Navarre, Agustín Ubieto Arteta referenced Berengaria as one of several Aragon-Navarrese royal women who held land, nominally hereditary, during the late eleventh and twelfth centuries.[28] However, Ubieto Arteta's discussion was mainly a preliminary work and from it we can only deduce that Berengaria was part of a wider pattern of Iberian women who held familial territories. Berengaria's holding of territory was intended to elevate her status as she began to appear in marriage negotiations. The strategic use of royal children for marital and political alliances was common from the advent of monarchy itself: the need for allies against a common enemy, or the neutralisation of an enemy, are but two reasons why a prince or princess could be utilised in marriage negotiations. Sancho VI's own marriage to Sancha of Castile was undoubtedly intended to neutralise Castile as an enemy, though it ultimately failed. In the context of the disputes between Aragon, León-Castile, and Navarre, marital alliances could be crucial in combining resources to tackle a common enemy. They were also important for maintaining the balance of power within the region, sometimes placating an enemy who feared reprisal if they attacked one part of an alliance. The Christian Iberian kingdoms had been in dispute with one another, as well as with the Islamic caliphate that dominated the southern Spanish regions since their emergence. As noted above, Navarre had recently broken away from its union with Aragon and was at the centre of disputes between the Aragonese and Castilian monarchs for control of the region, and therefore they were in need of allies.

Navarre in a Changing World

The shifting position of Navarre throughout the high medieval to the early modern period showed its centrality to Western European politics, and with it the reason why marital alliances, such as Berengaria and Richard's, were necessary. Marital alliances with other powers served to enhance Navarre's prestige and inclusion in international affairs. The lack of attention to Navarre in European, Anglophone, and royal historiographies goes some way to explaining why Berengaria of Navarre remains an unknown historical figure to so many. Navarre's independence from other kingdoms was to last less than a century, with the lack of surviving heirs borne to Sancho VII, resulting in the Navarrese crown passing to his nephew, Teobaldo IV, count of Champagne. The Champenois-Navarrese union was to endure until 1276, when the ascendancy of the minor queen Juana I, in 1274, led to a marital alliance with the kingdom of France, whereby Navarre was absorbed into a personal union with France until 1328. In 1328, Juana II, the only surviving child of Louis X, king of France (also known as Luis I of Navarre), acceded to the throne of Navarre with her husband, Philip of Évreux, as co-ruler. Thirteenth-century Navarre was thus beset with three changing dynasties, where alliances were short-lived amongst the conquering desires of its neighbouring kings. In the twelfth century, Sancho VI appeared primarily concerned with stabilising Navarre and defence rather than expansion, though his successor Sancho VII made modest gains and acquisitions, particularly in the north across the Pyrenees in the Ultrapuertos region.

The continued conquest and separation of the kingdom of Navarre through the medieval and early modern periods has left it as a region with little prominence outside of local and some national histories. It never reached the geographical breadth or international standing of some of the other Iberian kingdoms, like Aragon and Castile, and its ruling dynasties, such as the Jiménez, have never gained much in the way of popularity or notoriety in

Anglophone scholarship, with perhaps the notable exception of Carlos II due to his actions in the Hundred Years War. Although many prominent infantas and future queens came from Navarre, including Berengaria, they have remained understudied in the histories of queens of Western Europe.[29] Sancho VI was successful in bringing the kingdom of Navarre further into the orbit of Western Europe through his treaties and alliances, however, this was to be short-lived: Navarre never gained the long-term power and prestige of other European kingdoms through the later medieval and early modern periods, despite the fact that it remained an important part of French-Iberian relationships and disputes.

Richard I and the Plantagenet dynasty are well-known to many scholars and interested historians: however, the name of his queen is not. The alliance between the Plantagenets and the Navarrese – and Berengaria's position as the link between the two – was probably intended to mitigate tensions between the various polities of Western Europe. Across the Pyrenees from Navarre, there was a longstanding enmity between the Plantagenet rulers of the various surrounding duchies and counties, and the king of France, to whom the former owed homage. Henry II, king of England, and father of Richard I, engaged in conflict on the Continent at various points during his reign as duke of Normandy and king of England (1154–89), notably with the count of Toulouse in an attempt to claim the patrimony of Eleanor, his wife. Henry was also engaged in warfare with Louis VII, king of France (1137–80), and his son Philip Augustus, also known as Philip II, across the borders of the Angevin domains.

It was against this threat and for the prospect of harmony that Henry II and Louis VII arranged the marriage of Richard with Alys, Philip Augustus's sister, in 1169. The Treaty of Montmirail on 6 January 1169 saw Henry agree to divide his lands between his sons, with the exclusion of John, and for Richard to be betrothed to Alys, who was to have no dowry.[30] The peace conference came on the back of a year of failed talks and conflict, as Henry and Louis had been brought together at La Ferté Bernard in July 1168. This treaty was intended to resolve familial tensions regarding the inheritance of the Angevin domains, as well as resolve the ongoing conflicts between Henry and Louis, and

Henry and Thomas Becket. In both points it was a failure. Henry the Young King, Richard, and Geoffrey rose in rebellion in 1173 against Henry II, with Louis' support. Alys had been dispatched to England as Henry's ward in 1169 and was to be raised as such until the time of her marriage to Richard. However, rumours abounded in the 1170s and 1180s that Henry had engaged in an affair with Alys, and medieval chroniclers even speculated that Alys had a child by Henry.[31]

The twenty-two-year long betrothal was overly lengthy by any standards, and the continued desire by Louis VII and Philip Augustus for the marriage to take place is an indication of their pursuit for a permanent foothold in the Plantagenet court. We know little of Alys's character, and whether she would have held much sway in terms of political influence over her husband is unknown. However, her position at the centre of the Plantagenet court as a Plantagenet wife, and indeed her potential elevation as queen after the deaths of Henry the Young King and Henry II may have afforded a stable Plantagenet-Capetian alliance. This centricity was plausibly a motivation for the Capetians' continued pursuit of the marriage. In September 1177 at Nonancourt, Henry and Louis agreed that Richard was to marry Alys, and Henry argued for Margaret to be endowed with the French Vexin as the remainder of her dowry, and for Alys to be endowed with Bourges. Other than discussions regarding her dowry, Alys was left in an undetermined state. Alys's poor treatment at the hands of both Henry II and Richard demonstrated the lack of respect for both the personal and political aspects of the betrothal. Richard does not appear to have been particularly motivated by any chivalric duties towards Alys when he became king, instead moving towards an alliance with the Navarrese. His lack of concern for Alys is perhaps telling for how his relationship with Berengaria developed, as it appears he had relatively little concern for Berengaria's status and happiness during their marriage, as discussed in chapter two. Politically, Henry and Richard played a diplomatic game by repeatedly failing to ensure the marriage between Richard and Alys took place and tentatively keeping the Capetians allied to them. Berengaria and Richard's marriage broke the Anglo-French alliance with devastating consequences for the Plantagenets.

This rocky betrothal between Richard and Alys ran alongside another marital dispute between the Plantagenets and Capetians: that of Margaret of France, Philip Augustus's sister, who had been the wife of Henry the Young King, Henry II's eldest son who died in 1183. In December 1183 Philip agreed that Henry could keep the Norman Vexin on the conditions that he paid Margaret an annual pension of 2700 livres, and that the Norman Vexin was granted to 'whichever of his sons married Alice.'[32] Further discussions in March 1186 and February 1187 did little to clarify Alys's status, and that of the Vexin: there were certainly advantages to England for keeping Alys at hand, as it prevented Philip from gaining an alliance elsewhere. But it also meant that Philip had an arrow in his quiver when it came to disputes, as he sought a resolution to his sister's status.[33] The situation was finally resolved in a treaty at Messina between Richard and Philip in March 1191, when Richard was released from the betrothal in return for the sum of 10,000 marks, and the Norman Vexin was to belong to Richard and his male descendants, but would pass to Philip and his heirs should Richard die without a legitimate son. The original of this treaty is lost, with later records both by chroniclers and scribes varying on the details.[34] However, the treaty finalised the status of the betrothal of Alys and the Vexin, with Alys to return to France at last.

Further tensions between France and the Plantagenets escalated when Henry's younger son Geoffrey, duke of Brittany, died in 1186. Geoffrey's widow Constance was pregnant with the future Arthur I of Brittany, and Henry and Philip Augustus again disputed who should be the guardian of the duchy during the unborn duke's minority. With this, the issue of Alys's betrothal came to the fore once more since the marriage had still not taken place. Intermittent warfare followed with interim periods of truce. Philip Augustus employed friendships with the Angevin sons to foment rebellion against Henry II, but once the sons reached a position of power these friendships quickly soured. When Richard acceded to the throne in 1189, his relationship with Philip Augustus began to wane, even more so on the Third Crusade when news of Richard's betrothal to Berengaria broke. The instigation for the Anglo-Navarrese betrothal was likely mooted many years earlier

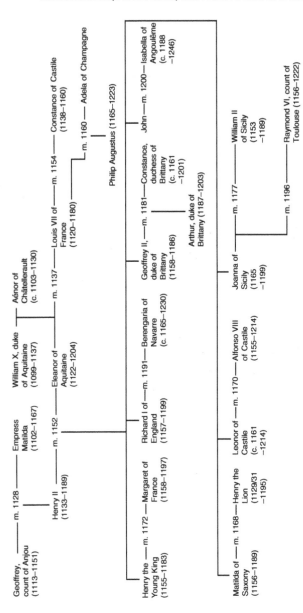

FIGURE 1.2   Family tree of Richard I

as Henry II and then Richard I realised that a marital alliance with the French was unlikely to be effective in neutralising France, and marriage to one of the French king's vassals also unlikely to yield enough power against the might of the Capetians. Thus, an alliance with the Navarrese served many purposes, providing an alliance against the count of Toulouse and protection of the Plantagenets' southern borders, as well as posing an additional threat to the kingdom of France.[35]

In the reign of Philip Augustus (1180–1223), Capetian expansion threatened many of the continental borders of the Plantagenets, and this looming threat contributed to the erosion of relationships between the Plantagenet and Capetian kings. With his venture on the Third Crusade looming, Richard needed a new ally – and the king of Navarre was an ideal protector of the Plantagenets' southern borders. The Plantagenets had made alliances with some of the other Iberian kingdoms during the rule of Henry II – most notably the marriage of his daughter Eleanor, or Leonor as she was later to be known, to Alfonso VIII of Castile, in 1170, to secure the Pyrenean borders.[36] The marriage between Leonor and Alfonso was productive in terms of partnership and heirs, producing four queens and a king of the surrounding kingdoms, and like her mother, Leonor wielded significant power. However, the marriage did little to assuage the territorial disputes between the kingdoms of Western Europe, particularly from the 1200s onwards – Alfonso wished to claim Gascony, one of the Angevin territories, which had allegedly been pledged as part of Leonor's dowry, however this claim has not been conclusively supported by the primary evidence.[37] Thus Castile became engaged in conflict with the Plantagenets over Gascony. Whether Richard wished to shore up the Pyrenean borders further with his alliance with Navarre because of unease regarding the Castilian alliance, in the late 1180s, is uncertain. Cloulas has posited – and I find this argument unconvincing – that upon the marriage of Berengaria and Richard, Berengaria was to receive Gascony on a provisional basis, until Eleanor of Aquitaine's death, when Leonor would receive all the dower lands Eleanor had been apportioned, but the primary evidence does not support this.[38] Cloulas based his argument on the supposition that Henry II had promised

Leonor the region of Gascony as her dowry for her marriage to Alfonso. However, given that the dowries of Leonor's sisters had been in cash and other material goods, not in lands, and the lack of contemporary evidence, this grant of Gascony is uncertain.[39] The issue of Berengaria's dower – which provisionally included that of Gascony – only heightened tensions in the area, which is discussed more in the following chapters.

The Angevin tactics of allying with their neighbours in the hope of gaining a comrade or neutralising an enemy were widespread practices, however, like several marital alliances during this period, not all were successful in securing their political or territorial objectives. The alliance with Castile ultimately did not lead to peace with the Plantagenets, with warfare erupting over Leonor's dowry in 1204 until Alfonso ceded the claim in 1208. The links with Castile through Leonor brought strong dynastic ties and the influence of Eleanor of Aquitaine can be seen most prominently with Leonor's rulership and through Leonor's daughters, including Blanche of Castile, who is discussed in more detail in chapter five.

Although the alliance with Navarre aided Richard whilst he was on the Third Crusade, as discussed in chapter two, it did not endure for more than a generation, as Berengaria was largely forgotten upon Richard's death. John, king of England (1199–1216), equally must have viewed Navarre as a useful ally owing to their negotiations shortly after Richard's death, but the Navarrese alliance never proved successful with regards to creating a dynastic alliance with heirs produced by the union. However, Sancho VII was an invaluable ally with regards to providing military support on the Angevin borders in the early 1190s, a provision that would not have materialised were it not for the Anglo-Navarrese alliance that was initially centred upon Berengaria and Richard's marriage. Sancho's brother Fernando was also part of the negotiations for Richard's release from captivity, offering himself as a hostage in Richard's place.[40] John's renewed treaty with the Navarrese in 1201 also brought military benefits, as Sancho VII intervened in Bayonne, a southern Gascon town.[41] John's hold on any lands on the mainland was for the most part lost during his reign, with Henry III (1216–72) inheriting only the region of

Gascony, from where he launched several successive campaigns during his tenure.[42]

Within the webs of dynastic and international politics, marital alliances, and political partnerships – whether between husband and wife, monarchs, or rulers and family members – were often crucial to ensuring longevity and success. Nowhere can this be seen more clearly than with Berengaria's mother-in-law, Eleanor of Aquitaine, and her second husband, Henry II. Their union made them very powerful and saw the expansion of their domains across what is now western France and the British Isles. Eleanor and Henry's partnership was remarkable, but not rare, although the personal success of the partnership waned after the 1173–4 rebellion by Eleanor and three of their sons against Henry. However, when considering the marital alliances of their children and the benefits these alliances brought to the wider Angevin domains, these partnerships had a varying level of success. The Anglo-Navarrese alliances under Richard and John brought military support at several key moments when their lands in France were under attack. Though the Anglo-Navarrese alliances did not turn into outright continued warfare, their usefulness began to wane in the reign of John's son, Henry III, eventually leading to conflict in 1243 between the two polities. Navarre proved a useful balance of power on both sides of the Pyrenees throughout the late twelfth and early thirteenth century, sometimes allying with England during the Hundred Years War.[43] Territorial disputes continued to dominate thereafter, and the marital alliance between Richard and Berengaria demonstrated that co-ruling partnerships that were weak or unbalanced did not produce successful political unions.

Negotiations and the Journey to Marriage

Understanding Berengaria's position and outlook, we now move to the negotiations for her marriage to Richard. Negotiations for Berengaria's marriage appear to have grown apace between 1187 and 1188. For this event, the main literary source is primarily the work of the troubadour Bertran de Born (c. 1140s–c. 1215), however, the dating of his poems has been debated by historians and literary scholars. Bertran de Born was one of the major Occitan troubadours of the twelfth–thirteenth centuries and was present at the Plantagenet courts. He was also in turn involved in revolts against Henry II, Richard I, and Philip Augustus. His proximity to the royal courts meant that he had access to a vast amount of information surrounding the marriage negotiations and refusal of Alys. He was also a baron and plausibly took interest in these negotiations when looking to the future and deciding where to ally himself next. The literary nature of Bertran's works is problematic, as Bertran writes with an air of exaggeration and with the intention of fomenting discord amongst the parties of whom he writes. Bertran's discussion of the marriage of Berengaria and Richard, and the political turmoil that surrounded it, can be seen in verse 35:

> And since Philip doesn't get angry about his lands, let him think of his sister and the overproud husband who throws her back, for Richard doesn't care to have her – this crime seems distasteful to me! – and who is continually perjuring himself, for the king of Navarre has given him as a husband to his daughter, so he has the greater shame.[44]

The initial negotiations took place amongst a backdrop of hostility surrounding the Plantagenets: Richard's relationship with Philip Augustus was on the downturn, and there was also Toulousian hostility on the Aquitanian borders. Henry II was fighting a lost cause towards the end of the 1180s: the marital alliance between Henry the Young King and Margaret of France had disintegrated upon the Young King's death, and the need to keep the Capetians onside with a marital alliance did not appear likely to succeed, given Philip Augustus's constant interference in Plantagenet affairs, even with the prospect of further Anglo-French marital alliances. However, by November 1188, Richard appeared to have resolved tensions with Philip Augustus and restored the agreement to marry Philip Augustus's sister, Alys.[45] The matter of Alys raised its head again at a conference on 4 July 1189, when Henry II, Richard, and Philip Augustus met at Ballon to negotiate terms after further conflict. Henry agreed to pay Philip 20,000 marks, Alys would be granted to a guardian of Richard's choosing, and

Richard would marry her after his return from crusade, the starting date of which was fixed for Lent 1190.[46] As a final blow to Henry, his subjects were to swear allegiance to Richard, and should Henry fail to meet these terms his barons ought to transfer their loyalties to Richard and Philip. Henry died only three days later on 6 July 1189.

There is little consensus among historians regarding the definitive reason for Berengaria and Richard's marriage, although many suggestions have been put forward.[47] John Gillingham argued that the marriage proposal must be viewed in the context of insecure borders, particularly around the county of Toulouse, which were likely to become a focal point for warfare whilst Richard was away from his kingdom and continental territories on crusade.[48] Toulouse was a frequent site for conflict in the high medieval period, as the counts of Toulouse had been in dispute with the dukes of Aquitaine since the late eleventh century. More recent tension had arisen over Eleanor's claim to the county through her paternal grandmother, Philippa, countess of Toulouse.[49] Philippa's cousin's son, Count Raymond V of Toulouse, married the sister of Louis VII, king of France, Constance, between 1154 and 1156, to strengthen the Capetian-Toulousian alliance against the Angevin-Toulousian rivalry. The Plantagenets had been engaged in warfare with the counts of Toulouse since at least 1159, and with no signs of the conflict reaching a truce the need for Richard to protect his southern border proved ever crucial.[50] Disputes and conflict over the rulership of Toulouse continued well into the reign of King John. Other motivations for the marriage include the proposition that it was a love match on the part of Richard, as noted by the Norman poet Ambroise: he stated that Berengaria and Richard may have met before their marriage, although this argument has been refuted and ignores the heavy traditions of the *chansons de geste* that Ambroise employed.[51] Ambroise's description is thus:

> She was a wise maiden, a fine lady, both noble and beautiful, with no falseness or treachery in her. Her name was Berengaria; the king of Navarre was her father. He had given her to the mother of King Richard who had made great efforts

to bring her that far. Then was she called queen and the king loved her greatly. Since the time when he was count of Poitiers she had been his heart's desire.[52]

The suggestion that Eleanor instigated the marriage arrangements has also been widely circulated.[53] It is most likely that the idea of a match, from the Plantagenet perspective, was negotiated due to the need to secure the southern borders from further incursion whilst Richard was away on military matters. However, the betrothal was not so simply arranged. Richard was already engaged to Alys, the sister of Philip Augustus, king of France. One fanciful idea is that Richard repudiated Alys due to her alleged liaison with her father Henry, although it is far more likely that Richard was aware of the strategic importance of Navarre as an ally.[54] The poet Bertan de Born commented on Richard's refusal of Alys, indicating that the match between Berengaria and Richard had been arranged as early as 1188, whilst some scholars have argued that the betrothal was arranged quickly.[55] In February 1190, Richard was at La Réole, Aquitaine, for a substantial meeting of the nobility and prelates to discuss the politics of the region in preparation for his departure on the crusade, which was a prelude to the March 1190 meeting in Nonancourt, Normandy, where he distributed roles for governance in anticipation of his absence. It is possible that the Navarrese negotiating party were at the La Réole meeting, as Richard did not meet Sancho VI to confirm the marital alliance arrangements until 6 June, in Bayonne.[56] Regardless of the timing of the arrangement, Philip Augustus was very much under the impression that a marriage would take place between Richard and his sister Alys, and as such the repudiation of Alys for Berengaria is heavily commented upon by the chroniclers.[57]

Richard's accession to the throne upon Henry II's death in 1189 saw tensions arise between Richard and Philip Augustus again, along with the resurrection of war between the Plantagenets and Toulouse in 1190. With one certain and one uncertain enemy on two fronts, the Navarrese alliance again seemed the solution to protecting the southern Angevin borders whilst Richard was on the Third Crusade. Thereafter the dowry of Berengaria, the castles of Saint-Pied-de-la-Port and Rocabruna were promised to Richard by Sancho VI, with Berengaria's dower to be shortly confirmed after her marriage, as will be discussed in more detail in chapters two and three. Richard's revelation that he was to marry Berengaria rather than Alys was a major affront to Philip Augustus, with whom Richard had been a close companion of prior to the Third Crusade. Although Philip was undoubtedly a smooth political negotiator, repudiating and playing off the Plantagenets against one another when suited him, the rejection of Alys in favour of Berengaria gave Philip the political leverage he needed to break ties with Richard and encourage the other French vassals to support his conquest of the Plantagenet territories on the Continent after the Third Crusade. Neither Berengaria nor Alys would have much say in the matter: marital alliances were primarily driven by kings or other royal males, though queen mothers with strong personalities, such as Sancha of Castile and Eleanor of Aquitaine, were involved on occasion. For princesses, marriages were not often an arena of choice. The notable contemporary instance where a royal woman refused a marital alliance was that of Joanna of Sicily, who strongly rejected Richard's proposal to marry al-'Âdil, Saladin's brother, in October 1191, as reported by three Arabic chroniclers and in the Lyon *Eracles* Continuation of William of Tyr.[58]

Berengaria, at the beginning of 1191 and on the eve of her marriage to Richard, was thus in a position similar to many of her contemporaries. Being used as a political pawn in marital alliances was the fate of many princesses, but this did not mean such young women were consigned to political and personal obscurity. Raised, one can assume, with the education afforded to many other infantas, with a strong sense of self, and surrounded by examples of strong female rulers, one may have expected Berengaria to follow in the footsteps of her mother-in-law Eleanor of Aquitaine and rule effectively alongside Richard, as Eleanor had done in the first fifteen years of her partnership with Henry II. However, as the following events in her life indicated, her path was to take an entirely different turn. The poor relationship between Berengaria and her husband and mother-in-law would leave her on the political precipice, relatively isolated, and lacking either resources or an heir to bolster her position. It is to this juncture in

Berengaria's life we now arrive, on the eve of her journey across the Pyrenees with her future mother-in-law, Eleanor, and a voyage to Sicily awaiting her, in April 1191.[59]

Notes

1 For an English history of Navarre, see Rachel Bard, *Navarra, the Durable Kingdom* (Reno: University of Nevada Press, 1982); Bard, *Navarra*, 38. Other histories in Spanish include: Jamie del Burgo, *Historia de Navarra: desde la prehistoria hasta su integración en la Monarquía Española (S. XVI)* (Madrid: Ediciones Académicas, 2012); Claudio Sánchez-Albornoz, *Vascos y navarros en su primera historia* (Madrid: Ediciones del Centro, 1974).

2 Further discussion of the complexities of Leonor's dowry and Berengaria's dower takes place in chapter 2.

3 Carmen Orcástegui Gros and Angel J. Martin Duque, eds., *Garci Lópes de Roncesvalles, Crónica de Garci López de Roncevalles. Estudio y Edición Crítica.* (Pamplona: Ediciones Universidad de Navarra, 1977); Carmen Orcástegui Gros, ed., *La Cronica de los Reyes de Navarra del Príncipe de Viana. Estudios, Fuentes y Edición Critica* (Pamplona: Diputación Foral de Navarra, Institución Príncipe de Viana, 1978), 145.

4 José Moret, *Anales del reino de Navarra, compuestos por el P. José Moret. Tomo Décimo*, ed. and trans. Manuel Silvestre de Arlegui. Additions by Francisco de Alesón (Tolosa: Establecimiento tipográfico y Casa Editorial de Eusebio Lopez, 1912); Susana Herreros Lopetegui, ed. *Anales del reino de Navarra / José de Moret; edición anotada e índices dirigida* (Pamplona: Institución Príncipe de Viana, 1987).

5 Louis Cooper, ed., *El Liber Regum: estudio linguistico* (Zaragoza: Institución 'Fernando el Católico', 1960), 37. '*El rei don Sancho de Nauarra priso muller la filla del emperador de Castiella & ouo d'ella fillos,/ el rei don Sancho, el ifant don Ferrando e la reina d'AnglaTerra, e la comtesse de Campanna/ e la ifant dona Costança, qui murie en Daroca.*'

6 Rodericus Xieménius de Rada, *Rerum Hispanicarum Scriptores Aliquot, quorum nomina versa pagina indicabit*, 3 vols. (Frankfurt: Andræ Wecheli, 1579–81), 225. '*Berengariam, quæ Ricardi Regis Angliæ fuit vxor. Quo mortuo sine prole, in viduitate laudabili diu vixit, & in ciuitate Cenomannis ex donation propter nuptias quam habebat, frequentius morabatur.*'

7 Henri Chardon, *Histoire de la reine Bérengère, femme de Richard Cœur-de-Lion et dame douairière du Mans, d'après des documents inédits sur son séjour en France* (Le Mans: Monnoyer, 1866), 5, 12.

8 Julia Baldó Alcóz, 'Sancha o Baecia (1139–1179), esposa de Sancho VI el Sabio,' in *Reinas de Navarra*, ed. Julia Pavón (Madrid: Sílex Ediciones, 2014), 316.

9 If Berengaria had been born around 1160, that would have made her 70 years old at the time of her death in 1230. Ghislain Baury and Vincent Corriol, *Bérengère de Navarre (v. 1160–1230). Histoire et mémoire d'une reine d'Angleterre* (Rennes: Presses Universitaires de Rennes, 2022), 28–30.

10 Tomás Urzainqui and Juan Maria Olaizola, *La Navarra marítima* (Pamplona: Pamiela, 1998), 94.

11 For more on these queens regnant, see Elena Woodacre, *The Queens Regnant of Navarre: Succession, Politics, and Partnership, 1274–1512* (Basingstoke: Palgrave Macmillan, 2013). Other queens sometimes counted as regnant are Blanca II and Jeanne d'Albret, however Blanca II never ruled, and Jeanne's control of Navarre was tenuous.

12 The Iberian peninsula in this context consists of the kingdoms of Portugal, Galicia, Navarra, Aragon, Castile, León, and Córdoba (the latter controlled by the Islamic caliphate). For Urraca see Therese Martin, *Queen as King: Politics and Architectural Propaganda in Twelfth-Century Spain* (Leiden: Brill, 2006); for Petronilla see Anaïs Waag, 'Rulership, Authority, and Power in the Middle Ages: The Proprietary Queen as Head of Dynasty,' *Anglo-Norman Studies* 44 (2022): 71–104.

13 Miriam Shadis, 'The First Queens of Portugal and the Building of the Realm,' in *Reassessing the Roles of Women as 'Makers' of Medieval Art and Architecture. Volume Two*, ed. Therese Martin (Leiden: Brill, 2012), 678.

14 Shadis, 'The First Queens of Portugal,' 701.

15 An important biographical collection of the queens of Navarre can be found in Pavón, *Reinas de Navarra*.

16 Alcóz, 'Sancha o Baecia,' 311, 313.

17 Dawn Bratsch-Prince, 'Pawn or Player?: Violant of Bar and the Game of Matrimonial Politics in the Crown of Aragon (1380–1396),' in *Marriage and Sexuality in Medieval and Early Modern Iberia*, ed. Eukene Lacarra Lanz (London: Routledge, 2002), 63–4; John Carmi Parsons, 'Mothers, Daughters, Marriage, Power: Some Plantagenet Evidence, 1150–1500,' in *Medieval Queenship*, ed. John Carmi Parsons (Stroud: Sutton Publishing, 1993), 63–78.

18 Santos A. García Larragueta, *El Gran Priorado de Navarra de la Orden de San Juan de Jerusalen*, 2 vols. (Pamplona: Institución Príncipe de Viana/Editorial Gomez, 1957), ii, no. 54.

19 Baury and Corriol, *Bérengère*, 40.

20 Eloísa Ramírez Vaquero, Susana Herreros Lopetegui, Roberto Ciganda Elizondo, and Fermín Miranda García, eds., *El Cartulario Magno del Archivo Real y General de Navarra. Tomo III* (Pamplona: Gobierno de Navarra, 2016), no. 163.

21 My thanks go to Eloísa Ramírez Vaquero for her guidance on the early status of Monreal and the relationships between the royal family and the region; I have also been fortunate to have viewed Eloísa's early work on this which is forthcoming, and the basis of my own suggestions.

22 Ángel J. Martín Duque, ed., *Documentación medieval de Leire* (Pamplona: Diputación Foral de Navarra, Institución Príncipe de Viana, 1983), nos. 123, 144; see Luis Javier Fortún Pérez de Ciriza, ed., *Leire, un señorio monástico en Navarra (siglos IX–XIX)* (Pamplona: Gobierno de Navarra, 1993) for a full analysis and history of Leire, and Luis Javier Fortún Pérez de Ciriza, 'San Sebastián en el dominio del Monasterio de Leire (Siglo IX – 1235),' in *Congresso el Fuero de San Sebastián y su época* (San Sebastián: Sociedad de Estudios Vascos, 1982), 451–68.

23 Fortún Pérez de Ciriza, *Leire*, 73–5.

24 Lucy K. Pick, *Her Father's Daughter. Gender, Power, and Religion in the Early Spanish Kingdoms* (Ithaca: Cornell University Press, 2017), 15.

25 For more on the *infantazgo* see Therese Martin, 'Hacia una clarificación del infantazgo en tiempos de la reina Urraca y su hija la infanta Sancha (ca. 1107–1159),' *e-Spania* 5 (2008). doi: 10.4000/e-spania.12163; Martin, *Queen as King*; Therese Martin, 'Sources of Power For Queens and Infantas: The Infantazgo in the Central Middle Ages,' *Anuario de Estudios Medievales* 46.1 (2016): 97–136; Janna Bianchini, 'The Infantazgo in the Reign of Alfonso VIII,' in *King Alfonso VIII of Castile: Government, Family, and War*, eds. Miguel Dolan Gómez, Kyle Lincoln, and Damian J. Smith (New York: Fordham University Press, 2019), 59–79. Teobaldo's second marriage to Agnes of Beaujeau bore one daughter, Blanche, in 1226, however there is a dearth of evidence for Agnes or Blanche's activities in Navarre in the 1220s and early 1230s.

26 Correspondence with Eloísa Ramírez Vaquero dated 19 April 2023.

27 Eloísa Ramírez Vaquero, 'La reina ha muerto: Memoria y representación en la Navarra medieval,' in *Espacios de memoria y representación: Reinas, infantas y damas de la corte ante la muerte en las monarquías ibéricas Medievales*, eds. Ángela Muñoz and Sonia Morales (forthcoming).

28 Agustín Ubieto Arteta, 'Aportación al estudio de la "tenencia" medieval: la mujer "tenente",' in *Estudios de Edad Media de la Corona de Aragon. Volume X*, ed. José María Lacarra, (Zaragoza: Consejo Superior de Investigaciones Científicas, Escuela de Estudios Medievales, 1975) 47–61, 53.

29 Pavón, *Reinas de Navarra*.

30 John Gillingham, *Richard the Lionheart*, 2nd ed. (London: Weidenfeld and Nicholson, 1989), 57.

31 Edward A. Bond, ed., *Chronica Monasterii de Melsa, A Fundatione Usque Ad Annum 1396, Auctore Thoma de Burton, Abbate. Accedit Continuatio Ad Annum 1406 A Monacho Quodam Ipsius Domus. Volume I.* (London: Longmans, Green, Reader, and Dyer, 1866), 256.

32 Gillingham, *Richard the Lionheart*, 100.

33 Gillingham, *Richard the Lionheart*, 105.

34 Henri-François Delaborde, ed., *Recueil des Actes de Philippe Auguste Roi de France. Tome I Années du Règne I à XV (1 Novembre 1179–31 Octobre 1194)* (Paris: Imprimerie Nationale, 1916), no. 376.

35 For more on Anglo-Navarrese relationships during the early Plantagenet era, see Nicholas Vincent, 'A Forgotten War?: England and Navarre, 1243–4,' in *Thirteenth Century England XI. Proceedings of the Gregynog Conference, 2005*, eds., Björn Weiler, Janet Burton, Phillip Schofield, and Karen Stöber (Woodbridge: Boydell & Brewer, 2007), 109–46.

36 For the daughters of Henry II and Eleanor of Aquitaine, see Colette Bowie, *The Daughters of Henry II and Eleanor of Aquitaine* (Turnhout: Brepols, 2014).

37 Ivan Cloulas, 'Le douaire de Bérengère de Navarre, veuve de Richard Cœur de Lion, et sa retraite au Mans,' in *La Cour Plantagenêt (1154–1204). Actes du colloque tenu à Thouars du 30 avril au 2 mai 1999*, ed. Martin Aurell (Poitiers: Université de Poitiers, Centre d'Études Supérieures de Civilisation Médiévale, 2004), 90; Julio González, ed., *El reino de Castilla en la época de Alfonso VIII*, 3 vols. (Madrid: Escuela de Estudios Medievales, 1960), i, 188.

38 Cloulas, 'Le douaire,' 90.

39 Jose Manuel Cerda, 'La dot gasconne d'Aliénor d'Angleterre: entre royaume de Castille, royaume de France et royaume d'Angleterre,' *Cahiers de civilisation médiévale* 54 (2011): 225–42; Vincent, 'A Forgotten War?'.

40 Doris Mary Stenton, ed., *Pipe Rolls Richard I, 2ⁿᵈ to 10ᵗʰ Years*, 8 vols. (Burlington: TannerRitchie Publishing, 2015–6), v, 205, vi, 19–20. Note this reference includes the Chancellor's Roll of 1196.

41 J.-A. Brutails, ed., *Documents des archives de la chambre des comptes de Navarre (1196–1384)* (Paris, 1890), no. 3; José Maria Jimeno Jurio and Roldán Jimeno Aranguren, eds., *Archivo General de Navarra (1194–1234)* (San Sebastián: Sociedad de Estudios Vascos, 1998), no. 44.

42 David Carpenter, *Henry III. The Rise to Power and Personal Rule. 1207–1258* (London: Yale University Press, 2020), 39–40.

43 Fabia Ann Gray, 'Formal and informal contacts between the House of Navarre and the English during the fourteenth-century phase of the Hundred Years War' (PhD Thesis, University of East Anglia, 2005).

44 Bertran de Born, *The poems of the troubadour Bertran de Born*, eds. William D. Paden, Jr., Tilde Sankovitch, and Patricia H. Stäblein (Berkeley: University of California Press, 1986), no. 35, verse 5. '*E pueis per terras non torna iros/ membre'l sa sor e'l maritz ergulhos,/ qe la laissa, qe non la vol tener –/ aqest forfaitz mi sembla desplazer! –/ e tot ades qe vaia pejuran,/ qe'l reis navars l'a donat ad espos/ a sa filha, per qe l'ant'a plus gran.*'

45 See discussion of this reconciliation and the implications it had for rumours around Richard's sexuality in chapter 2.

46 Gillingham, *Richard the Lionheart*, 123.

47 For an outline of the various arguments, see John Gillingham, 'Richard I and Berengaria of Navarre,' *Historical Research* 53 (1980): 157–73.

48 Gillingham, 'Berengaria,' 167.

49 Ralph V. Turner, *Eleanor of Aquitaine* (London: Yale University Press, 2009), 61–2, 134.
50 Richard Benjamin, 'Toulouse and the Plantagenets, 1156–96,' in *Medieval Warfare, 1000–1300*, ed. John France (Abingdon: Routledge, 2006), 324.
51 Trindade, *Berengaria. In Search of Richard the Lionheart's Queen* (Dublin: Four Courts Press, 1999), 67; Gillingham, 'Berengaria,' 166.
52 Marianne Ailes and Malcolm Barber, eds. and trans., *The History of the Holy War. Ambroise's Estoire de la Guerre Sainte*, 2 vols. (Woodbridge: The Boydell Press, 2002), i, l. 1138–49, 19; ii, 47. 'Ço estoit une sage pucele/ E gentilz femme e preuz e bele, Non pas fause ne losengere;/ Si avoit a non Berengiere;/ Le rei de Navare ot a pere,/ Qui l'aveit baillé a la mere/ Li reis Richard, qui s'en pena/ Tant que jusquë la li mena. Puis fud el reïne clamee/ E li reis l'aveit multa mee/ Desque il esteit coens de Peitiers,/ La coveita sis coveitiers.' Ailes and Barber's translations.
53 Elizabeth A. R. Brown, 'Eleanor of Aquitaine: Parent, Queen, and Duchess,' in *Eleanor of Aquitaine: Patron and Politician*, ed. William W. Kibler (Austin: University of Texas Press, 1975), 20–1; Alfred Richard, *Histoire des comtes de Poitou, 778–1204*, 6 vols. (Pau: Princi Negue, 1903, 2005), vi, 28.
54 Trindade, *Berengaria*, 79.
55 Bertran de Born, *The Poems of the Troubadour Bertran de Born*, 376.
56 Frédéric Boutoulle, 'Richard Cœur de Lion à Bayonne et dans le Labourd,' *Annales du Midi* 123.275 (2011): 339.
57 Paul Webster, ed., and Janet Shirley, trans., *The History of the Dukes of Normandy and the Kings of England by the Anonymous of Béthune* (Abingdon: Routledge, 2021), 99.
58 For more discussion on this event, see Martin Aurell, 'Joan of England and al-'Âdil's Harem: The Impossible Marriage between Christians and Muslims (Eleventh–Twelfth Centuries),' *Anglo-Norman Studies* 43 (2021): 1–14; Peter W. Edbury, ed. and trans., 'The Old French Continuation of William of Tyr,' in *The Conquest of Jerusalem and the Third Crusade. Sources in Translation* (London: Routledge, 1999), 120.
59 *The Chronicle of Richard of Devizes of the Time of King Richard the First*, ed. and trans. John T. Appleby (London: Thomas Nelson and Sons, 1963), 25; *The Annals of Roger de Hoveden Comprising the History of England and of Other Countries of Europe from A.D. 732 to A.D. 1201*, ed. and trans. Henry Thomas Riley, 2 vols. (London: H. G. Bohn, 1853), ii, 193, 196; *Roger of Wendover's Flowers of History Comprising The History of England from the Descent of the Saxons to A. D. 1235, Formerly Ascribed to Matthew Paris*, ed. and trans. John Allen Giles, 2 vols. (London: George Bell & Sons, 1892), ii, 95.

QUEEN

To the Holy Land and Plantagenet Country

Berengaria's arrival in Sicily in the spring of 1191 brought her to new horizons. She was about to meet her future husband, and from Sicily they would take the often-perilous journey to the Holy Land for the Third Crusade. The marriage of Berengaria to Richard I has formed a focal point for most historians of the Plantagenet domains, in part due to its significance for Western European politics in the 1190s, but also due to a lack of consensus regarding the origins of the betrothal. This chapter discusses Berengaria's use of titles throughout her time as consort and dowager, as this lays the foundation for discussions throughout the rest of the text. It then moves to outline the context and alliance between England and Navarre from the Plantagenet perspective in the lead-up to Berengaria and Richard's marriage, as well as a wider examination of co-rulership and queenly authority in the twelfth and thirteenth centuries. It will then look at her tenure, including her position as a childless queen and how this could have negatively affected Berengaria's access to power. As we shall see, a queen without resources and children had to turn to other avenues to access and exercise power.

Plans for Marriage

Of Berengaria's travels to Sicily, we only know a rough itinerary with her future mother-in-law, Eleanor of Aquitaine; it seems unlikely that any great companionship was created between the pair in light of Eleanor's domination of rulership and later events.

DOI: 10.4324/9781003223306-3

Both the sea and overland journeys were dangerous: travelling overland meant passing through enemy territory, that of the counts of Toulouse and Provence; travelling by sea was a risky undertaking owing to maritime disasters. We know that Eleanor and Berengaria travelled at least partially overland due to their presence at Lodi, near Milan, where they witnessed a charter of the Holy Roman Emperor Henry VI.[1] The presence of both women is important. This is not the only time Berengaria and Eleanor appeared together in a charter, and it indicates Berengaria's introduction on to the international and diplomatic stage alongside her future mother-in-law. The occasion was a key opportunity for Berengaria to show herself and import her status more widely, and transform herself from an unknown Navarrese princess to a more central figure in Western European politics. It was also a moment where Berengaria and Eleanor could more widely indicate what their political partnership may have been like, whether they worked together or remained wholly independent figures. Berengaria immediately found herself in the midst of political tensions at the imperial court: Eleanor's daughter, Matilda, had been married to Henry the Lion, duke of Saxony, until her death in 1189. The Welf dynasty, of which Henry the Lion was part, had long been a rival to the now ruling Hohenstaufen dynasty, to which Henry VI belonged. Emperor Henry VI had his eye on further imperial expansion, particularly the conquest of Sicily which had a history of being a contested polity. Henry's claim to Sicily came through his marriage to Constance, daughter of Roger II, king of Sicily, and aunt of William II, king of Sicily and husband to Joanna of Sicily, Richard's sister. William's death on 11 November 1189 had thrown the rulership of the island into dispute, with Henry and Constance, and Tancred, pressing claims to rule. At the time of Berengaria's journey to Sicily, Constance had been imprisoned since September 1190, having been captured by her illegitimate nephew, Tancred. Thus, Richard's arrival in Sicily with a large army, en route to the Holy Land, was a cause for concern. Gillingham notes Richard was also keen to collect the substantial bequest granted by William II to Henry II of money, gold plate, and war galleys in order to finance a crusading expedition.[2] As Henry's heir, Richard viewed the testament as valid despite Henry's death four months prior to William's. The meeting between Eleanor, Berengaria, and Henry VI was likely intended to assuage any political tensions and arrange an agreement of non-enmity between the Plantagenets and Hohenstaufens, and to ensure political stability whilst Richard was on crusade.

The interactions between Eleanor and Berengaria as they travelled to Messina, Sicily are unknown. Eleanor's primary concerns were probably the survival of the Plantagenet dynasty and the smooth governance of the realms, rather than extolling further affection for another royal daughter-in-law. Although Eleanor was undoubtedly close to her own daughters from surviving evidence, primarily in the form of letters and the continuance of familial traditions, evidence of affection towards any of her daughters-in-law does not survive. Although Eleanor appears to have been affectionate with her children, like her mother-in-law, the Empress Matilda, and other royal women of the period, her day-to-day responsibilities focused on political events and aspects of governance rather than solely childcare. Royal children were often raised with their own households and tutors.[3] It has been argued that Richard was Eleanor's favourite son: indeed, her desire to have Richard inherit Aquitaine caused much disruption and antagonism between the four Plantagenet sons, Eleanor, and her husband, Henry II. After Richard's enthronement as duke of Aquitaine and count of Poitou in 1170, two-thirds of the acts issued by Eleanor from this point until 1174 associated Richard with herself, as 'I and Richard my son.'[4] Regardless of any undue favouritism, Eleanor was a determined woman who worked continuously to ensure her sons succeeded to the throne and ruled.

Eleanor's actions during the reigns of Richard I and John cast Berengaria and her sisters-in-law, Isabella of Gloucester and Isabella of Angoulême, to the sidelines. Eleanor's immediate concerns were with her own power and that of her children: her true feelings to Berengaria are unknown, and it is difficult to surmise whether she may have viewed Berengaria with some suspicion as a potential threat to her power or was welcoming towards her. Eleanor's escort of Berengaria may suggest she gave her approval to the match as it was unlikely she did so under duress. Whether their relationship was initially harmonious or not, what is evident is that Eleanor's influence and position held dominance through-out Berengaria's reign. Eleanor's strong relationship with Richard was to have a significant impact on Berengaria, and Berengaria's ability to rule as queen consort.

The *Itinerarium Peregrinorum et Gesta Regis Ricardi* recorded Berengaria and Eleanor's journey to Reggio, Italy, and then Be-rengaria's journey onwards to Sicily and Cyprus.[5] The second part of the *Itinerarium*, often referred to as IP2, was probably authored by Richard de Templo, prior of the Augustinian priory of Holy Trinity, London, and composed between 1217–22. Be-rengaria's arrival is also recorded in the thirteenth-century Castil-ian chronicle *Gran Conquista de Ultramar*, though with several inaccuracies on the circumstances surrounding her arrival, draw-ing upon the literary traditions of the *chansons de geste* which is known for its flair.[6] Richard I had established a court in Sicily en route to the Third Crusade, stopping to ensure the protection and restitution of the dower rights of his sister, Joanna, the queen of Sicily who had been widowed in 1189 and deprived of her lands and revenues by the new king, Tancred. Richard's campaign in Sicily did little to gain support for his endeavours, though Tan-cred eventually ceded to Richard's demands. After Berengaria had been safely delivered, Eleanor returned to England, with the royal court making progress to Cyprus. On their journey to Cyprus, Berengaria and her soon-to-be sister-in-law, Joanna, having been sent to travel in the first line of ships by Richard and thus travel-ling in different vessels from Richard and the army, were ship-wrecked. Richard made landfall at Crete, but the two women fell into the sphere of Isaac Comnenus, the tyrannical ruler of Cyprus. Isaac attempted to seize Berengaria and Joanna and take them hostage.[7] The author of the *Itinerarium Peregrinorum* wrote,

On the day after his arrival the emperor sent a message to the queens couched in amicable but fraudulent words. He in-formed them that they could come ashore safely, and by his unconditional decision they could be assured of suffering no trouble or difficulty from any of his people. They refused … On the third day, a Sunday, he again tried to get round the queens and seduce them with flattery and deceit.[8]

The queens were defiant and prevaricated to evade capture:

> The queens were in a tight spot. They began to waver, anxious
> that if they submitted to the emperor's persuasions they would
> be taken captive. On the other hand, they were afraid that he
> would attack them if they persisted in their refusals – they had
> not yet been informed of the king's [Richard's] arrival and the
> success of the royal fleet. In order to hold the emperor off for a
> while they gave a noncommittal reply, assuring him that they
> would disembark on the following day and entrust themselves
> to the emperor's judgement. On the basis of this promise the
> emperor held back.[9]

The chronicler Roger of Howden, a twelfth-century English historian who was in service at the courts of Henry II and Richard,
and accompanied Richard on the Third Crusade until the departure of Philip Augustus, presents a different perspective of this
episode, stating that the queens were simply forced to wait in
the harbour for rescue.[10] This incident demonstrates the political astuteness and the agency of both women, as they managed
to avoid falling into Isaac's clutches until Richard and his forces
arrived. Richard de Templo ascribed agency to Joanna and Berengaria, who acted in their own interests and exercised political
and diplomatic agency when negotiating for their release: they
were not simply depicted as damsels in distress awaiting rescue by
Richard. Isaac's rule in the eyes of many Latin – and some of the
Greek – chroniclers was despotic and violent, with the inhabit-
ants of Cyprus suffering much under his reign.[11] After Richard
captured Isaac, Isaac was imprisoned, and Richard quickly sold
the island to the Knights Templar.

Marriage, Cyprus, and a New Era

Once the situation was resolved and Berengaria had safely reached
Limassol on Cyprus, she and Joanna were initially lodged in the
town where 'they relaxed in peace and security.'[12] Berengaria and
Richard were married at St George's Chapel on 12 May 1191.[13]
Described by the author of the *Itinerarium Peregrinorum* as a

lady of 'graceful manner and high birth' and as 'very wise and of good character,' Berengaria's attributes as a bride are made clear.[14] Interestingly the characteristic of wisdom was typically attributed to men and therefore this unusual compliment shows Berengaria's importance as a queen consort as well as the wider political advantages of the match. Shortly after the marriage ceremony, Berengaria was crowned queen of England by the bishop of Evreux, who was assisted by the archbishops of Apamea and Auxienne and the bishop of Bayonne, ecclesiastical travellers accompanying Richard as part of his court.[15] Coronation was a significant ritual for various reasons, not least the literal and symbolic power and authority it granted. For Berengaria, her coronation was the only connection she had to England and her subjects as their symbolic figurehead. The reality of the situation was that Berengaria's mother-in-law, Eleanor, continued to hold the status and powers of queen, as she had before her imprisonment, despite being queen dowager. Though this situation was not uncommon, the king would be required to make suitable provisions for both the queen consort and queen dowager and agree an arrangement which would allow the queen consort to exercise rulership accordingly. By choosing to crown Berengaria in Cyprus rather than England, Richard could quickly grant Berengaria symbolic power as queen consort, as well as secure the Anglo-Navarrese alliance, which Richard needed to maintain security around the Plantagenet borders whilst on crusade. This symbolic power did not turn into actual power for Berengaria, as the coronation ceremony, far from her English and many of her Plantagenet subjects, did little to acknowledge her position as a visible queen of the English.

Once their marriage ceremony had taken place, Richard confirmed Berengaria's dower grant, sealed by Philip of Poitou, and in so doing established her position as queen consort.[16] Dower in England during this period was land and property granted to queens for personal use during their lifetime, not just their widowhood as would later become the case. For noblewomen and below, and as was the case in Western Europe, dower was a widow's share of her dead husband's estates. Richard was faced with a delicate situation in which Eleanor was entitled to dower lands as queen dowager, but he also needed to provide for his new wife, a not altogether unusual situation amongst the nobility. Eleanor did not appear willing to return and solely rule Aquitaine without access to her dower, reluctant to limit herself and her energies as duchess whilst Richard ruled.[17] The granting of dower by the king during a consort's tenure is evidence that the king expected the queen to establish her power base through controlling and administering her own lands, which would enable her to create networks and grant patronage. However, Berengaria's dower situation was not only complicated by her rivalry with Eleanor for control of these particular lands, but also with a potential claim from her sister-in-law, Leonor. This left Berengaria's initial dower agreement as provisional until Eleanor's death. Unfortunately for Berengaria, Eleanor was to outlive Richard – she lived into the reign of a third Angevin queen consort, Isabella of Angoulême, heightening the competition between the three queens for access to dower.

Dower was typically granted to women at the time of their marriage, and ought to have encompassed a third of their husband's lands unless assigned less at the church door. The situation with queens was quite different from that of noblewomen. The timing of the grant was not always at the date of marriage, and the value and size of the grant varied considerably.[18] Dower was an instrumental part of queenly revenues and finances, and if a consort did not have access to familial lands or inheritance, dower constituted a major part of their income. Although the queens of England had some consistency in the lands they received, at least with regards to area if not value, no dower grant was exactly the same.[19] The lands that constituted a queen's dower remained at the king's disposal, even though they were apportioned to the consort. This became much more apparent after 1200, when the kings of England regularly granted land away to top up the royal coffers or create alliances, but this was not solely the preserve of men – Berengaria's mother-in-law, Eleanor, also granted away lands from her dower which were meant to be preserved for Berengaria.[20] Dower was an important stream of income, and this was even more the case for Berengaria who did not have other resources as an heiress, or networks to depend upon for power.

Berengaria's dower arrangements have previously been out-lined by Ivan Cloulas, who noted that Berengaria was to receive all that had belonged to Eleanor, which consisted of Domfront, Falaise, and Bonneville-sur-Tocques in Normandy, two towns and castles in Touraine, Château-du-Loir in Maine, the castle and land of Mervent, Januay, and Oléron in Poitou, as well as several manors and castles in England.[21] The 1191 grant was wit-nessed by the archbishop of York, Garnerio of Napoli, magis-trate of the Knights Hospitallers, Andreas of Chaliron, Geoffrey of Perche, and Robert of Sablé, Sablé being an area within the diocese of Le Mans.[22] Nearly all of these men would retain con-nections with Berengaria throughout her life, appearing in later charters or connections with the queen. There is no evidence that Berengaria administered her dower lands whilst queen, and there is evidence to support Eleanor retaining income from them dur-ing Richard's reign.[23] In this situation, with her dower lands being contested or held by her mother-in-law, Eleanor, and sister-in-law, Leonor, Berengaria had no opportunity to administer her lands, establish networks, and exert queenly agency, or collect revenues. Berengaria's lack of access to her dower lands as queen consort impacted not only her power, but also public perceptions of her activity as a consort because she was not involved in political or diplomatic activities in England nor acted as a patron. Even as a dowager queen herself after 1199, Berengaria was still unsuccess-ful in accessing her dower lands, as will be discussed below.

Reign: Expectations and Reality

After their marriage ceremony on 12 May 1191, Richard wasted little time in progressing with the crusade, departing on 5 June after the sale of Cyprus to the Knights Templar, with Berengaria, Joanna, and the unnamed daughter of Isaac Comnenus having left Cyprus on 1 June 1191.[24] Richard and his entourage landed in Acre on 8 June, and the Anglo-French forces were instrumental in the successful capture of the city, which was surrendered to the crusaders shortly after Richard's arrival. An alliance between Richard I and Guy de Lusignan, husband of the former queen of Jerusalem, Sibylla, led to Richard's sale of Cyprus to Guy after the Templars returned it in April 1192.[25] From the histories of Pierre Langtoft (d. c. 1305) and Roger of Howden (d. 1201), we know that the three women remained together in Acre at the main camp, undoubtedly with as much comfort as a besieging force could provide. The *Itinerarium Peregrinorum* also records Berengaria and Joanna's entrance to Acre:

> In addition the king of France had the Templars' noble palace and all that went with it for his share, while King Richard had the royal palace in which he placed his queens with their girls and maids.[26]

The first two parts of Langtoft's history are drawn from a number of earlier sources, some of which are unknown, as well as some of his own additions in the third part of the history. It is plausible that the three women then joined Richard at the royal palace in northern Acre from 21 August after the city had been captured and left in the care of Bertram de Verdun.[27] The presence of women on crusade was nothing unusual at this stage: previous queens and noblewomen had accompanied their kings and husbands, notably as seen with Eleanor of Aquitaine during the Second Crusade. Other women worked in the camps as washerwomen, cooks, or prostitutes, amongst other professions. Without a distinctive itinerary for Berengaria, it is difficult to conclusively state that she was alongside Richard for all his military endeavours – indeed much of the time it would have been unsafe for the queens to have been so close to the action. The author of the *Itinerarium Peregrinorum* records Berengaria and Joanna's progress to the bustling port of Jaffa at the end of September 1191.[28] Much like Acre, the port of Jaffa was a melting pot of communities and goods, with markets selling products from across Europe and Asia, including indigo, glass, and local perfumes.[29] Berengaria's presence at the Christmas celebrations at Toron des Chevaliers, in the lordship of Toron, part of the kingdom of Jerusalem's fiefs, in December 1191 was marked by Roger of Howden, placing her on the boundaries of the holy city.[30]

The roles of queens and noblewomen, such as Berengaria and Joanna, whilst on the Third Crusade is traditionally thought to

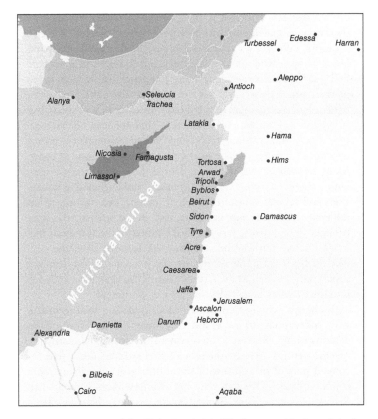

FIGURE 2.1   Map of the Holy Land. Modified map, with the original
material © ExploreTheMed.

have been that of wives and mothers, however we can clearly
see political participation and leadership by a number of women,
such as Eleanor of Aquitaine, Eleanor of Castile, and Marguerite
of Provence. Likewise, the many queens regnant of Jerusalem including Sibylla, Isabella I, Maria, and Isabella II demonstrated
that women did wield power, even when the records did not note
this in as much detail as they often did for kings regnant. The
twelfth and thirteenth centuries are a period where we can see
royal and noblewomen participating in the crusades and ruling

crusader states, and this is the context in which Berengaria's own time as queen ought to be seen. In comparison to the two Eleanors, Berengaria's activities as a queen on crusade are sparse but not uneventful, as seen with her and Joanna's near capture by Isaac Comnenus. Berengaria and Joanna plausibly spent much of their time in the royal palaces in Acre and Jaffa, and given neither had a contingent to merit their presence in war councils it is difficult to estimate how much time they spent in official matters of governance: though this is not to underestimate the power of female influence outside of the political mechanisms of court. Many of their days may have mirrored those of Western courts, with time spent sewing, reading, gaming, and engaging in discussions and debates, albeit in a different setting. Jaffa was somewhat different from Acre: supplies abounded, as did women who were brought in to provide services to the army, but it was nevertheless an active fortification and thus not isolated from the conflict. Such residences for Berengaria and Joanna plausibly brought some comforts, and as the Crusade continued they ultimately fell into the rhythms of daily life in a new environment.

Richard's activities on the Third Crusade are well-recorded, with the capture of Acre and the battles of Arsuf and Jaffa demonstrating Richard's involvement in front-line activities. Twelfth-century Acre by the time of Richard's residence had become a port of pleasure, with sinful indulgence becoming more commonplace.[31] One can only imagine how Acre compared to Berengaria's experiences at the Navarrese court: the camps were often sites of sickness, with an epidemic having struck the crusaders' camp in 1190 from which Sibylla, queen of Jerusalem, died. The mixture of warfare and illness on campaign contrasted with the boisterous and lively intermingling of the multifaith and multicultural communities that resided across the crusader states and was certainly a change from the Navarrese courts of Berengaria's youth. The Third Crusade was plausibly not Berengaria's first experience with Jews and Muslims (themselves split into Mozarabs and Mudejares), with both faiths having concentrated populations in Navarrese society.

With continued political and military activity for their two years in the Holy Land, it is perhaps unsurprising that Berengaria features little in the historical narrative of the crusades. Berengaria does not appear to have been an active diplomat, negotiator, or leader, like some of her queenly predecessors and contemporaries, but was plausibly involved in running her household away from the fighting and looking to the care of the unnamed Byzantine princess. Her contemporaries also suffered from a lack of visibility in the historical record and male interference in their political activities. As seen with Isabella I of Jerusalem, both Richard and Philip Augustus had input into who married Isabella. The succession dispute in Jerusalem was between the previous queen Sibylla's consort, Guy de Lusignan, Isabella's first husband, Humphrey of Toron, and Conrad of Montferrat. Richard I allegedly opted for Conrad due to his popularity amongst the army, and placated Guy with Cyprus, however, Conrad's popularity quickly waned amongst the nobility and he was scathingly criticised by Latin and Arab chroniclers alike.[32] Their involvement with marital alliances across Europe demonstrates the importance of controlling the marriages of heiresses and queens in particular, as these women affected the control of resources and policies on a national and sometimes international scale. Berengaria was but one of another political pawns on the Western European marriage market and both royal and noblewomen were fortunate if the match was personally successful and they were afforded the affection, status, and resources to prosper.

Evidence for Berengaria's reign is sparse besides her appearances in chronicle narratives, but her activity is attested in a letter that confirms how she and Joanna of Sicily witnessed a loan granted in Rome on their return journey from the Holy Land in 1193. Berengaria and Joanna left Acre on 29 September, and they were once again joined on their travels by the unnamed daughter of Isaac Comemnus. Berengaria and Joanna travelled independently from Richard en route to Italy. According to the anonymous of Béthune, they took separate routes because scouts from the king of France were watching for Richard's arrival. Unlike the women, Richard took to sea once more, and was then shipwrecked between Venice and Aquileia.[33] Richard and his party were then forced to take the dangerous land route through central Europe, and Richard was captured shortly before Christmas 1192 near Vienna by Leopold of Austria, who accused Richard of arranging the murder of his cousin Conrad of Montferrat, Isabella I's second husband. Richard was held prisoner at Dürnstein Castle, Austria, and Leopold was excommunicated for his detention of a crusader. On 28 March 1193, Richard was brought to Speyer as part of an exchange, and handed to the Holy Roman Emperor Henry VI, who imprisoned him at Trifels Castle, angered by the Plantagenets' support of Henry the Lion. Henry VI demanded a ransom for Richard's release, and against this backdrop it is unsurprising that Berengaria remained in Rome, plausibly both for protection and to intercede on Richard's behalf.

The letter witnessed by Berengaria and her sister-in-law explained how a loan of 150 marks was made by Roman citizens to Adam, son of Adam of Taleworth, and John de Tolosa, canon of Hereford. The letter also implies that the women persuaded the Bishop of Porto to stand as surety for the loan, a clear sign of Berengaria's influence with senior ecclesiastical figures outside of her domains as a Plantagenet queen.[34] It is worth noting that the title used to refer to Berengaria indicates her importance in terms of corporate rulership: she is listed as 'queen of the English, duchess of the Normans and Aquitanians, countess of the Angevins.' This is also evidence that she considered herself to have been fully established as queen of England and was recognised as such in the eyes of her contemporaries.[35] Berengaria's position as the first witness in this charter, ahead of Joanna, demonstrates her position as one of the most pre-eminent women of the Plantagenet realms. Conversely, her appearance further down the witness list in later charters demonstrates the superiority of Eleanor, her mother-in-law, over Berengaria during their dowager periods, even if Berengaria's presence in such documents still evidences her status as queen even after Richard's death.

The 1193 charter contains some ambiguity with regards to how the bishop of Porto was persuaded to stand as surety, although both Adam and John are recorded as having appointed the bishop as a guarantor 'at the prayer and witness of us [both queens].'[36] Ensuring the involvement of the bishop in the procurement of the loan may be viewed as an example of Berengaria's effective queenly diplomacy and intercession. There are no known connections between Berengaria and Richard and the canon of Hereford, although there was a longstanding relationship between the Plantagenets and the bishops of Hereford, including Richard FitzNeal and his father, Nigel. This link between Hereford and the Plantagenet royal family may be why Berengaria witnessed and was involved with the transaction. Berengaria represented the Crown here, acting in her official capacity as queen consort. This is the only evidence we have for her acting as a royal official during her tenure, so it is especially significant since it shows Berengaria's awareness of her royal duties, and her abilities: she enacts and carries out royal powers on the international scene.

Of the other witnesses listed in the charter, five are named as companions of the king of England. Walter de Coutances, archbishop of Rouen, and the co-justiciars of England are also listed in order to compel the sureties to pay the loan in the event Adam and John were unable to do so, or in the last resort to pay the money back from the royal treasury.[37] Walter had travelled with Richard to Sicily and remained with him until April 1191, when Richard dispatched Coutances back to England to settle disputes. Coutances became justiciar after the exile of William Longchamp and was thus in a pre-eminent position in England and well-placed to join Berengaria as another representative of the English Crown. The close links to the English Crown and royal finances, in addition to the prominence of Adam and John in Richard's court, can indicate why Berengaria was involved in this confirmation, as she had no other known links to the sureties or Adam or John. This is the only known instance of her standing in the capacity of the English Crown and is plausibly due to the convenience of her six-month stay in Rome during her journey to the Plantagenet domains.[38]

It is plausible that Berengaria would have used her time in Rome to persuade the papacy to send assistance to Richard who, as discussed in the next section, had been captured upon his return from the Third Crusade: how effective any requests were is unknown, though we know that her mother-in-law Eleanor also petitioned Celestine III (1191–8) for aid. From Rome, Celestine provided an escort for Berengaria, Joanna, and the unnamed princess to journey onwards to Pisa.[39] Thereafter we can only surmise the itinerary of their return journey, plausibly overland but along the coast and avoiding the imperial territories where possible until her arrival in France.

Return from Crusade

Where Berengaria resided upon her return from the crusade is difficult to ascertain. She came back to the Plantagenet domains via a different route to her husband, and thus avoided capture since she did not cross enemy lands. At this juncture it is possible that she remained in the Angevin heartlands, possibly at Chinon, Saumur, or Beaufort-en-Vallée as Ann Trindade has suggested, though there is no evidence to prove her residence in any of these places conclusively.[40] Similarly Baury and Corriol have discussed the likelihood of the three castles as one of her primary residences, though without a definitive answer.[41] Given that her sister did not arrive at the Champenois court until 1199 it is unlikely that Berengaria lived there during her consort period.

We do not know with any certainty whether Berengaria and Richard met again after Richard's return from the Third Crusade. Roger of Howden reported that after Richard was remonstrated with by a hermit for his sins in 1195, Berengaria and Richard were reunited after their separation due to Richard's travels and capture on his return from the Third Crusade.[42]

> For on that day, the Lord scourged him with a severe attack of illness, so that, calling religious men before him, he was not ashamed to confess the guiltiness of his life, and, after receiving absolution, he took back his wife, whom for a long time he had not known: and, putting away all illicit intercourse, he remained constant to his wife, and they two became one flesh, and the Lord gave him health both of body and soul.[43]

Howden's account is useful as it is often an eyewitness or near eyewitness account, however, as with many medieval chroniclers, his religious background is influential when it comes to matters of sin and misdeeds. The telling of the hermit's remonstration appears to be a golden opportunity for the chronicler Roger of Howden and the hagiographer Adam of Eynsham to flagellate Richard for his sexual excesses prior to his reunion with Berengaria, though the finer details of the story are difficult to ascertain. Richard's reputation in the eyes of his contemporaries was one indulgent of sexual excess: whether Berengaria was as stoic as Eleanor when it came to extramarital affairs is unclear, but it would certainly bring further pressure on Berengaria for 'failing' to entice Richard and beget an heir. Due to the fact we know little of Berengaria's location during the second half of Richard's reign, and we know that Richard was engaged in military affairs, predominantly in Normandy, during this period, it does seem unlikely that a reconciliation between Berengaria and Richard took place. Richard was far more concerned with military matters than with rulership and marital affairs, and nor did he care how others viewed him and his piety. As such, the remonstration that characterises Adam's and Roger's accounts casts doubt on the authenticity of the events.

Upon his return from crusade, Richard was crowned for a second time at Winchester Cathedral on 17 April 1194. This was a prime opportunity for Richard to introduce Berengaria to her English subjects, and to reinforce her authority and power as queen consort after her coronation in Cyprus in 1191. However, Richard instead chose to have his mother Eleanor at his side. Berengaria's absence may have been due to the short amount of time between the organisation of the coronation and the actual ceremony, which was insufficient for her to reach Winchester on time.[44] Yet, given that Richard had a significant amount of trust in Eleanor to co-rule with him and act as a regent in his stead, it is far more plausible that he chose to have Eleanor at his coronation to highlight her importance, not only in the governance of England but also the wider Plantagenet territories, and to confirm her position as his co-ruler. This public acknowledgement of Eleanor's status is particularly significant given Richard's departure for the Continent shortly after his return. The coronation was doubly significant for Richard since it also heralded his own reassumption of power, reinforcing the royal authority he had plausibly lost when he was captured.

Undoubtedly, Berengaria's absence from Richard's second coronation and the lack of public coronation for her in England negatively impacted her ability to exercise power as a consort. Berengaria's position was weakened further by Eleanor's position as Richard's co-ruler, and Eleanor's continued access to queenly revenues. That Berengaria and Richard's marriage produced no heirs, and their lack of personal affinity for one another, as discussed in the following section, also disadvantaged her. These circumstances meant that Berengaria had little opportunity to establish her own networks and power base, unlike many of her queenly predecessors. The evidence from the English Pipe Rolls states that she received sporadic annual income, as well as lists her debts, from the counties of Devon and Surrey from 1196 to 1204, although there is no indication that she collected the queen's gold or any other revenues she may have been owed as queen of England or duchess of Normandy, with these instead being collected by Eleanor.[45] Two payments from 1195, one for Berengaria's clothes amounting to 30 pounds in the Pipe Rolls, and another for messengers to the queen who travelled between Normandy and Argentan, indicate that Richard was contributing somewhat to her upkeep.[46] In 1196, Richard allotted 200 marks from the purchase of tin in Devon to one Puntius Arnald, in payment of a debt owed by Berengaria: the roll records that she owed the money and therefore this allotted sum was not a gift.[47] Berengaria's partial payment of the 200 marks is recorded in the following three years, with the debt having accrued interest.[48] Berengaria received 20 shillings from land formerly belonging to Postelli, in Surrey, for several years, however, she also regularly owed 10 shillings.[49] In 1204, this income was reduced to 5 shillings to be received in one quarter of the year, with Isabella to receive 15 shillings from the same lands for the other three-quarters of the year, and she still owed 10 shillings.[50] This low income, sporadic as it was, likely enabled Berengaria's household and livelihood, however, there is no evidence for her granting land and revenues to institutions or individuals as patronage, or for her administration of lands in Devon and Surrey.

As noted above, one of the most significant reasons for Berengaria's lack of power was that she and Richard did not produce an heir. Their alliance may have been viewed as politically successful because of her brother Sancho's defence of the Angevin borders against Toulousian and French conquest whilst Richard was on crusade. However, by 1196 the peace treaty made between Richard and Raymond VI, count of Toulouse, including the marriage of Joanna of Sicily to Raymond, nullified the political value of an Anglo-Navarrese alliance, and with a lack of heir from Berengaria perhaps its personal value as well.[51] Furthermore, the same year, a payment of 100 marks and 100 shillings was made to 'Fernando, son of the king of Navarre,' where he had been held hostage for Richard's release (note the transcription error here, as Fernando was Berengaria's brother, not nephew).[52] Lastly, as discussed in chapter five, Sancho VII had also been slow in granting Berengaria's dowry to Richard. The Anglo-Navarrese alliance otherwise was not personally or politically successful for the couple themselves, with no compelling evidence of a personal connection between the pair. Due to a lack of heirs being produced, Berengaria's position as queen consort can be viewed as ultimately unsuccessful in historical memory as she did not fulfil one of the primary roles of a queen, that of bearing an (preferably male) heir to continue the dynasty. The lack of heir between Berengaria and Richard in turn led to John's succession and his largely unsuccessful reign may have been averted had a son been produced and survived to adulthood. The production of an heir was a fundamental part of being queen consort, however, the blame cannot be entirely apportioned to Berengaria. Richard appears to have spent little time with her and showed no inclination to do so to enable an heir to be conceived. Richard's itinerary and the chronicles are indicative that Richard instead showed more interest in campaigning and foreign affairs, with no reports of Berengaria appearing alongside him after their respective returns from the Third Crusade. Whether this was because Richard believed he had more time to arrange the reproduction of an heir – Eleanor pressed Richard at several points to name an heir in case of military misadventure – the lack of heir did Berengaria's political career no favours, which was already suffering from the effects of a poor marital relationship, a successful mother-in-law, and a lack of resources from which to exercise any power and authority.

As is evident from the discussion so far, during her time as queen consort, Berengaria was neglected by both her marital and natal family, in particular by the kinsmen who ought to have been her partners and protectors. The 1193 charter mentioned above at least indicates that, given the opportunity, Berengaria was able to exercise aspects of queenly power and perform royal duties. That Richard did not provide Berengaria with the opportunity to be regent in the Plantagenet domains may be understandable due to her lack of previous experience as a consort or ruler, however there were several opportunities where Richard could have provided Berengaria with revenues or administration in order to gain experience and act as a co-ruler later in his reign. Thus, Berengaria's experience of co-rulership was markedly different to her Angevin predecessors, the Empress Matilda and Eleanor of Aquitaine. Berengaria was also younger than her predecessor when she became queen consort of England: assuming a birth date of c. 1165, she was twenty-six in comparison with Eleanor, who was thirty when she became queen of England (though she had become queen of France at the age of fifteen) and had a wealth of previous experience behind her which placed her in a better position to rule. Berengaria's younger age – and she was younger than her husband – may have further contributed to her political inactivity.

Berengaria's most likely residence upon her return from the Holy Land is within Anjou, perhaps Beaufort-en-Vallée or Chinon, however, Howden only listed Berengaria's journey to Poitou.[53] The English writer Adam of Eynsham recorded that he travelled to Beaufort-en-Vallée to comfort Berengaria upon Richard's death, but this is not conclusive evidence that Berengaria resided there for the entire duration of her time as queen consort after returning to Western Europe.[54] At all times where one would expect to find Berengaria during Richard's reign, Eleanor was there: receiving revenues, standing side by side at Richard's second coronation, negotiating with the nobility and the church. It is little surprise that Berengaria has been largely lost from historical memory of the Plantagenet period.

Ignored, politically and personally, Berengaria's position on Richard's deathbed was precarious. Seemingly isolated from her natal family and unable to construct any networks or alliances within the Plantagenet realms, this could easily have been the moment that Berengaria vanished from the historical record. But she did not disappear. Berengaria did not have had the same opportunities to co-rule and bear children as Eleanor, or other queenly predecessors both in France and England. However, Berengaria's experience of co-rulership was part of a wider pattern of approaches to co-rulership undertaken by the Plantagenets. Once a widow, Berengaria had a significant chance to take a role on the Anglo-French political scene, rather than disappear into obscurity. And seize the opportunity she did.

Notes

1 Bettina Pferschy-Maleczek and Heinrich Appelt, eds., *Die Urkunden Heinrichs VI. für deutsche, französische und italienische Empfänger. Monumenta Germanie Historica* (online edition, 2020), no. 116.

2 John Gillingham, *Richard the Lionheart*, 2ⁿᵈ ed. (London: Weidenfeld and Nicholson, 1989), 151.

3 See Charles Beem,'"Greatest in Her Offspring": Motherhood and the Empress Matilda,' in *Virtuous or Villainess? The Image of the Royal Mother from the Early Medieval to the Early Modern Era*, eds. Carey Fleiner and Elena Woodacre (Basingstoke: Palgrave Macmillan, 2016), 85–99. Further discussion around royal medieval motherhood can be found in Elena Woodacre and Carey Fleiner, eds., *Royal Mothers and their Ruling Children, Wielding Political Authority from Antiquity to the Early Modern Era* (Basingstoke: Palgrave Macmillan, 2015).

4 Marie Hivergneaux, 'Queen Eleanor and Aquitaine, 1137–1189,' in *Eleanor of Aquitaine: Lord and Lady*, eds. Bonnie Wheeler and John Carmi Parsons (Basingstoke: Palgrave Macmillan, 2003), 67. '*Ego et Ricardus filius meus.*'

5 *The Chronicle of the Third Crusade: The Itinerarium Peregrinorum et Gesta Regis Ricardi*, ed. and trans. Helen J. Nicholson (Abingdon: Routledge, 2016), 173. For discussions of its authorship, see *Itinerarium Peregrinorum*, 1–20.

6 Louis Cooper, ed., *La Gran Conquista de Ultramar. Edición Crítica con Introducción, Notas y Glosario*. 4 vols. (Bogotá: Imprenta Patriótica del Instituto Caro y Cuervo, 1979), iv, 11–12.

7 *The Annals of Roger de Hoveden Comprising the History of England and of Other Countries of Europe from A.D. 732 to A.D. 1201*, ed. and trans. Henry Thomas Riley, 2 vols. (London: H. G. Bohn, 1853), ii, 200; Gabrielle Storey, 'Berengaria of Navarre and Joanna of Sicily as crusading queens: Manipulation, reputation, and agency,' in *Forgotten Queens in Medieval and Early Modern Europe, Political Agency, Myth-making, and Patronage*, eds. Estelle Paranque and Valerie Schutte (Abingdon: Routledge, 2018), 48–50.

8 *Itinerarium Peregrinorum*, 182. Nicholson's translation.

9 *Itinerarium Peregrinorum*, 182. Nicholson's translation.

10 *Roger de Hoveden*, ii, 200.

11 For a full analysis of Isaac's image in the chronicles, see Savvas Neocleous, 'Imaging Isaak Komnenos of Cyprus (1184–1191) and

the Cypriots: Evidence from the Latin historiography of the Third Crusade,' *Byzantion* 83 (2013): 297–337.

12 *Itinerarium Peregrinorum*, 185. Nicholson's translation.

13 *Roger de Hoveden*, ii, 204; *Wendover*, ii, 103; Peter W. Edbury, 'The Old French Continuation of William of Tyr,' in *The Conquest of Jerusalem and the Third Crusade. Sources in Translation*, ed. Peter W. Edbury (Abingdon: Routledge, 1999), 104.

14 *Itinerarium Peregrinorum*, 172, 189. Nicholson's translation.

15 *Roger de Hoveden*, ii, 204.

16 Master Philip became Richard's premier clerk on the Third Crusade after the drowning of the vice-chancellor, and keeper of the king's seal, Roger Malus Catalus, on 24 April 1191; see Jane E. Sayers, 'English Charters from the Third Crusade,' in *Law and Records in Medieval England. Studies on the Medieval Papacy, Monasteries and Records*, ed. Jane E. Sayers (London: Variorum, 1988), 196.

17 In John's reign, Eleanor appears to have been keen to withdraw from political life. See Jane Martindale, 'Eleanor of Aquitaine: The Last Years,' in *King John: New Interpretations*, ed. Stephen D. Church (Woodbridge: Boydell Press, 1999), 136–64; Ralph V. Turner, 'Eleanor of Aquitaine in the Governments of Her Sons Richard and John,' in *Eleanor of Aquitaine: Lord and Lady*, eds. Bonnie Wheeler and John Carmi Parsons (Basingstoke: Palgrave Macmillan, 2003), 77–95. For more on Eleanor's and Berengaria's dowers, see the section below.

18 Katia Wright, 'A Dower for Life: Understanding the Dowers of England's Medieval Queens,' in *Later Plantagenets and the Wars of the Roses Consorts. Power, Influence, and Dynasty*, eds. Aidan Norrie, Carolyn Harris, Joanna L. Laynesmith, Danna R. Messer, and Elena Woodacre (Cham: Palgrave Macmillan, 2023), 147.

19 Gabrielle Storey, 'Co-Operation, Co-Rulership and Competition: Queenship in the Angevin Domains, 1135–1230' (PhD thesis, University of Winchester, 2020),' ch. 5; Katia Wright, 'Female Lordship,'.

20 Nicholas Vincent, 'Isabella of Angoulême: John's Jezebel,' in *King John: New Interpretations*, ed. Stephen D. Church (Woodbridge: The Boydell Press, 1999), 188–9.

21 Cloulas, 'Le douaire,' 89–90. See appendix for full list of lands.

22 Edmond Martène and Ursin Durand, eds., *Veterum Scriptorum et Monumentorum, Historicorum, Dogmaticorum, Moralium Amplissima Collectio*, 9 vols. (Paris: 1724–33), i, cols. 995–7.

23 Marie Hivergneaux, 'Aliénor d'Aquitaine: le pouvoir d'une femme à la lumière de ses chartes (1152–1204),' in *La Cour Plantagênet (1154–1204): Actes du Colloque tenu à Thouars du 30 avril au 2 mai 1999*, ed. Martin Aurell (Poitiers: Université de Poitiers, 2000), ed. Martin Aurell (Poitiers: Université de Poitiers, 2000), 78.

24 *Itinerarium Peregrinorum*, 195. Much of Berengaria and Joanna's participation on the Third Crusade has been discussed at length in Storey, 'Berengaria of Navarre and Joanna of Sicily.'

25 Peter W. Edbury, *The Kingdom of Cyprus and the Crusades, 1191–1374* (Cambridge: Cambridge University Press, 1991), 28. Richard's

quick sale of the island and the lack of title given to Berengaria is indicative that he had no long-term interest in holding it; Angel Nicolaou-Konnari, 'The Conquest of Cyprus by Richard the Lionheart and its Aftermath: A Study of the Sources and Legend, Politics and Attitudes in the year 1191–1192,' Επετηρίδα Κέντρου Επιστημονικών Ερευνών, 26 (2000): 60.

26 *Itinerarium Peregrinorum*, 221; also in attendance we can surmise was the unnamed Byzantine princess, who Richard had entrusted to Berengaria's care for her wellbeing and education, 195. Nicholson's translation.

27 *Roger de Hoveden*, ii, 220.

28 *Itinerarium Peregrinorum*, 265. Nicholson's translation.

29 *The Chronicle of Ibn al-Athir for the Crusading Period from* al-Kamil fi'l-Ta'rikh. *Part 2. The Years 541–589/1146–1193: The Age of Nur al-Din and Saladin*, trans. D. S. Richards (Farnham: Ashgate, 2010), 325.

30 *Gesta Regis Henrici Secundi Benedicti Abbatis. The Chronicle of the Reigns of Henry II. and Richard I. A.D. 1169–1192; known commonly under the name of Benedict of Peterborough*, ed. William Stubbs, 2 vols. (London: Longmans, Green, Reader, and Dyer, 1867), ii, 235.

31 Thomas Asbridge, *The Crusades. The War for the Holy Land* (London: Pocket Books, 2010), 460.

32 Elena Woodacre, 'Questionable Authority: Female Sovereigns and their Consorts in Medieval and Renaissance Chronicles,' in *Authority and Gender in Medieval and Renaissance Chronicles*, eds. Juliana Dresvina and Nicholas Sparks (Newcastle upon Tyne: Cambridge Scholars Publishing, 2012), 398–402.

33 Webster, *History*, 99.

34 AD Seine-Maritime, Cote 7H57 (1193); John Horace Round, ed. and trans., *Calendar of Documents preserved in France, Illustrative of the History of Great Britain and Ireland, I, 918–1206* (London: Her Majesty's Stationery Office, 1899), 94, no. 278.

35 AD Seine-Maritime, Cote 7H57. '*Berengaria dei gratia regina Anglorum, ducissa Normannorum et Aquitannorum, comitissa Andegavorum.*'

36 AD Seine-Maritime, Cote 7H57. '*ad preces nostras sub nostro testimonio fideiussorum.*'

37 AD Seine-Maritime, Cote 7H57.

38 Of Berengaria's relationship with Joanna, we know little. They spent a substantial amount of time together during their journeys to and from the Holy Land, however, there are no surviving letters between the pair to indicate whether a close relationship had been formed. Indeed, of Joanna's early life and marriages we know as little as Berengaria's: she was married first to William, King of Sicily and then to Raymond VI, Count of Toulouse, before dying in childbirth in 1199. For more on Joanna, see: Colette Bowie, *The Daughters of Henry II and Eleanor of Aquitaine* (Turnhout: Brepols, 2014).

39 Baury and Corriol, *Bérengère*, 76.

40 Trindade, *Berengaria*, 118.

41 Baury and Corriol, *Bérengère*, 83.

42 *Roger de Hoveden*, ii, 356–7; *Chronica magistri Rogeri de Houedene*, ed. William Stubbs, 4 vols. (London: Longmans, Green, Reader, and Dyer, 1868–1871), iii, 288–90; Elizabeth Hallam, 'Bérengère de Navarre,' *La Province du Maine* 93 (1991): 230–1.

43 *Chronica magistri Rogeri de Houedene*, iii, 289.

44 As suggested in Trindade, *Berengaria*, 112–13.

45 More detail on the financial records of Berengaria's reign can be found in ch. 3; Doris Mary Stenton, ed., *The Chancellor's Roll for the Eighth Year of the Reign of King Richard the First: Michaelmas 1196* (Burlington: TannerRitchie, 2016), 150; Doris Mary Stenton, ed., *The Great Roll of the Pipe for the 9th Year of the Reign of King Richard the First* (Burlington: TannerRitchie, 2016), 8; Doris Mary Stenton, ed., *The Great Roll of the Pipe for the 10th Year of the Reign of King Richard the First* (Burlington: TannerRitchie, 2016), 180; *The Great Roll of the Pipe for the First Year of the Reign of King John: Michaelmas 1199* (Burlington: TannerRitchie, 2015), 57, 190; Doris Mary Stenton, ed., *The Great Rolls of the Pipe for the 2nd to 4th Years of the Reign of King John*, 3 vols. (Burlington: TannerRitchie, 2016), I, 227; iii, 218; iv, 247; Doris Mary Stenton, ed., *The Great Roll of the Pipe for the Fifth Year of the Reign of King John: Michaelmas 1203* (Burlington: TannerRitchie, 2015), 73.

46 Doris M. Stenton, *The Great Roll of the Pipe for the 7th Year of the Reign of King Richard the First: Michaelmas 1195* (Burlington: TannerRitchie, 2016), 113; Thomas Stapleton, ed., *Magni Rotuli Scaccarii Normanniæ. Tomus I* (London: London Society of Antiquaries, 1840), 138. Note that Stapleton has mistranscribed 'hernesio' for 'hermesio' here.

47 Stenton, *Chancellor's Roll*, 150.

48 Stenton, *9th Year*, 8–9; Stenton, *10th Year*, 180; *First Year of the Reign of King John*, 190.

49 Stenton, *Chancellor's Roll*, 31; Stenton, *9th Year*, 217; Stenton, *10th Year*, 148; *First Year of the Reign of King John*, 57; Stenton, *Second Year of the Reign of King John*, 217; Stenton, *Third Year of the Reign of King John*, 226; Stenton, *Fourth Year of the Reign of King John*, 13.

50 Doris M. Stenton, ed., *The Great Roll of the Pipe for the Sixth Year of the Reign of King John: Michaelmas 1204* (Burlington: TannerRitchie, 2016), 103.

51 Gillingham, 'Richard I and Berengaria,' 172.

52 Stenton, *Chancellor's Roll*, 19–20.

53 Trindade, *Berengaria*, 111, 118; *Roger de Hoveden*, ii, 307.

54 Adam of Eynsham, *Magna Vita Sancti Hugonis. The Life of St Hugh of Lincoln*, eds. and trans. Decima L. Douie and David Hugh Farmer, 2 vols. (Oxford: The Clarendon Press, 1985), ii, 136.

DOWAGER

The Lost Years?

The death of Richard on 6 April 1199 left Berengaria in the shadows of the political scene. Richard's demise was a shock to the Plantagenet realms, as Richard was the first king of England to die of a battle wound since Harold at the battle of Hastings, 133 years prior. It was Eleanor who was at Richard's deathbed, not Berengaria, though this may be due to proximity rather than any hostility on Berengaria's part. Equally, Richard's sister Joanna, already overcome with grief after her expulsion from Toulouse, upon learning of Richard's death resolved to retire to Fontevraud according to a later eighteenth-century chronicler.[1] Berengaria's emotional response according to the hagiographer Adam of Eynsham is explored in more detail below, however, her lack of strong response is perhaps indicative of the lack of affection in her relationship with Richard. Given Berengaria's dowager period (1199–1230) lasted nearly four times the length of her marriage, she spent most of her life as a widow. This does not mean she was forever consigned to obscurity however. Her mother-in-law, Eleanor of Aquitaine, was quick to move in to ensure her son John's succession against the factions which supported her grandson, Arthur I, duke of Brittany (1196–1203), as heir, as well as against movements from Philip Augustus, king of France, who remained a threat on the horizon. Queen consorts were often important to help facilitate a smooth succession from the king to his son, however, given that Berengaria and Richard had no children together, it is perhaps unsurprising that she was left out of the transition of power. Richard's death provided Berengaria

DOI: 10.4324/9781003223306-4

with the opportunity to step forward into the political arena: although she may have been neglected as a consort, she now stood at the crossroads of Western Europe, with several options available to her. This chapter will consider these lost years of her early widowhood and provide an examination of the financial records of medieval England and France to lay the foundations for the examination of her dower campaign in chapter five.

Queen at the Crossroads

Firstly, Berengaria could have returned to her natal home of Navarre. We know little of her relationship with her brother Sancho VII, as noted in the previous chapter, but Berengaria may not have desired to return to her Navarrese homelands given that Sancho appears to have prioritised affairs with the Plantagenets over the personal wellbeing of his sister during her marriage.[2] There was also the risk that Berengaria may have been remarried, as was the case with her sisters-in-law Margaret of France and Joanna of Sicily. Even when Henry III (1216–72), king of England and Berengaria's nephew, granted her safe passage to Navarre in March 1219, there is no certainty that she returned even at this moment. Going to Navarre in 1199 would have placed her under Sancho's protection but it could also have seen her return to the marriage market as a pawn in political alliances, much as she had been a decade earlier when she was betrothed to Richard. Later letters demonstrate that Berengaria retained a close friendship with her sister Blanca, who married Thibaut III, count of Champagne, within a few weeks of Richard's death. The marriage took place on 1 July 1199, in Chartres, and Berengaria was witness to the ceremony and marriage settlement.[3] Also present at the wedding was Geoffrey III, count of Perche, who had been a witness at Berengaria's own marriage and dower settlement. It has been posited that Blanca travelled from Navarre through Aquitaine and met Berengaria at Fontevraud, or in Maine, accompanied by the counts of Perche and Brienne.[4] No definitive evidence supports this hypothesis given that we do not have a conclusive itinerary for either woman, but it is plausible that Blanca took the opportunity to reunite with her sister for the first time in eight years. The wedding of Blanca and Thibaut high-lighted the close connections between the nobility of northern and central France, with Rotrou, the bishop of Châlons and Geof-frey's brother, also present.[5] Berengaria may have been resident at the court of Champagne until 1204, plausibly joining her sister after Thibaut III's death in May 1201. It is uncertain whether Berengaria had any strong inclination to reside in Champagne in the immediate aftermath of her husband's death.[6] What is also of note is that, similar to Berengaria, Blanca utilised her position as a vulnerable widow two years later to appeal for papal protection in the aftermath of Thibaut's death.[7]

Remarriage would have appeared an obvious solution for a young, widowed heiress like Berengaria, yet neither Sancho nor John showed any inclination in securing her future alliance with another noble or prince. At best, Sancho's concern for his sister appears to have been perfunctory. Why Sancho showed such lit-tle interest in the most pragmatic option of utilising his sister for a political alliance is unclear; John at the very least had a series of conflicts, both internally and externally, to remedy. Medieval widows were often under societal pressure to remarry, and thus once again come under the control of a male family member, where her reputation and activities would fall under those of wife and mother.[8] Given that Berengaria was in her mid-thirties when Richard died, her potential options for remarriage were plausibly affected by concerns regarding her fertility: women were less fer-tile from their mid-thirties onwards, and Berengaria had not yet produced a child to give an indication of strong fertility either. Like many medieval widows, Berengaria could have chosen the religious life and lived out her days in one of France's many abbeys or nunneries, an alternative path that was usually met with con-temporary approval if a widow did not remarry. Royal and elite women often held strong ties with religious institutions during their lives, sometimes because these communities had been respon-sible, in part, for their upbringing, in other cases because of ties of patronage (notably seen with Berengaria and her foundation of L'Abbaye de L'Épau in 1230). Religious houses could also serve as places for retirement and residency. Not all women took vows to enter a religious institution – Isabella of Angoulême, John's second wife and Berengaria's sister-in-law, spent much of her final years at Fontevraud Abbey, although she remained married to her second husband, Hugh X de Lusignan. Religious institutions could offer a place to retire from the world and provide a safe haven, as well as being a site of residence for those royal and elite women who did wish to remain politically active even if not living at court. Had Berengaria chosen to either reside or take vows at an ecclesiastical institution, it would have removed her from the eyes of the Plantagenet-Capetian-Jiménez courts, and she would have remained a dowager queen of obscurity. Piety may have been important to Berengaria, since we have evidence for her religious patronage and interactions during her time in Le Mans, as will be explored in chapter six. This piety did not extend to taking any religious vows, however, although this was a path chosen by other royal women such as Mary of Boulogne, Matilda of Anjou, and Eleanor's granddaughter Alix, daughter of Alix of France and Thibaut V, count of Blois. Instead, it was at this stage of her life that Berengaria decided to move into political life more fully, demonstrating her freedom, to an extent, to decide her own future.

From Richard's death in 1199 until she exchanged her Norman dower lands for Le Mans in a transaction with Philip Augustus in the autumn of 1204, Berengaria was undoubtedly in a precarious situation as she decided her next political move. Her presence at Fontevraud Abbey, the site of Richard's burial, on 21 April 1199, suggests that she probably attended the funeral, perhaps with an eye to centring herself in the Plantagenet orbit. Bishop Hugh of Lincoln is reported to have travelled to visit Berengaria at Beaufort-en-Vallée upon receiving the news of Richard's death in order to comfort her, and Hugh's hagiographer, Adam of Eynsham, reports that the bishop encountered a 'sorrowing and almost heart-broken widow.'[9] Adam was Hugh's chaplain and spent the last three years of Hugh's life with him, and therefore had first-hand access to the finer details of Hugh's life.[10] Reports of Berengaria's grief ought, however, to be treated with some caution: there are no reports of a particular closeness of the royal couple, and given the shoddiness with which Berengaria was treated it is unlikely she was heartbroken at the news. Instead, it is much more likely that Adam of Eynsham utilised a gendered trope to construct Berengaria's position as a vulnerable widow in need of episcopal solace and protection. Eynsham's construction here served a hagiographical purpose, whereby Hugh would appear to embody Christ's care for the less fortunate and appear as a benevolent figure. Berengaria herself utilised this trope of a vulnerable widow when later asking the papacy to intervene on her behalf in disputes concerning her dower. Whilst at Fontevraud, Berengaria witnessed a charter issued by Eleanor on 21 April 1199, in which she granted, together with John, a pool at Langeais and the king's rights to the mills there to the abbey of Saint Mary, Torpenay, in return for prayers and the commemoration of Richard's death.[11] This charter is unusual, documenting the grant and attestation of two queens in one record, as well as recording the presence of both women.[12] Berengaria's presence at Fontevraud had a multitude of personal and political objectives. She carried out her commemorative responsibilities towards Richard as a widow by her presence, as well as continuing to associate herself with the Plantagenets, namely Eleanor and John. Doing so strengthened the line of succession as she gave her tacit approval as Richard's widow to John as his heir, rather than granting support to John's nephew and rival, Arthur I, duke of Brittany. After Eleanor's delivery of Berengaria to Richard in 1191, we do not know if there was any further interaction between the pair while Berengaria focussed on life with Richard and resided in the Angevin heartlands, and Eleanor predominantly involved herself in affairs in England and Aquitaine. Consequently, the meeting at Fontevraud may have been the first time the two women had seen each other in nearly a decade.

The funeral presented an opportunity for Berengaria to try and secure the resources she would need as a widowed queen. It was highly unlikely that Eleanor would miss the burial of her *carissimi filii*, her 'dearest son,' and therefore Berengaria had a chance to press her case to be granted her dower lands and gain some financial security.[13] Whatever undocumented conversations may have taken place between Berengaria and Eleanor, they do not appear to have resulted in any increase in Berengaria's revenues or helped her achieve the security she sought. From Fontevraud, Berengaria likely returned to her previous residence, probably somewhere in the Angevin heartlands, and thereafter commenced her campaign for the restitution of her dower lands and achievement of a modest income to enable her to live comfortably in widowhood.

Following Richard's burial and Blanca's marriage, we have little knowledge of Berengaria's whereabouts and activities until 1201. It is plausible that she may have attended the funeral of another Plantagenet – her sister-in-law Joanna, queen of Sicily and countess of Toulouse, was buried on 4 September 1199, likewise at Fontevraud Abbey. Berengaria's travels with Joanna on the Third Crusade and their return journey may have engendered a friendship to develop. Joanna had an affinity for Fontevraud Abbey, having been consecrated as a nun there, despite being married and pregnant at the time. Her will, and the recorded heartfelt execution by Eleanor thereof, demonstrates Joanna's continued commitment to the abbey, as it confirmed a donation of 1000 shillings from the salt pans in her dower lands at Agen for the maintenance of the nun's kitchen, as well as new bequests of 300 marks to the abbey's convents, a rent of 10 marks to its infirmary, and a further rent of 10 marks for buying fish at Lent on an annual basis.[14] There were also further bequests to two nuns at Fontevraud, Agatha and Alice, who had a rent of 6 marks for the rest of their lives, as well as 900 marks to pay off the debts of Fontevraud's abbess. Fontevraud held an important status as a royal necropolis for the Plantagenet dynasty. Joanna's will made no reference to her sister-in-law; however, it is entirely plausible that Berengaria could have attended the funeral even if she was otherwise adrift on the outskirts of the Plantagenet court.

John's succession to the Plantagenet domains in April 1199 was set against the aspirations of his nephew Arthur I, duke of Brittany, son of his brother Geoffrey and Constance, duchess of Brittany, as Arthur also sought the throne. Arthur had a stronger hereditary claim to the throne by right of his father, Geoffrey, duke of Brittany, and second eldest son of Henry II and Eleanor of Aquitaine. John, as the youngest son of Henry II, had a weaker claim as rules of primogeniture dictated that the throne pass through the senior line before the junior. It is evident that there was no intended place for Berengaria to take up as a dowager queen in the Plantagenet court, bereft of a child and any avenue to power as she was, and that the attentions of the Plantagenet dynasty were firmly diverted elsewhere.[15] There was localised pockets of disloyalty in Anjou, Maine, and Touraine, due to taxes and the longer-term results of Richard's absentee kingship, as well as the ever-increasing success of Philip Augustus on the Norman and Angevin borders. Groups of Angevins, Poitevins, and Bretons were largely favourable towards Arthur as well, and Philip repeatedly threw his support behind Arthur, undoubtedly intending to destabilise John and ensure that the new king was his pawn. With a new contender for the throne, the ever-precarious Angevin Union threatened to split with many of the nobles tentative about outlining their support for John.[16] The Treaty of Le Goulet, agreed between John and Philip Augustus in May 1200, was intended to bring peace to Normandy.[17] It redrew the borders of the Plantagenet and Capetian domains, with John acknowledging Philip Augustus's control of a considerable portion of Normandy. The boundary between the territories now lay between the cities of Le Neubourg and Évreux, and the treaty also resolved the tenacious Vexin territory dispute in Philip's favour.[18] Philip Augustus finally acknowledged John as heir to the Plantagenet domains, while withdrawing his support for Arthur. John was also obligated to pay 20,000 marks for the suzerainty of Anjou and Brittany. To seal the contract, a marriage betrothal was arranged between Blanche of Castile, John's niece and daughter of his sister Leonor, and Louis (the future Louis VIII), son of Philip Augustus. The ever-stoic Eleanor of Aquitaine traversed the Pyrenees to select the bride, and chose Blanche. Eleanor repeated the journey she undertook to escort Berengaria nearly a decade earlier, and brought the Castilian princess north to her new court and husband. Eleanor remained an ever-present figure on the international political stage late into her dowager period.[19]

Peace between the Plantagenets and the Capetians was not particularly long-lasting, with outbreaks of rebellion in Aquitaine later that year. The political situation in France had also been made more unstable by John's decision to annul his first marriage to Isabella of Gloucester, and then marry Isabella, heiress to the county of Angoulême in August 1200. Isabella of Angoulême was already betrothed to one of John's vassals, Hugh IX of Lusignan, whose lands were of strategic importance for trade and supply routes across Aquitaine. John's quick decision and fast marriage to Isabella caused a rift with Hugh, leading to a Lusignan uprising the same year. Although John suppressed this rebellion, the Lusignans were able to appeal to Philip Augustus owing to his overlordship of John's territories in France, which they did the following year. Philip summoned John to court in Paris in 1202 to discuss the matter, but he refused to attend, not wishing to appear weak. Philip's summons were of dubious legality: John's offences had been undertaken in his capacity as duke of Aquitaine, who did not typically perform homage to the kings of France at this time.[20] As a result of John's refusal to attend, Philip declared John in breach of his responsibilities as count of Poitou and duke of Normandy, and once again instigated warfare against the Plantagenets. The French king also granted John's territories to John's nephew Arthur of Brittany, except for Normandy which Philip claimed for himself. Throughout these initial years of turmoil at the beginning of the thirteenth century, Eleanor remained a central presence in issuing orders and decrees and advising John on the best path forward.

Against this wider political backdrop, Berengaria remained more concerned with issues of a local and personal matter. In 1201, the initial stages of her campaign for her dower became apparent. Roger of Howden noted that Berengaria travelled to Chinon to meet with John, who stated that he would make satisfaction for the dower she had been granted upon marriage, an arrangement confirmed by Philip, bishop of Durham, and those present at Berengaria's marriage ceremony and this meeting at Chinon.[21] Without her dower, Berengaria enjoyed little income with which to support herself and her household. By legal rights, the dower lands granted to Berengaria did belong to Eleanor, as they had originally been granted for Eleanor's subsistence during and after her tenure as queen consort. Until Eleanor's death, Berengaria was to hold the duchy of Gascony, however, this was complicated by the fact that Gascony had been promised as part of the dowry of Leonor, daughter of Eleanor and Henry II, for her marriage to Alfonso VIII, king of Castile.[22] Berengaria's initial agreement with John entitled her to be paid 1000 marks per year,

150 Angevin pounds of which she was to receive from the income of Segré, Anjou, and the remainder in two parts, half from Caen, Normandy within eight days of the feast of Saint Michael, and the other half within eight days of Easter.[23] Berengaria was also to receive the city of Bayeux, two mansions in Torrea, and the forest of Bur.[24] Evidence from the Pipe Rolls also indicates that Berengaria received a yearly income from the county of Surrey of 20 shillings from 1196 to 1204.[25] This income would have provided a little relief for Berengaria, if she actually received it. During John's reign, he gradually absorbed the incomes of the queen's household into his own, with Isabella of Angoulême receiving little by way of financial revenues that were directly for her use, and as Berengaria's dower campaign reveals, John was not particularly forthcoming with money.[26]

There is scant record for Berengaria's expenses in the early years of the 1200s, and it is evident from her actions in 1204 that her situation had become untenable. The argument usually posited by historians is that Berengaria remained at either Chinon, in the county of Poitou, Beaufort-en-Vallée, Anjou, or Saumur, Touraine, however, without substantive evidence or records of expenditure her whereabouts are uncertain. It is unlikely she would have resided in the duchy of Aquitaine, homeland of her mother-in-law with whom she had a competitive relationship. It is also unlikely that she would have resided in Normandy, which was the nexus of the fighting between the Plantagenets and the Capetians during this period. There is no record to indicate that she came to England until 1220, and given she had never visited the kingdom whilst queen consort, it is implausible that her widowhood would have driven her to take up residence there at this juncture. Given that many of her English dower lands were either under Eleanor's direct control or had been bartered away by her to favourites and nobles to maintain alliances, Berengaria had nowhere in England that would have offered a comfortable residence. Therefore, it has been argued that Berengaria's likely residences were within the counties of Anjou, Maine, or Touraine, plausibly within the key locations of Angers, Chinon, Le Mans, Saumur, and Tours, or some smaller residences. The suggestion that her primary residence was within Greater Anjou has been made by Baury and Corriol, by a process of eliminating other locations, but without reference to Champagne.[27] As noted above, it is plausible that Berengaria resided with her sister Blanca in Champagne between 1199 and 1204. Berengaria's residence in an Angevin heartland castle in the first two years of her dowager period kept her away from much of the border disputes and rebellions, but with the growing conquests of Philip Augustus by 1202 her situation may have become precarious in terms of allegiance. There is no evidence that Berengaria was utilised as a political hostage or bargaining chip, unlike her earlier experience with Isaac Comnenus on the Third Crusade.[28]

By 1204, the power dynamics between the Plantagenets and the Capetians had been dramatically altered. The success of Philip Augustus's campaigns in the latter 1190s and early 1200s saw the expansion of the kingdom of France and the demise of the majority of the Plantagenet domains on the Continent barring the duchy of Gascony. The unexpected death of Arthur of Brittany in 1203 was blamed on John, who had taken Arthur captive after the battle of Mirebeau in July 1202. This disappearance caused further dissension amongst an already fraught conglomeration of territories, with both Brittany and Anjou rebelling against John. The fall of Normandy, a key connecting territory between England and the continental lands of its kings, by August 1204, in particular marked the ascendancy of the Capetians. John's beleaguered campaigns to ensure the survival of Anjou and Poitou were unsuccessful, and the death of Eleanor on 1 April 1204 was the loss of not only a crucial political advisor but also a strong co-ruler in the south. Aquitaine and its rebellious barons now had a choice to ally with John or Philip. John had maintained his hold on Aquitaine largely due to the survival of his mother. After Eleanor's death, Aquitaine rapidly slipped into Capetian hands. Living amidst this political and territorial change, Berengaria needed to make a decision to ensure her own survival. Even if John had been in a position to support Berengaria, it seems unlikely he would have offered to do so, with no strong motivation or any evidence of a harmonious relationship between the two.

And decide she did. By August 1204, Berengaria had evidently made a decision about her political affiliation in the future, since several documents from this date attest to the exchange she made with Philip Augustus, trading her Norman dower lands for the city and lordship of Le Mans. Le Mans, in Maine, had been part of the dominions of the Angevin counts, brought with the marriage of Erembourg, countess of Maine, upon the death of her father, Elias I, to Fulk V, count of Anjou, and grandfather to Henry II of England.[29] Fulk ruled over Maine from 1110 onwards, with the agreement that he would perform homage to the duke of Normandy as his overlord. At that time, the king of England, Henry I, was also the Norman duke, and thus Fulk's lord. When Maine passed to Fulk's son, Geoffrey, upon Fulk's death in 1129, it then became subsumed into the wider Plantagenet domains. Maine had been under the command of the seneschal of Anjou, William des Roches, since 1199, who had initially been appointed by Arthur of Brittany, but then had his position reconfirmed by John. William changed sides after the battle of Mirebeau in August 1202, and later made homage to Philip Augustus alongside several other barons. William's switch of allegiance emboldened Philip to attack Maine, and the French king had successfully captured the territory by the end of 1203. In 1204, William agreed to exchange his lordship of Le Mans (although he remained in post as seneschal) for the property of Château-du-Loir, which had been granted to Berengaria as part of her dower.[30]

The circumstances behind this exchange are of interest, as it was a highly unusual situation. Philip's conquest of Normandy meant he had no reason to uphold Berengaria's rights to her Norman dower lands – by rights of conquest the duchy now belonged to him. Berengaria's land exchange demonstrated how the power balance had shifted across France: Philip had successfully captured Maine, and he was therefore exchanging a set of lands from William to Philip, and then from Philip to Berengaria.[31] The reasoning behind Philip's motivation to exchange these lands with Berengaria and grant her the lordship cannot be confirmed but is worth considering. The changing allegiance of William de Roches, seneschal of Maine, may have been a factor. By positioning Berengaria as lord of Le Mans, Philip was placing someone in charge who was unlikely to rebel against him and disrupt the newly emerging kingdom of France with all its gains from the Plantagenets. Philip may

FIGURE 3.1 Map of France showing possessions of the king of England and the king of the Franks in 1154. At the time of Berengaria's death in 1230, only the duchy of Gascony remained under the control of the king of England, Henry III.

have also been motivated by the reasoning that Berengaria was unlikely to have been attacked by John as his widowed sister-in-law and someone protected by the Church. Alternatively, there may have been a sense of respect between Berengaria and Philip that motivated him to act in her interests and secure her future in Le

Mans, as is perhaps suggested by Philip addressing Berengaria as '*dilecte*' or 'beloved' in the 1204 grant.[32] Berengaria's sister Blanca was the widow of Philip Augustus's nephew, Thibaut III, count of Champagne, and this familial connection may have encouraged a closer relationship between Philip and Berengaria as well, or at least a more harmonious one. Without extant evidence, Philip's reasoning cannot be proven conclusively, but it is highly plausible that he wanted a resolution that was in both his and Berengaria's interests. This exchange between Berengaria and Philip demonstrates her agency as she pushed for recompense from Philip when no such compensation was forthcoming from John, and she may potentially have instigated the exchange. Through the acquisition of Le Mans, Berengaria gained the power of lordship, and established herself as a semi-independent vassal of the king of France who was able to act in her own interests, an impressive feat for a woman without an intercessor.

It needs to be acknowledged that Berengaria's exchange with Philip was probably driven by personal desperation at her financial situation. With no apparent support from her natal family, and John facing political instability both in England and on the Continent, it was evident that her dower revenues would not be forthcoming imminently. Although historians have readily castigated John for being a 'bad' king, and his treatment of both Berengaria and Isabella was undoubtedly shoddy, the financial and political pressures on John, especially in the early 1200s, meant he faced a series of unpalatable options to try and protect England and the wider Plantagenet domains from Capetian conquest whilst balancing the domestic situation.[33] Thus, in the autumn of 1204, Berengaria exchanged her Norman dower lands of Falaise, Domfront, and Bonneville-sur-Tocques with Philip for the lordship of Le Mans.[34] With this transaction Berengaria removed herself firmly from the Plantagenet sphere of influence, choosing to acknowledge Philip as her overlord. By establishing herself as lord of Le Mans, Berengaria was no longer dependent on Sancho or John to control her future, nor did she have to consign herself to religious life. Her action at this juncture is one of the clearest examples we have of Berengaria's agency, and it was a remarkable turning point in her path to power. Although she

may not have had the ability to influence and intercede successfully with John and Sancho, the young widow negotiated with,
and gained assistance from, Philip Augustus. Berengaria was not
lacking other protectors, since a series of popes, respectively Innocent III (1198–1216), Honorius III (1216–27), and Gregory IX
(1227–41), all upheld their role as protector of the vulnerable,
including widows, against the might of rulers and overlords. Berengaria never realised the power that she should have exercised
as queen consort, but she established herself in widowhood as a
semi-independent member of the ruling elite of Western Europe,
outside the remaining spheres of conflict between the kings of
England, France, and Navarre.

Berengaria's Financial Affairs

As seen in the discussion above, Berengaria's documented access
to revenues – important whilst she was queen, but even more so
now she was politically independent – was limited and contested.
Difficulties with access to queenly revenues endured: Berengaria's
queenly successors Philippa of Hainault and Isabella of France
struggled financially even with established access to lands, as
debts accrued and lands were granted and bartered away dependent on the king's need for allies and security.[35] As will be discussed
in chapter six, Berengaria's fight for her dower lands and revenues
dominated her tenure as lord, and the majority of her dowager
period, lasting through the reigns of John and his son, Henry III,
king of England. The evidence for the finances of queens in this
period is inconsistent and scant at points, with such records becoming more consistent towards the end of the thirteenth century,
owing in part to the increasing reliance on administrative systems
first documented during John's reign. The piecemeal records for
the Angevin queens, including Berengaria, largely consist of entries in the records of the English royal exchequer and chancery,
as well as surviving letters from the kings of England and the pope
to individual queens.

During the reigns of the early Plantagenets, administrative
systems underwent a period of sustained development: by John's
reign royal administration largely centred around the chancery,

the exchequer, and the *curia regis*.[36] These governmental bodies maintained records of the monarch's expenditure and income on several different types of rolls. Those most relevant to Berengaria's financial affairs include: the Pipe Rolls, the earliest of which dates to 1129–30 and note payments made to the Crown, as well as Crown expenditure and debts owed; and the Patent Rolls (1199 onwards) which record royal grants, amongst other matters concerned with the monarch's interests. Alongside these are scattered entries in the Charter, Close, Fine, and Liberate Rolls which note some queenly revenue and expenditure, alongside the king's income and expenses which are documented in more detail.[37] As Adrian Jobson and Thomas F. Tout have noted, the lack of commitment to retaining records concerned with the royal household meant that many of these records have since been lost, and with them, further information recording queenly finances and, possibly, additional insights into Berengaria's finances. Comparisons between royal women can help shed further light on aspects of queenly income and expenses during the twelfth and early thirteenth centuries, as I have shown elsewhere.[38] Such analyses need to be contextualised against the disparity in records. It is entirely plausible that queens prior to Isabella of Angoulême received more revenue than the records depict, however, this administrative dearth may be due to the lack of surviving records rather than lack of record-keeping or, as I argue, due to the lack of provision of income for some queens.[39] It is evident from the work undertaken on later medieval queens such as Eleanor of Provence and Philippa of Hainault that they possessed an array of lands from which they received revenues, as well as other forms of royal income. As frustrating as the lack of evidence can be for the earlier and high Middle Ages, a longue durée approach to financial records and comparative studies can furnish a deeper understanding of how the maintenance and survival of medieval records contribute to our knowledge of queenly finances and thus, women's ability to wield and exercise power.

Queens in England in the twelfth and thirteenth centuries could expect income from two sources: firstly, the queen's gold, a surcharge of one tenth on all voluntary fines paid to the king and, secondly, dower lands.[40] The examination of queen's gold in the medieval period has been undertaken by Hilda Johnstone, Kristin Geaman, and Louise Tingle.[41] Whilst Eleanor of Aquitaine was queen consort, queen's gold became a fixed source of income, though it was not collected consistently, as the sporadic references in the Pipe Rolls evidence. The financial records also note that Eleanor continued to collect queen's gold in her dowager period when such revenues ought instead to have been provided to Berengaria. This exacerbated Berengaria's financial situation as Eleanor continued to receive income from the queenly dower lands as well, in addition to her own income from the duchy of Aquitaine. Although the revenue was not substantial, the queen's gold was a source of income that Berengaria did not receive, and this therefore affected her ability to exercise authority.

Eleanor's death in April 1204 did not mean that the competition regarding access to queen's gold was over. Berengaria was a dowager from 1199, but being a dowager had not thwarted her mother-in-law's claim to the income traditionally apportioned to a consort. Nevertheless, Berengaria focussed her attentions on the revenues owed to her from her dower lands, leaving the revenue from queen's gold to be passed directly to her queenly successor, Isabella of Angoulême. However, Isabella was also unable to benefit from the queen's gold, initially due to Eleanor's continued collection of the revenue, but even after her death, the Pipe Rolls record that the revenue passed directly to John instead of his queen. Without access to this stream of revenue, royal consorts lacked an avenue to power, since they required income to build networks and power bases, exercise patronage, and support themselves and their household. It was the latter financial burden which became a significant concern for Berengaria between 1199 and 1204.

In the Angevin period (1154–1216), it was expected that the queen would hold her dower lands from her husband's death until her own death, but this practice caused issues for new kings needing to provide lands for their own queen consort as well as a dowager queen. Between 1200 and 1204, John had the unfortunate situation of providing lands and revenues for his queen consort, Isabella of Angoulême, his dowager sister-in-law, Berengaria, and his mother, the dowager queen Eleanor, all at a time

when his own lands were diminishing in the face of Capetian conquests. What constituted the dower lands of the twelfth- and early
thirteenth-century queens of England has been examined and debated by a number of historians.[42] As discussed in chapter two,
the dower grant to Berengaria on her wedding day comprised the
lands of Domfront, Falaise, and Bonneville-sur-Tocques, Normandy, as well as further lands in Maine, Poitou, and Touraine.[43]
In England, she was granted lands from Berkshire, Devonshire,
Northamptonshire, Oxfordshire, Rutland, Somerset, and Sussex.
The main difference between the copy of Berengaria's dower charter and the lands that Eleanor held as dower is that of Lillebonne,
Normandy, which was under Eleanor's authority but does not
appear in the copy of Berengaria's dower grant.

Like the queen's gold, Eleanor continued to collect revenues
from the dower lands into her dowager period. Although this
was not without due cause, as the lands were apportioned to her
until her death, it removed another source of income for Berengaria. Discussion of Berengaria's petition for the restitution of her
dower lands and income will follow in chapter six, however, during the early 1200s, Berengaria was cut off from the main sources
of queenly revenue which could have supported her as a dowager.
Unlike Eleanor and Isabella, Berengaria did not have access to
lands of her own as an heiress which could support her. Although
she was heiress of Navarre, it was ruled by her brother and it was
only upon his death, if no other heirs were apparent, that Berengaria could have accessed Navarrese revenues. It is no surprise,
then, that she turned to Philip Augustus to barter for her Norman
dower lands in return for a place that would provide a stable income and which she could rule in her own right without the need
to depend on her natal or marital family.

The financial records help us uncover more about queens' lives
than was previously thought possible. Sometimes we encounter
details of a queen's clothing, jewellery expenses and preference for
certain items, the size and cost of her household, her gift-giving
and patronage. Such records can also shed light on the various
incomes queens did, or did not, receive. Income was imperative to
enable women to act with independent agency and exercise power;
without money, queens were dependent on their natal and marital

families, or their overlord, for support. Berengaria's poor relationships with both her families meant that she had to carve her own place in the world – although she maintained some correspondence with her sister, Blanca, there is no extant evidence that Blanca provided any fiscal support for Berengaria. The importance of finances can be seen by Berengaria's prolonged campaign for her dower lands, as discussed in chapter six, as well as her disputes with ecclesiastical officials in Le Mans as she maintained her rights and incomes with determination. Although Berengaria undoubtedly endured struggles in the period 1199–1204, her cause was not entirely without support, with both Philip Augustus and the papacy using their political power to assist her survival and grant her protection. It is to Berengaria's experience as queen consort, her expectations, and reality, that the next chapter now explores.

Notes

1 Joseph Vaissete, *Abregé de l'histoire générale de Languedoc. Tome III* (Paris: Jacques Vincent, 1749), 248.
2 See John Gillingham, 'Richard I and Berengaria of Navarre,' *Bulletin of the Institute of Historical Research* 53 (1980): 157–73 for discussion of the Anglo-Navarrese relationship in the context of Berengaria and Richard's marriage; evidence of the continued partnership between John and Sancho VII can be found in Carlos Marichalar, ed., *Colección Diplomática del Rey de Sancho el Fuerte de Navarra* (Pamplona: Aramburu, 1934), 173, 187–8, accessed 17 July 2022, www.euskomedia.org/PDFAnlt/cmn/1934153222.pdf, and Thomas Rymer, ed., *Foedera, Conventiones, Literæ, Et Cujuscunque Generis Acta Publica inter Reges Angliæ et alios quosuis(?) imperatores, reges, pontifices, principes, vel communitates, ab ineunte sæculo duodecimo, viz ab anno 1101, ad nostra usque Tempora, Habita aut Tractatal ex autographis, infra secretiores archivorum regiorum thesaurarias, per multa sæcula recondita, fideliter exscripta, Tomus I* (London: J. Tonson, 1727), 126–7.
3 AN, J 198 (1199); Alexandre Teulet, ed., *Layettes du Trésor des Chartes*, 2 vols. (Paris: Henri Plon, 1863–6) i, no. 497.
4 Luis Javier Fortún Pérez de Ciriza, *Sancho VII El Fuerte (1194–1234)* (Iruna: Editorial Mintzoa, 1986), 128.
5 Ghislain Baury and Vincent Corriol, *Bérengère de Navarre (v. 1160–1230). Histoire et mémoire d'une reine d'Angleterre* (Rennes: Presses Universitaires de Rennes, 2022), 100.
6 Nicholas Vincent, 'Isabella of Angoulême: John's Jezebel,' in *King John: New Interpretations* (Woodbridge: Boydell, 1999), ed. Stephen D. Church, 188. Vincent notes that Berengaria was in Champagne

in 1204 according to C. R. Cheney and Mary G. Cheney, eds., *The Letters of Pope Innocent III (1198–1216) concerning England and Wales. A Calendar with an appendix of texts* (Oxford; The Clarendon Press, 1967), no. 531. Theodore Evergates records that Berengaria was at Sens with Philip Augustus in May 1201: Theodore Evergates, *The Aristocracy in the County of Champagne, 1100–1300* (Philadelphia: University of Pennsylvania Press, 2007), 36, presumably in reference to Theodore Evergates, *The Cartulary of Countess Blanche of Champagne* (Toronto: University of Toronto Press, 2009), no. 449, when Blanca makes homage to Philip Augustus. Berengaria appears in Philip's charter of the same date: Henri-François Delaborde, Charles Petit-Dutaillis and J. Monicat, eds., *Recueil des Actes de Philippe Auguste Roi de France. Tome II Années Règne XVI à XXVII (1 Novembre 1194–31 Octobre 1206)* (Paris: Imprimerie Nationale, 1943), 235–8, no. 679.

7 Teulet, *Layettes*, i, no. 615.
8 Ann Trindade, *Berengaria, In Search of Richard the Lionheart's Queen* (Dublin: Four Courts Press, 1999), 138; Sara McDougall, 'Women and Gender in Canon Law,' in Judith M. Bennett and Ruth Mazo Karras, eds., *The Oxford Handbook of Women & Gender in Medieval Europe* (Oxford: Oxford University Press, 2013), 168–9; Michel Parisse, ed., *Veuves et veuvage dans le haut Moyen Âge* (Paris: Picard, 1993); Sandra Cavallo and Lyndan Warner, eds., *Widowhood in medieval and early modern Europe* (Harlow: Longman, 1999).
9 Adam of Eynsham, *Magna Vita Sancti Hugonis. The Life of St Hugh of Lincoln*, eds. and trans. Decima L. Douie and David Hugh Farmer, 2 vols. (Oxford: Clarendon Press, 1985), ii, 136. '*Locutusque ad cor uidue merentis et usque ad animam pene consternate, miro modo spiritum eius deliniuit.*' Douie and Farmer's translation.
10 Adam of Eynsham, *Magna Vita*, i, viii.
11 AN, J 460, no. 4 (1199); John Horace Round, ed. and trans., *Calendar of Documents preserved in France, Illustrative of the History of Great Britain and Ireland, I, 918–1206* (London: Her Majesty's Stationery Office, 1899), no. 1301. '*Alienor dei gratia regina Angliae … hiis testibus … Regina Berengaria*'; Teulet, *Layettes*, i, no. 489.
12 The appearance of multiple queens in one charter has precedents to the early English period: thanks go to Florence H. R. Scott, Katherine Weikert, Mary Blanchard, and Matthew Firth for providing the references for these; Pauline Stafford, *Queen Emma & Queen Edith, Queenship and Women's Power in Eleventh-Century England* (Oxford: Blackwell Publishers, 1997), 254: charters referenced are S 364; S 745/746; S 1011.
13 Colette Bowie, *The Daughters of Henry II and Eleanor of Aquitaine* (Turnhout: Brepols, 2014), 45–7.
14 Round, *Calendar of Documents*, no. 1105; Bowie, *The Daughters of Henry II and Eleanor of Aquitaine*, 186–7.
15 Jane Martindale, 'Eleanor of Aquitaine: The Last Years,' in *King John: New Interpretations*, ed. Stephen D. Church (Woodbridge: Boydell and Brewer, 1999), 163.

16 For the coining of the term Angevin Union, see Stephen D. Church, 'The "Angevin Empire" (1150–1204): A Twelfth-Century Union,' in *Unions and Divisions: New Forms of Rule in Medieval and Renaissance Europe*, eds. P. Srodecki, N. Kersken, and R. Petrauskas (Abingdon: Routledge, 2022), 68–82.

17 AN, J 628 (1200).

18 Stephen Church, *King John. England, Magna Carta and the Making of a Tyrant* (London: Pan Books, 2016), 86–7.

19 Martindale, 'Eleanor of Aquitaine,' 145; John Gillingham, *Richard the Lionheart*, 2nd ed. (London: Weidenfeld and Nicholson, 1989), 159–61.

20 Michael Clanchy, *England and Its Rulers. 1066–1307*, 4th ed. (Oxford: John Wiley & Sons, 2014), 204.

21 *The Annals of Roger de Hoveden Comprising The History of England and of Other Countries of Europe from A.D. 732 to A.D. 1201*, ed. and trans. Henry Thomas Riley, 2 vols. (London: H. G. Bohn, 1853), ii, 523; for Berengaria's dower grant, see ch. 2/appendix.

22 Ivan Cloulas, 'Le douaire de Bérengère de Navarre, veuve de Richard Cœur de Lion, et sa retraite au Mans,' in *La Cour Plantagenêt (1154–1204). Actes du Colloque tenu à Thouars du 30 avril au 2 mai 1999*, ed. Martin Aurell (Poitiers: Université de Poitiers, 2000), 89; Bowie, *The Daughters of Henry II and Eleanor of Aquitaine*, 123–4. Gascony was recorded as part of Berengaria's dower grant on 20 May 1191; see John W. Baldwin, François Gasparri, Michel Nortier, and Elisabeth Lalou, eds., *Recueil des historiens de la France. Documents financiers et administratifs. Tome VII. Les Registres de Philippe Auguste, publiés par John W. Baldwin avec le concours de François Gasparri, Michel Nortier et Elisabeth Lalou sous la direction de Robert-Henri Bautier. Volume I: Texte* (Paris: Imprimerie Nationale, 1992), 469–70; Edmond Martène and Ursin Durand, eds., *Veterum Scriptorum et Monumentorum, Historicorum, Dogmaticorum, Moralium Amplissima Collectio*, 9 vols. (Paris: 1724–33), col. 996, accessed 18 July 2022, https://archive.org/veterum_scriptorum.

23 *Registres de Philippe-Auguste*, 488–90; Thomas Duffy Hardy, ed., *Rotuli Literrarum Patentium in Turri Londinensi Asservati. Volume I. Part I* (London: Public Record Office, 1835), 2–3.

24 *Registres de Philippe-Auguste*, 488–90. 'Preterea concessimus ei castrum de Baiocis et civitatem nostraam Baiocensem integre, intra muros et extra, et etiam placita de spada ibidem, retenta nobis donatione episcopatus, et de foresta nostra de Bur calfagium suum et domus sue, et quod necessarium fuerit ad edificationem et reparationem domorum predicti castri per visum forestariorum nostrorum.'

25 TNA, E 372/45 (1199–1200); E 372/46 (1200–1), E 372/47 (1201–2); E 372/48 (1202–3); E 372/49 (1203–4); compared with Doris M. Stenton, ed., *The Great Roll of the Pipe For the First Year of the Reign of King John, Michaelmas 1199* (Burlington: TannerRitchie Publishing, 2015), 190; Doris M. Stenton, ed., *The Great Roll of the Pipe for the Second Year of the Reign of King John, Michaelmas 1200*

(Burlington: TannerRitchie Publishing, 2016), 247; Doris M. Stenton, ed., *The Great Roll of the Pipe for the Third Year of the Reign of King John, Michaelmas 1201* (Burlington: TannerRitchie Publishing, 2016), 218; Doris M. Stenton, ed., *The Great Roll of the Pipe for the Fourth Year of the Reign of King John, Michaelmas 1202* (Burlington: TannerRitchie Publishing, 2016), 247.

26 Gabrielle Storey, 'Co-Operation, Co-Rulership and Competition: Queenship in the Angevin Domains, 1135–1230' (PhD Thesis, University of Winchester, 2020), ch. 5; Vincent, 'Isabella of Angoulême,' 189–92.

27 Baury and Corriol, *Bérengère*, 102.

28 For Berengaria on the Third Crusade, see chapter 2 and Gabrielle Storey, 'Berengaria of Navarre and Joanna of Sicily,' in *Forgotten Queens in Medieval and Early Modern Europe, Political Agency, Myth Making, and Patronage*, eds. Estelle Paranque and Valerie Schutte (Abingdon: Routledge, 2018), 41–59.

29 For more on the Plantagenets and Maine, see Martin Aurell, Ghislain Baury, Vincent Corriol, and Laurent Maillet, eds., *Les Plantagenêts et le Maine* (Rennes: Presses Universitaires de Rennes, 2022).

30 *Recueil des Actes de Philippe-Auguste*, 419–20.

31 Jacques Boussard, 'Philippe-Auguste et Les Plantagenêts,' in *La France de Philippe-Auguste. Le Temps des Mutations. Actes du Colloque international organisé par le C.N.R.S. (Paris, 29 septembre–4 octobre 1980)*, ed. Robert-Henri Bautier (Paris: C.N.R.S., 1982), 282.

32 *Recueil des Actes de Philippe-Auguste*, 419–20. Note that Berengaria is also referred to as beloved cousin, or '*dilectisime consanguinee*' by Philip Augustus's son Louis IX, when Louis grants Berengaria the land for the establishment of L'Abbaye de L'Épau in 1230, in BNF, Latin 17124, 26–7 (1230). '*nos dilectisime consanguinee ut fideli nostre Berengaria Regine Anglorum illustri dedissemus ut concessimus in perpetuum lorum illum qui vulgariter consueverat appellam Espal juxta Cenomanum.*'

33 For a recent assessment of John's reputation, see Stephen D. Church, *King John. England, Magna Carta and the Making of a Tyrant* (London: Pan Books, 2016).

34 *Registres de Phillipe-Auguste*, 493–4. '*Noverit universitas vestraa quod he sunt conventiones inter nos et dominum nosstrum Philippum, illustrem regem Francorum, quod nos, castrum Falesie et villam cum appenditiis, castrum de Danfront et villam cum appenditiis, castrum et villam de Bonavilla super Toscam cum appenditiis et omnibus forestis trium castrorum, quitta clamamus ipsi et heredibus suis in perpetuum, que Richardus quondam rex Anglie, maritus noster nobis assignavit in dotalitium, ita quod nec in predictis castris nec in eorum appendiciis nec in forestis aliquid reclamabimus nec per nos nec per alium; et insuper instrumentis et omnibus cartis et scriptis que de dotalitio predicto trium castrorum, sicut predictum est, habebamus, renuntiamus.*'

35 Katia Wright, 'The Queen's Lands: Examining the role of queens as female lords in fourteenth century England' (PhD Thesis, University of Winchester, 2022).

36 Adrian Jobson, 'Introduction,' in *English Government in Thirteenth Century England*, ed. Adrian Jobson (Woodbridge: Boydell Press, 2004), 1.

37 For an introduction to the rolls of medieval England, see Jobson, *English Government in the Thirteenth Century*; Thomas Frederick Tout, *Chapters in the Administrative History of medieval England*, 6 vols. (Manchester: Manchester University Press, 1920–33); TNA, accessed 17 July 2022, www.nationalarchives.gov.uk/help-with-your-research/research-guides/royal-grants-letters-patent-charters-from-1199/; The National Archives, accessed 17 July 2022, www.nationalarchives.gov.uk/help-with-your-research/research-guides/medieval-financial-records-pipe-rolls-1130–1300/.

38 Storey, 'Co-Operation,' ch. 5.

39 Nicholas Vincent, 'Why 1199? Bureaucracy and Enrolment under John and his Contemporaries,' in *English Government in the Thirteenth Century*, ed. Adrian Jobson (Woodbridge: Boydell & Brewer, 2004), 33–4.

40 For more on queens' finances during the Angevin period, see Storey, 'Co-Operation,' ch. 5. For broader discussions on dower in medieval England, see Katia Wright, 'A Dower for Life: Understanding the Dowers of England's Medieval Queens,' in *Later Plantagenet and the Wars of the Roses Consorts. Power, Influence, and Dynasty*, eds. Aidan Norrie, Carolyn Harris, J. L. Laynesmith, Danna R. Messer, and Elena Woodacre (Cham: Palgrave Macmillan, 2022), 145–64. See also Kristin Geaman, 'Queen's Gold and Intercession: The Case of Eleanor of Aquitaine,' *Medieval Feminist Forum. A Journal of Gender and Sexuality* 46 (2010): 10–33.

41 Geaman 'Queen's Gold,' 10–33; Louise Tingle, '*Aurum reginae*: Queen's Gold in Late Fourteenth-Century England,' *Royal Studies Journal* 7.1 (2020): 77–90; Hilda Johnstone, 'The Queen's Household,' in *Chapters in the Administrative History of Medieval England*, ed. Thomas Frederick Tout, 6 vols. (Manchester: Manchester University Press, 1930), v, 262–7. See more recent work by Amalie Fößel, 'The Queen's Wealth in the Middle Ages,' *Maiestas* 13 (2005): 23–45 and Attila Bárány, 'Medieval Queens and Queenship: A Retrospective on Income and Power,' *Annual of Medieval Studies at CEU* 19 (2013): 149–200.

42 Cloulas, 'Le douaire,' 89–94; Lois L. Huneycutt, '*Alianor Regina Anglorum*. Eleanor of Aquitaine and Her Anglo-Norman Predecessors as Queens of England,' in *Eleanor of Aquitaine: Lord and Lady*, eds. Bonnie Wheeler and John Carmi Parsons (Basingstoke: Palgrave Macmillan, 2003), 115–32; Heather J. Tanner, 'Queenship: Office, Custom, or Ad Hoc? The Case of Queen Matilda III of England (1135–1152),' in *Eleanor of Aquitaine: Lord and Lady*, eds. Bonnie Wheeler and John Carmi Parsons (Basingstoke: Palgrave Macmillan, 2003), 133–58; see appendix for list of dower lands.

43 *Veterum Scriptorum*, i, cols. 995–7.

QUEEN

Power, Prospects, Rulership, and Reality

For most women, access to queenship as a consort came from marriage to a (co-)ruling king, or being opted into a co-ruling partnership with the reigning monarch. Berengaria's position as queen of England came through her marriage to Richard I, and she undoubtedly brought her own expectations of power and rulership, framed by her early experiences in Navarre and influenced by the actions of her contemporaries. Berengaria's experiences of and her understanding of queenship are considered through an examination of female succession and rulership from a broader Western European framework, before moving on to consider her access to titles and the importance these had on perceptions of one's status as queen, both by the public and by the queen herself. The third section of this chapter explores Berengaria's time as queen consort and her ability to co-rule with Richard, and then looks at her personal partnership with him and the wider implications it had for the exercise of monarchical powers in the Angevin Union. Lastly, this chapter considers how being a childless queen affected one's avenues to power, and how some – but not all – queen consorts were able to adapt in this situation to their benefit.

Female Succession and Rulership

The marital alliance between Berengaria and Richard discussed in chapter one highlighted Navarre's importance as a continental ally. However, it is necessary to understand more of Berengaria's background as a Navarrese and Iberian princess, and the impact

DOI: 10.4324/9781003223306-5

that had on her attitude to power. After the deaths of her other brothers (at dates unknown), Berengaria was theoretically heiress of Navarre during the reign of her brother Sancho, though her own lack of an heir made her less likely to succeed in reality. Eventually, the Navarrese throne passed through her sister Blanca's line instead, with Blanca's son Teobaldo (1234–53) inheriting, after Berengaria (d. 1230) and Blanca (d. 1229) both predeceased Sancho (d. 1234). Female succession in the Iberian peninsula was more commonplace than in England and France and appears to have been far more successful across the medieval period. One of the most famous instances of female succession and rule before Berengaria was that of Urraca, who succeeded her father as queen regnant, and thus ruled in her own right, in León, Castile, and Galicia in 1109, as well as reigning as queen consort through marriage in Aragon and Navarre.[1] As with many other regnant queens of the medieval period, Urraca's succession and rule were not without dispute. However, her rule for seventeen years as the first European queen regnant laid the foundations for future female heiresses to claim their own thrones. More recent work is being undertaken by Anaïs Waag on the many queens regnant of the period and the challenges they faced to succeed in medieval Europe, and her case studies are indicative of the fact that female heiresses were not unusual or always unsuccessful, as has commonly been presumed.[2]

But what of Iberia? Urraca's case was far from singular, even if she was the first queen regnant in the Iberian peninsula. Many noblewomen across Iberia were able to successfully inherit estates on their own merits, and female landholding and administration, on behalf of a male family member or as a sole agent, were more frequent than previously assumed. This acceptance of female inheritance was translated across royal and noble families, and although it was by no means universally popular, Berengaria and Blanca may have faced less opposition and obstacles to ruling in Navarre than their English counterparts, as seen most evidently with the Empress Matilda and the civil war between 1135–48. A multiplicity of circumstances was needed to ensure successful female rule, particularly when a primary concern of the vassals was military strength and leadership in times of conquest and warfare. In Navarre, and Iberia more broadly, Berengaria was surrounded with strong examples of female leadership in her own time and before. Urraca, the many queens regent of and from Castile, the regnant queens of Jerusalem, and Eleanor of Aquitaine (1137–1204) demonstrated that female succession to duchies, counties, and kingdoms could succeed and was able to flourish and prosper in the high Middle Ages.

Berengaria's position as heiress came amidst a lack of other male heirs. With his surviving son, Sancho, Sancho VI was undoubtedly aware of the risk that came with dynastic transmission to one male heir. The phrase 'heir and a spare' is rightly popular as the need for a second son was vital in case any illness or misfortune befell the eldest male heir. However, Sancho VII, at the age of thirty-seven, succeeded to the Navarrese throne in 1194 upon the death of his father. Sancho VII married Constance of Toulouse the following year, although he repudiated her for unknown reasons by 1200, perhaps due to a lack of a son. He is known to have taken a second wife, even if her identity and the longevity of this marriage is disputed: one chronicler, Carlos, príncipe de Viana, also stated that the couple had a son who died in an accident aged fifteen, however, no other chroniclers have substantiated this.

As such, by the 1220s, Berengaria, as the eldest surviving sister, was theoretically the (unnamed) heir to Navarre. Given that she did not return to Navarre at any stage after her marriage to Richard I, and did not produce a (male) heir or remarry after Richard's death, the choice of her as successor was unrealistic. From surviving evidence, Berengaria showed little interest in supporting Sancho during his infirmity, the succession of the kingdom, or ruling Navarre. Blanca was in support of female rule and succession, given her implementation of the custom formally enabling women to inherit if there was no surviving son in Champagne.[3] Therefore, it seemed more plausible for Blanca, or at least her line, to inherit Navarre. As noted above both Blanca and Berengaria predeceased Sancho and thus the throne was to be transmitted to his nephew, Blanca's son, Teobaldo. Though Teobaldo was of Champenois descent, and thus slightly unpopular with the Navarrese, as the primary surviving male heir he was at least the best dynastic choice to avoid any further conquest from neighbouring Iberian or French kingdoms.

The positions of Blanca and Berengaria as heiresses to the Navarrese throne are theoretical due to the lack of surviving evidence formally naming them as regent or heiress. It is uncertain whether Blanca ruled in Navarre in the 1220s prior to her death; she was a successful and experienced regent in Champagne, having ruled and negotiated with Philip Augustus, king of France (1180–1223) during Teobaldo's minority, and it is highly plausible her successes in Champagne made her an ideal candidate for rulership in Navarre. Unfortunately, documentation from Sancho VII's reign is scarce, and evidence indicating the range of activity that Blanca may have enacted as regent is unknown. Her retirement in 1222 to the convent at Argensolles, Champagne, which she founded, adds further weight to the notion that Blanca did not return to Navarre to act as regent.[4] From Blanca's rule in Champagne, we can see that she was an effective and progressive ruler, working to ensure the smooth transition of power to Teobaldo, and like her sister, a successful negotiator and diplomat. Similarly, Berengaria's governance of Le Mans was strong and effective, with the lack of evidence pointing towards a very different picture of her time as queen consort.

Titles: Symbols of Power

A queen's use and choice of title was crucial to how they could display and exercise power. A coronation ceremony bestowed symbolic power and authority, whereas the use of titles in documentation demonstrated the extent of a person's access to power. Berengaria's coronation in Limassol, the same day as her wedding, would undoubtedly have enhanced her status symbolically and in front of some of her new subjects, but the lack of ceremony in her queenly realms ultimately did her a disservice with regards to visibility and authority. Coronations and other rituals were one of the dominant ways that monarchs could connect with and be visible to their subjects, and without further evidence it is difficult to conclude why Berengaria never came to England to be crowned during her reign. As discussed above, it was a missed opportunity for both Berengaria and Richard not to have her present, or indeed recrowned at Richard's second coronation ceremony in Winchester Cathedral in 1194. Richard understandably wanted to confirm Eleanor's position and authority in the Angevin realms, and her wealth of experience explains why she was chosen over Berengaria to rule as regent. However, this coronation ceremony was another opportunity to present Berengaria to her English subjects, to have her crowned in front of them, and at least afford her some status as queen consort, even if it remained symbolic whilst Eleanor continued to rule.

With both her coronation and marital ceremony taking place outside the Plantagenet territories, Berengaria had few opportunities to present herself to her subjects either in England or in the continental domains. As Berengaria lacked financial and political resources it is unlikely she was able to present herself as a patron of ecclesiastical institutions or the arts and literature, nor could she establish networks which gave her further visibility in that manner, as so many queens before her had done. The extent to which her queenly household was of Navarrese origin, or indeed her initial entourage to the crusader states, is unclear. Often a lack of representation in the primary sources can be due to a dominant focus on motherhood and marital duties, but this is not the case with Berengaria either. It is not known whether Berengaria regularly appeared at or held court in the Plantagenet territories, which would have equally provided further reasoning to document her activity in the medieval record. There is always the possibility of (re)discovering new documentation in unlikely places, as is the case with the 1209 and 1212 charters to the Templars recently presented by Nicholas Vincent.[5] However, for the most part, we can safely assume that it is unlikely a large trove of material for Berengaria's time as queen consort will be unearthed.

Berengaria undoubtedly held the title of *regina*, and ought to have been able to fully exercise the powers associated with this title whilst consort.[6] The absence of surviving evidence cannot be taken as definite proof that Berengaria lacked access to these powers. She did not use the titles of duchess of Normandy or countess of Anjou, Maine, or Touraine in charters she issued as dowager, which is surprising considering her residence in the continental Plantagenet domains as her usage of these titles might have brought some sense of connection with her subjects.

From surviving evidence it is difficult to ascertain whether Berengaria's household included a chancery whilst queen: more evidence survives for her dowager period.

As her brother Sancho did not leave a surviving heir, Berengaria was theoretically heiress to Navarre, although it was her sister Blanca who took over the administration of the kingdom when Sancho went into seclusion after illness. Despite this position, Berengaria did not utilise the title associated with Navarrese royal power, that of *reginula*, the female equivalent of *regulus*, meaning 'little king,' or *primogenita*. The latter is a title which was later employed by royal Navarrese heiresses. The absence of these titles in any of her extant charters is perhaps a further indication of her distance from her family in Navarre.[7] The titles employed by heiresses were variable: some, such as the Empress Matilda and Melisende of Jerusalem, listed *heres Angliae* and *heres regni* respectively in their charters, giving an indication of the variable practice amongst royal medieval heiresses in the twelfth century.[8]

The evidence from during Berengaria's reign shows that she was aware of the importance of utilising her title, even if she did not have access to the power and authority associated with it. When contrasting with her dowager period, Berengaria's employment of titles makes an interesting case study. Her common epithet, lady of Le Mans, was not a formal title, although it does appear in an undated charter between 1204 and 1230, in which Berengaria confirmed the sale of the vineyards of the Jew Désirée to the abbey of Saint Vincent.[9] Regardless of her lack of powers as a Plantagenet royal – and then as a former ruler – during her consort and dowager periods, Berengaria does not appear to have been restricted in authority in Le Mans. Berengaria's employment of her title *regina* in her dowager period demonstrates she understood the authority that was associated with the title and used it to try and wield the authority she had been denied as consort. As demonstrated in chapters four and five, Berengaria was able to successfully exercise this authority.

What is interesting to note is Berengaria's self-representation in primarily French charters after her consort period, whereby she referred to herself as *quondam regina Angliae*, the former queen of England, rather than solely as *regina* as her predecessors and successors did. Berengaria's decision here is one of agency, whereby she acknowledged that continuing to use the title of *regina* granted her status and authority, even if her use of *quondam* indicates some distance from the title. In the particular case of the charters issued from Le Mans, Berengaria, even if not the grantor, would have had oversight of her representation and taken an active role in curating her image.[10] This phrasing does not appear in all charters concerned with Berengaria during her time in Le Mans, though Trindade asserted Berengaria always styled herself as *quondam*.[11] The charter Berengaria grants concerned with the Abbey of Saint Vincent, Le Mans, noted above, lists her as queen of England, however, the *Registres de Philippe-Auguste*, one of several later editions of documents from Philip Augustus's reign, refer to her as *quondam* only when John confirms a charter regarding her dower.[12] The documents collated in the *Recueil des Actes de Philippe-Auguste* and *Registres* otherwise list Berengaria as '*jadis*', nominally 'once' queen of England when discussing the negotiations for Le Mans.[13] The *Enquête de Saint-Julien* only records Berengaria as queen of England.[14] It is plausible the charters Berengaria had more control over issuing are the ones in which she referred to herself as *quondam*, which is seen in two sets of documents: British Library Additional Charter 46402 (1230), and the collection of six charters in the Bibliothèque Nationale de France Latin 17124. Both are concerned with grants to L'Épau by Berengaria and the transferral of the land to Berengaria from Louis IX, king of France. One later document from shortly after Berengaria's death, explored in more detail in chapter five, sees her labelled as '*reginae Cenomanis*.'[15] The last set of documents wherein we can see variances in Berengaria's title is the cartulary of St Pierre-de-la-Cour whereby Berengaria is referred to as both *quondam regina* and *regina*.[16] The choice of titles is inconsistent, as it does not appear to be attached to a particular period, type of patronage, or institution. Berengaria does not refer to herself as 'formerly queen' in all the charters she issued and there is no one title that became a consistent way of referring to her in groups of documents. In most English records such as the Pipe Rolls, Berengaria continues to feature as queen. The change in her title therefore appears to be a mostly French phenomenon. In the forty-five French documents issued between 1204 and 1230 examined here, Berengaria appears as queen thirty-two times and as formerly queen twenty-two times.[17]

It may appear an obvious choice that Berengaria would continue correspondence with her natal family as consort, particularly as the success of the Anglo-Navarrese alliance depended on her successful partnership with Richard and the bearing of an heir. Such communication would grant an insight into her perception of herself as queen and the potential titles used. However, during her time as queen there appears to be little evidence to support any continued relationship. Richard was in regular contact with Sancho, however, there is no reference to Berengaria in these letters. Berengaria does not appear to have reached out to either Sancho VII or Blanca during her reign. Surviving letters indicate a closeness with her sister Blanca, regent of Champagne from 1199 onwards, though no communications between Berengaria and Sancho are extant.[18] The only record which suggests Berengaria may have returned to her homeland is a letter from Henry III granting her safe conduct to travel to Navarre in 1219.[19]

Due to her position as a single woman lacking other titles – duchess, empress, countess, or princess – one would expect that Berengaria continue to use the title of *regina* as a symbol of her status and authority. The addition of *quondam* beforehand indicates the distance Berengaria wished to place from her previous position: after all, the position did not bring her much success. She may have chosen to use this descriptor as she did not fulfil the role of queen mother, because she did not bear children. It is also plausible she wanted to disassociate herself from the Plantagenets as she carved out her new life in France. From the extant evidence Berengaria possessed little power as consort; however, as the title held symbolic authority Berengaria may have chosen to use it to reinforce her authority when required.

The titles by which Berengaria addressed herself as in letters are also a crucial indicator of her self-representation. They can be compared to charters she issued during her dowager period, and contrasted with how her predecessors and successors, notably her mother-in-law Eleanor of Aquitaine and future sister-in-law

Isabella of Angoulême, presented themselves. The titles in documents both issued by and in which Berengaria appears provide an insight into her perceived status as queen.[20] Berengaria continued to use her title of queen throughout her dowager period, although she used the phrase *quondam regina*, rather than solely *regina*.[21] Even more important are the cases in which she represented herself as 'the humble queen of England,' in letters to Peter des Roches, bishop of Winchester in 1220, and Henry III, king of England, in 1225.[22] This is in stark contrast to her mother-in-law Eleanor, although both Berengaria's successors Isabella of Angoulême and Eleanor of Provence utilised 'humble' as a descriptor in their letters to respective kings.[23] Berengaria's awareness of the precarity of her position and her embodiment of the queenly values of humility and simplicity demonstrate that she wanted to fulfil her role as queen, exhibiting a specific type of model of queenship. In her position as queen, she could be seen as a chaste, obedient wife, however, it may well be that this contributed to her lack of visibility and status in the eyes of her subjects and contemporary chroniclers.

Another important facet of queenship and representations of power were rituals and ceremonies. Berengaria's access to visible rituals in front of her Plantagenet subjects – rituals which granted substantial power and authority, symbolically and typically in reality – was limited by her location at the time of her marriage to Richard, and Eleanor of Aquitaine's dominance in the Plantagenet domains. Competition – namely the vying for power and resources – does not mean hostility between the two women. Equally, it is also impossible to know the true power Berengaria exercised as queen consort. Surviving evidence from Berengaria's reign demonstrates that Eleanor continued to administer her own dower lands and featured at royal ceremonies including Richard's second coronation in 1194; she also played a leading role in the governance of the Plantagenet domains as regent whilst Richard was on crusade. Eleanor's prominence in the government of England during Richard's reign explains both Berengaria's absence from the contemporary chronicles and documentary records focusing on English, Norman, and Angevin affairs. Instead, the records which provide the substantive evidence for Berengaria are crusading accounts which document her wedding and journey to the Holy Land.

The crusading records alone, however, cannot explain why Eleanor was so prominent in the first place. The strong and close relationship between Richard and Eleanor has often been posited as one of the reasons why Eleanor was chosen to rule on Richard's behalf. Eleanor was already an experienced and competent ruler, as well as demonstrating unwavering loyalty to her son and the Plantagenet dynasty. Eleanor's quashing of the rebellion involving her youngest son John in 1193–4 was strong proof of such loyalty. John had proved a disloyal and troublesome brother from early on in Richard's reign, initially in conflict with key officials in Richard's regency, namely William de Longchamp, before allying with Philip Augustus and agreeing to hand over part of eastern Normandy and act as the vassal of the king of France in return for Philip's support and acknowledgement of John as heir to the Plantagenet realms. It was Eleanor who raised the defences against John's forces, mediated during the civil war in England, and further mediated between Richard and John upon Richard's release from his capture in 1194.

Eleanor's vast experience as queen consort of England and France, and as countess and duchess across the Plantagenet domains, is a more plausible reason for why Richard chose her as co-ruler than simply her devotion to him. By contrast, Berengaria, both at the time of her accession and likely during her reign, simply did not have the expertise, connections, or the assets to rule in a similar fashion to her mother-in-law. It is unlikely that Berengaria would have been deployed as regent when Richard had a regency council and a loyal mother to rule in his stead. Another significant factor may have been the need for Berengaria and Richard to bear an heir and likely prompted their close companionship initially.

Rulership: To Be or Not To Be?

The expectations that Berengaria had for her marriage to Richard are unknown. Given the strong examples of female rulership in Iberia, as regnants and co-rulers, however, and the prominent involvement of her mother-in-law Eleanor in the governance and rule of the Plantagenet domains, it would not be surprising if Berengaria envisioned a similar role for herself. Before considering Berengaria's reign as queen consort, it is necessary to consider the existing power structures within the Plantagenet territories, and what Berengaria's place may have been within them.

Studies of monarchy across the Middle Ages show that royal power does not reside in individuals alone: power is shared, dispersed, granted, and taken back. No ruler was able to rule in isolation: they depended on co-rulers or the machinery of government to exercise power with or for them. Berengaria's position as queen therefore needs to be viewed within the context of widespread practices of co-rulership. Since 'all queens are co-rulers,' as Elena Woodacre has explained so adroitly, queenly power is significant, even if it fluctuated and is not always immediately visible in the sources.[24] In Berengaria's case, it is questions concerning her marital co-rulership that dominate, but these must also be placed alongside an examination of regencies and the idea of co-rulership between a monarch and other parties. Such an approach reveals that queens always held agency, even when, at times, their access to genuine power was limited. The ability to access aspects of power, such as control of one's subjects, patronage, and diplomacy, could crucially depend on the success of their co-ruling partnership with the king. Access to resources and a strong partnership were vital for these aspects to materialise. Outside Navarre, successful co-ruling partnerships can be seen elsewhere which Berengaria could look to for a model or guidance, notably with Alfonso VIII and Leonor of England.[25]

Berengaria's experience of co-rulership with Richard was dependent on the model of co-rulership he embodied with her. There were several options available to Richard for the type of political partnership to enact with Berengaria. Elsewhere, I have outlined three models of co-rulership. Divide and Rule, whereby co-rulers focused on specific spheres to exercise influence and power but worked towards the same goals; Collaborative Union, where the co-rulers worked fully together and shared powers across domains; and Lord Rules All, where the male monarch/dominant ruler held the majority of the power and did not share it, and on occasion accessed the co-ruler's power for his own.[26] The Lord Rules All approach isolated the wife and queen, instead of effectively utilising her for co-rule. The notion of joint rulership in medieval Europe is not entirely novel: it had been the case that shared royal authority was evident in Iberia from the tenth century onwards.[27] Thus, Berengaria may have expected to have been involved in rulership with Richard but was faced with a Lord Rules All approach.

Berengaria's marriage brought her into a dynasty with a long history of ruling multiple domains. The Plantagenet domains, composed of kingdoms, principalities, duchies, and counties, formed a composite monarchy ruled over by a primary monarch where local customs were in force and each territory was ruled separately. Composite rule had to be flexible to enable different laws and forms of governance within what remained a unified monarchy.[28] The marriage of Henry and Eleanor in 1152 and their accession to the English throne at the end of 1154 only increased the composite nature of the Plantagenet domains, since the ruling couple were together responsible for governing seven distinct and separate territories. Such a union did not bring harmony across the domains: Aquitaine had always been, and remained, difficult to rule by anyone except its native duke or duchess. The duchy remained firmly out of the control of Berengaria and even, to an extent, Richard. The counties of Maine, Touraine, and Anjou had been ruled as a unit since 1109 following the marriage of Fulk V, count of Anjou, and Ermengarde of Maine, and they displayed little dissent against the Plantagenet rulers. By contrast, the Anglo-Norman and Welsh domains proved a sticking point for the Angevin kings to fully exercise control at several points over the twelfth and thirteenth centuries. For co-rulership to work successfully, it was necessary for the elites from the various parts of a composite monarchy to be willing to engage with the government and administration.[29] The Norman nobility had risen up, or sided with forces against the Plantagenet monarch, in 1173, 1193–5, and between 1200 and 1204, although the appointment of William FitzRalph as its seneschal (and thus an integral part of the composite monarchy) in c. 1178 did much to stabilise Plantagenet power in the region. The extent of the Plantagenet domains could have furnished multiple opportunities for Berengaria to learn skills of administration and act as co-ruler, if Richard had afforded her the opportunity. There was a precedent for female regents or 'deputies' in England, with Edith-Matilda, Matilda of Boulogne, and Eleanor of Aquitaine all serving as co-rulers and acting on their husbands' behalf whilst queen consort.

Composite monarchy was not always a success, however, and nowhere can this be seen more clearly than with John's reign, particularly during the Barons' War and in the face of successful French conquests. A centralised approach to rulership, with its origins in the reign of Henry I, was developed further through Richard's and John's reigns as it became apparent that adhering to local customs was not as effective. The Angevin kings were incredibly itinerant, needing to travel with their court. Due to the breadth of their domains, they also needed to install representatives, namely co-rulers, in the form of justiciars, seneschals, or in longer periods of absentee kingship, regents, in different regions. This could lead to instability, however, as it did in the reigns of Henry II, Richard I, and John.[30] Issues of royal absenteeism also affected the effective governance of the realms, and despite the multiple models of co-rulership employed by Richard and John, the Angevin realms did disintegrate due to successful Capetian invasions.[31]

It is useful to consider the notions of corporate monarchy and rulership, as this lays the foundations for what Berengaria experienced as a co-ruler. Theresa Earenfight's discussion of rulership as a partnership, in a concept she terms as the 'flexible sack,' is useful for this. The flexible sack of rulership incorporates both the king and queen, allowing the circumstances around their rulership as well as their personalities to be analysed in full, which allows us to gain a broader understanding and knowledge of how kings and queens co-ruled.[32] Considering co-rulers as operating within a flexible sack is useful as it can be applied to all the partnerships in this period. It also allowed the king to deploy the queen, either consort or dowager, to rule other places as part of the composite monarchy. With so many territories to rule, it would have been an ideal opportunity to deploy Berengaria as a co-ruler – even of a smaller or less troublesome territory, such as Anjou, whilst

Richard and Eleanor focused on the larger or more complex territories of England and Aquitaine. By sharing governance of the territories, the co-rulers were able to deal with the challenges they faced as a composite monarchy and increase their dynastic representation. Although some partnerships operated well with shared governance – as seen with Eleanor and Richard – not sharing power could be to the monarch's disadvantage, and we will never know how effective Berengaria would have been as a consort if able to rule with Richard. Additionally, although these theories have been developed for later medieval European royal studies, they are just as pertinent for high medieval figures, such as Berengaria, because high medieval royals still had multiple territories to govern and ruled in similar ways. What this discussion of co-rulership has demonstrated is that there were several options available to Richard when sharing power whilst monarch. The fact he opted not to include Berengaria in this power-sharing is slightly unusual, and it is likely she would have expected to have participated in governance and rule.

Personal Partnership

Berengaria's legacy and memory have also suffered due to a perceived lack of successful partnership between her and Richard. As noted in chapter two, several chroniclers record their marriage, but further details of co-operation or dissension are harder to discern. The three models of co-rulership I mentioned above are applicable here to better understand Berengaria and Richard's partnership.[33] Richard employed two very different co-ruling partnerships with his wife and mother. With Berengaria, he opted for a Lord Rules All approach whereby he maintained control and did not share power with his wife, leaving her without favour. With Eleanor, Richard operated a Collaborative Union, working together with his mother to ensure stability and governance across the Plantagenet domains.

The partnership between Berengaria and Richard and our interpretations of it have been tempered by the myths of Richard's sexuality: the impact of this on Berengaria has been hitherto missing from discussion. Much speculation has been raised by historians on the nature of Richard's sexuality, based on spurious evidence, and it is impossible to consider Berengaria without considering her relationship with Richard too – personally disconnected they may have been, but for all intents and purposes they were tied together. Disputes surrounding Richard's sexuality have been discussed by several scholars, and I have recently contested the need to definitively categorise Richard's sexual identity.[34] Regardless of his sexual interests, the surviving evidence indicates a preference on Richard's part for his male companions and friendship rather than spending time cultivating marital affection. Although the reasons why Berengaria and Richard may not have produced an heir will be considered below, at the very least, it is clear that Richard did not wish to reside and co-rule with Berengaria on his return from the Third Crusade, choosing Eleanor as his co-ruler before embarking on military campaigns in France shortly thereafter. Whether the lack of personal partnership between the pair was due to differing personalities or disinterest from one or both parties, it had significant implications for Berengaria's authority and activities as queen consort. She was left on the sidelines and only able to hold symbolic power. Since her nearest kin were in Navarre and Champagne, and we know little of her household, it is impossible to assert whether she would have had the resources to patronise close relatives and develop further networks as consort at court.

Allegations of Richard's homosexuality, to use an anachronism, or same-sex relations, have formed part of his legacy and reputation not only amongst historians, but also in the mind of the general public. The popular modern image of Richard is as a crusading hero and chivalric warrior, hailed as semi-legendary due to his military prowess. During the twelfth and thirteenth centuries an atmosphere of 'compulsory heterosexuality' had developed around knights, which was only publicly avoided through the taking of monastic vows, as the Teutonic Knights and Knights Templar did.[35] Both Mathew Kuefler and Ruth Mazo Karras have shown the likelihood of increased male same-sex activity whilst men were engaging in military activities, and the implications such activities could have on authority and power outside the military sphere.[36] Homosociality, in the form of male friendships, and devotion and loyalty between men were not simply topics occupying contemporary writers, but were very much part of everyday life. Richard's homosocial activities were not untypical of male monarchs but choosing to spend time with male companions instead of Berengaria led to her further absence personally and politically from events at court and in the chronicles.

The Angevin chronicler Roger of Howden is the most commonly cited source of Richard's alleged same-sex activities. Howden reports that a hermit rebuked Richard with the words 'remember the destruction of Sodom and abstain from illicit acts, for if you do not God will punish you in a fitting manner.'[37] Howden's supporting 'evidence' was a statement that Philip Augustus and Richard shared a bed, and several modern historians have taken this at face value as evidence of both homosociality and homosexuality. Both medieval chroniclers and modern historians have often discussed sexuality and sexual activities from a binary perspective, although the discourse is gradually moving to a more fluid understanding of premodern sexualities. Contemporary chroniclers viewed acts of male same-sex activity as too French, or as something committed by heretics and followers of Islam.[38] It is worth remembering that the act of sharing a bed is viewed as an act of political closeness and was not uncommon between rulers. It was not always inherently sexual. Medieval chroniclers may not have explicitly described the act in detail, but there are other cases that demonstrate the politicalness of the act, such as when Henry II of England and his knight, William Marshal, shared a bed. It is plausible that the religious background of both Howden and his hermit source influenced their views of Richard's activities, whether acts of sexual immorality or a lack of hospitality and chivalry, neither of which behaviours aligned with Christian values of the period. When the hermit rebuking Richard speaks of Sodom, the exact quote that he alludes to is that in Genesis 19:5: 'Where are the men which came in to thee this night? Bring them out unto us, that we may know them.'[39] It is a stretch of the imagination to go from knowing a person to knowing them sexually.[40] Liberties with both translation and interpretation have conflated the meaning of this rebuke to become highly sexualised and shape understanding of Richard's legacy, and with it our understanding of Berengaria and Richard's relationship.

As so little has been reported on Berengaria and her life, even less is known of her sexuality and preferences. The discussion in the previous section focused on Howden's recording of 'sodomy' in relation to Richard. Therefore, any assertions regarding Richard's behaviour would not have impacted contemporary beliefs of Berengaria. Indeed, it is modern perceptions of Richard's sexuality which have done further harm to our view of Berengaria. She does not appear to have behaved inappropriately during or after her marriage and may have chosen not to remarry: the latter is a potential indication of her strength of character, although equally Berengaria may not have had the option to marry again. Historians have also claimed she was barren, or lacked sexual interest, which may have affected her marital choices.[41] She lived as a chaste queen and widow, fulfilling an ideal role through which she gained respect and authority. One reason for the lack of record on Berengaria is perhaps an indication of how well she fulfilled this role of chaste queen, and thus in the eyes of the chronicler she merited no comment.[42] Even though she did not bear children, she can be viewed as a successful role model for chaste queens.

In the eighteenth century, when Laurence Echard spoke of a great intimacy and closeness between Richard and Philip Augustus, he described their relationship as an 'unnatural impurity,' imparting his own assertions about the monarchs' sexualities.[43] By the mid-twentieth century, John H. Harvey claimed he was breaking the cycle of silence around Richard's sexuality and based his interpretation on the exclusion of women from the coronation ceremony, something that was hardly unusual.[44] It is Harvey's work which has spurred the modern myth of Richard's alleged same-sex activities. John Gillingham interpreted Howden's account as Richard avoiding illicit intercourse and focussing on sexual relations with Berengaria.[45] If this was the case, the marriage did not prove fruitful. Gillingham readily dismissed the allegations, stating that thirteenth-century chroniclers would be strongly aware of Richard's heterosexuality, and then discusses several cases of Richard's lustful nature, including an illegitimate son.[46] By the 1190s the use of 'Sodom' by medieval writers had become linked to sexual intimacy between men. By utilising a hermit, who had the authority to criticise a monarch, Howden added weight to this rumour whilst distancing himself from being its originator.[47] We cannot confidently assert Richard's homosexuality or bisexuality.

By contrast, Berengaria's sexuality does not appear to have been remarkable by the standards of Plantagenet chroniclers, as she is not recorded as having conducted extramarital relations with anyone or had a particularly voracious sexual appetite. This was in direct contrast with both her queenly predecessor, Eleanor of Aquitaine, and successor, Isabella of Angoulême, who suffered from the common chronicler trope of assigning sexual scandal to women who, in their eyes, contravened societal gendered boundaries.[48] Berengaria has been unfairly apportioned the majority of the blame for the failed political partnership with Richard and the lack of heir, whether due to her looks, infertility, or lack of attraction and being unable to draw Richard away from his male companions: Richard of Devizes listed her as 'a maid more accomplished than beautiful.'[49] We will never know with certainty why Berengaria and Richard were unsuitable marital companions: it is entirely plausible that Berengaria was at fault as much as Richard. However, their marriage needs to be viewed as a partnership, and both parties held responsible for the lack of marital harmony. Had the marriage and partnership been more successful – and lasted longer – it is plausible that Berengaria would have had more opportunities to wield power and been given further opportunities. In the face of the decisions made by her more powerful co-ruler and husband, namely Richard's focus on establishing and continuing a co-ruling partnership with Eleanor and conducting military campaigns, instead of building a power-sharing relationship with his wife, Berengaria and Richard's partnership undoubtedly fits the Lord Rules All framework I have established. This model left Berengaria with little opportunity to rule.

Unless historians can prove one way or another that Richard did or did not engage in same-sex affections and activities, we will continue to wonder and speculate about his sexuality and identity. It is my view that when considering royal sexualities, we ought to move away from binaries and strict categorisation, as well as avoiding anachronisms where possible, unless appropriately nuanced. With regards to Berengaria, she may have been neglected both maritally and by the historical record, but she was a sexual being and plausibly made significant, decisive choices regarding her future by choosing to remain a widow. As noted above, the evidence does not indicate Berengaria (or her natal or marital families) was approached for a marital alliance. Equally she does not appear to have actively sought such an alliance either.

Given the focus on Richard's sexuality, rather than a more nuanced concentration on his marriage and relationship with Berengaria, these allegations have contributed to Berengaria's erasure. We cannot assert either figure's sexuality with confidence. What can be asserted is that focusing on Richard's sexuality has moved historical attention away from Berengaria and affected our understanding of her and Richard's partnership. It is clear that the time apart did harm Berengaria and Richard's relationship. Although separation and travel were hardly unusual for medieval couples, there was very little prior foundation upon which to build a relationship, or any time spent together to remedy this. This left Berengaria little opportunity to co-rule with Richard or be provided with opportunities and resources to engage in governance, which could have been offered. What Richard and Berengaria's partnership tells us is that a king, whether intentionally or through lack of attention, could obscure his queen's visibility, power, and activity, and directly impact female rule and success. However, we choose (or not) to define Richard, it is irrefutable that his lack of closeness with Berengaria had a dire impact for both their marriage and the dynasty. Without a child of their own who could succeed as Richard's heir, the Plantagenet domains passed to John upon Richard's death in 1199, and this had significant implications for the future of the Angevin dynasty.

Childless Queen

The production of an heir was an essential part of a queen consort's role, and becoming a mother was one of the primary responsibilities a queen was expected to fulfil. There have been many suggestions as to why Berengaria did not bear a child, and there were several factors at play. The fact that she spent most of her marriage apart from Richard, not even residing in the same domain as him after 1193, left little time for the couple to produce an heir. Fertility issues on one or both partners' parts could also have played a role, though we know that Richard had at least one natural-born child. A lack of marital harmony may also have impacted the willingness of both parties to further the dynasty.

Unpicking the details of royal personal lives is rarely simple: marital relationships rarely merit attention from chroniclers, who are typically more attentive to great deeds of kings and military exploits. In stark contrast to her queenly successors and predecessors, who bore several children and held lands in their own right, Berengaria was unable to dominate the political scene. The act of giving birth was a life cycle event and a significant political development which would often appear in the chronicles for female royal figures. Being a royal mother gave women the opportunities to network and to intercede. Motherhood also offered royal women the opportunity to rule on behalf of and be influential over their children, establishing networks and alliances, as well as other paths to rulership.[50] As will be shown chapters five and six, Berengaria wielded significant diplomatic and intercessory power in her dowager period as lord of Le Mans even though she did not have access to royal domains or children.

Although childless queens were able to exercise power in their consortship or dowager period, a lack of heirs could restrict the exercise of patronage for queen consorts. Without children, a female ruler could disappear from the historical narrative and, even if they issued charters and appeared in letters, they could be obscured.[51] To succeed, childless queens 'depended on their personalities, their talent for governance and their natal families.'[52] In Berengaria's case, we know starkly little about the first two aspects during her time as queen consort, and we have already seen the lack of evidence indicating natal support before 1199. Childless queens can and indeed did succeed, as evident with one of Berengaria's later successors, Anne of Bohemia. As a dowager, Berengaria appears to have been tenacious and determined, so why did she struggle to exert her personality in her favour during her marriage? Perhaps Berengaria's lack of experience at this juncture impacted her decision not to force her hand as consort, or perhaps she viewed Eleanor as an imposing barrier to her own exercise of power at this stage. Either way, Berengaria's strong personality does not appear forthcoming during her reign, much to her disadvantage.

As will become clear in later chapters, Berengaria had an aptitude for governance that can be seen most prominently in the stability and success of her rule in Le Mans. The earlier absence of a similar aptitude – or at least potential opportunities to demonstrate it – can be attributed to Richard's lack of delegation and co-rulership with Berengaria, as well as Eleanor's primacy in political matters. Even if queen consorts were not active in diplomatic matters at court, they often possessed enough wealth and resources to make regular donations and exercise patronage to religious institutions. This was not the case for Berengaria or for John's queen, Isabella of Angoulême, and the lack of evidence for their patronage starkly contrasts with the wealth of religious donations by queens such as Matilda of Boulogne, Empress Matilda, and Eleanor of Aquitaine.[53] Across the Channel in France, and also in the Iberian peninsula, there is a veritable trove of material to demonstrate the patronage and power of queens, but for Berengaria this evidence is sorely lacking. The following chapter will explore her familial and political relationships in more detail, focusing especially on Berengaria's strongest immediate familial ally, her sister, Blanca, countess of Champagne. Together the two women were able to balance personal and political needs and desires with the duties and relationship they had with the king (and queen mother) of France. It is to Le Mans, and Berengaria's triumph as a lord, to which we now turn.

Notes

1 Roger Collins, 'Queens-Dowager and Queens-Regent in Tenth Century León and Navarre,' in *Medieval Queenship*, ed. John Carmi Parsons (Stroud: Sutton Publishing, 1998), 79–92.

2 Anaïs Waag, 'Female Royal Rulership in Theory and Practice: Queens Regnant, 1109–1328' (Leverhulme Postdoctoral Fellowship, University of Lincoln, 2020–3).

3 Theodore Evergates, 'Aristocratic Women in the County of Champagne,' in *Aristocratic Women in Medieval France*, ed. Theodore Evergates (Philadelphia: University of Pennsylvania Press, 1999), 85.

4 Theodore Evergates, 'Countess Blanche, Philip Augustus, and the War of Succession in Champagne, 1201–1222,' in *Political Ritual and Practice in Capetian France. Studies in Honour of Elizabeth A. R. Brown*, eds. M. Cecilia Gaposchkin and Jay Rubenstein (Turnhout: Brepols, 2021), 77.

5 The charter will be discussed in more detail in chapter 5; my sincere thanks to Nicholas Vincent for making me aware of it, and more on his discovery of the document can be found in his preface to Ghislain Baury and Vincent Corriol, *Bérengère de Navarre (v. 1160–1230). Histoire et mémoire d'une reine d'Angleterre* (Rennes: Presses Universitaires de Rennes, 2022), 12.

6 For a charter of Berengaria's use of *regina* see BL, Additional Charter 46402 (1230) and discussion below.

7 Charles Cawley, 'Foundation for Medieval Genealogy, Kings of Navarre,' accessed 14 May 2023, http://fmg.ac/Projects/MedLands/NAVARRE.htm#_ftn396, 4.1, 4.2.

8 Hans Eberhard Mayer, 'The Succession to Baldwin II of Jerusalem: English Impact on the East,' *Dumbarton Oaks Papers* 39 (1985): 144–5.

9 André Chédville, ed., *Liber Controversiarum Sancti Vincentii Cenomannensis ou Second Cartulaire de l'Abbaye de Saint-Vincent Du Mans. Texte édité avec introduction, notes et index par A. Chédville* (Paris: Institut de Recherches Historiques de Rennes, 1968), no. 97. Discussed in further detail in chapter 5.

10 By Le Mans charters I here mean the charters issued by Berengaria or concerning her and issued from France and not by the English court: this pertains to the series of documents held by AN, BNF, and AD Sarthe and are discussed in chapters 5 and 6.

11 Ann Trindade, *Berengaria, In Search of Richard the Lionheart's Queen* (Dublin: Four Courts Press, 1999), 147.

12 Chédville, *Liber Controversiarum*, no. 97; John W. Baldwin, François Gasparri, Michel Nortier and Elisabeth Lalou, eds., *Recueil des historiens de la France. Documents financiers et administratifs. Tome VII. Les Registres de Philippe Auguste. Volume I: Texte* (Paris: Imprimerie Nationale, 1992), no. 42.

13 Henri-François Delaborde, Charles Petit-Dutaillis and J. Monicat, eds., *Recueil des Actes de Philippe Auguste Roi de France. Tome II Années du Règne XVI à XXVII (1 Novembre 1194-31 Octobre 1206)* (Paris: Imprimerie Nationale, 1943), nos. 837, 840; *Registres de Philippe Auguste*, no. 47.

14 Julien Chappée, A. Ledru and Louis J. Denis, eds., *Enquête de 1245 relative aux droits du Chapitre Saint-Julien du Mans* (Paris: Honoré Champion, 1922), 32–3, 41–2, 56–7, 59–61.

15 Léopold Delisle and Natalis de Wailly, eds. *Recueil des historiens des Gaules et de la France. Tome Vingt-Deuxième contenant la troisième*

livraison des monuments des règnes de Saint Louis, de Philippe le Hardi, de Philippe le Bel, de Louis X, de Philippe V, et de Charles IV, depuis MCCXXVI jusqu'en MCCCXXVIII (Paris: Imprimerie Royale, 1855), 577.

16 Menjot D'Elbenne and L.-J. Denis, eds. *Cartulaire du Chapitre Royal de Saint-Pierre-de-la-Cour, du Mans* (Le Mans: Siège de la Société, 1907), nos. 44, 45.

17 This has not included letters sent to or from Berengaria, grants in which she is mentioned but not the recipient or grantor, and charters which include Berengaria but without a complete title.

18 Trindade, *Berengaria*, 179; Félix Bourquelot, 'Fragments des comptes du XIIIe siècle,' *Bibliothèque de l'École des Chartes* 5th séries 4 (1863): 51–79, accessed 14 May 2023, www.persee.fr/doc/bec_0373–6237_1863_num_24_1_445869. For more on Berengaria and Blanca, see chapter 5.

19 TNA, C 66/20, m. 4 (1219).

20 For discussion of Berengaria's titles during her dowager period, see chapters five and six.

21 For further discussion of Berengaria's titles, see Storey, 'Co-Operation,' ch. 5.

22 TNA, SC 1/1/23 (1220); TNA, SC 1/2/156 (1225). *'humilis quondam Angliae Regina.'*

23 TNA, SC 1/2/5 (1218–9); TNA, SC 1/3/81 (1244–5).

24 Elena Woodacre, *Queens and Queenship* (Leeds: Arc Humanities Press, 2021).

25 See Julio González, ed., *El reino de Castilla en la época de Alfonso VIII*, 3 vols. (Madrid: Escuela de Estudios Medievales, 1960), for numerous entries of Alfonso and Leonor appearing in documents together and sharing power.

26 Storey, 'Co-Operation,' ch. 3.

27 Roger Collins, 'Queens-Dowager and Queens-Regent in Tenth Century León and Navarre,' in *Medieval Queenship*, ed. John Carmi Parsons (Stroud: Sutton Publishing, 1998), 90.

28 Charlotte Backerra, 'Personal Union, Composite Monarchy and 'Multiple Rule',' in *The Routledge History of Monarchy*, eds. Elena Woodacre, Lucinda H. S. Dean, Chris Jones, Russell E. Martin, and Zita Eva Rohr (Abingdon: Routledge, 2019), 89.

29 Backerra, 'Personal Union,' 96.

30 Backerra, 'Personal Union,' 104.

31 John Huxtable Elliott, 'A Europe of Composite Monarchies,' *Past & Present* 137 (1992): 55, 68.

32 Theresa Earenfight, 'Without the Persona of the Prince: Kings, Queens and the Idea of Monarchy in Late Medieval Europe,' *Gender & History* 19 (2007): 10.

33 Storey, 'Co-Operation,' ch. 3.

34 Gabrielle Storey, 'Questioning Terminologies: Homosocial and "Homosexual" Bonds in the Royal Bedchamber and Kingship in Medieval England and France,' *Royal Studies Journal* 9.1 (2022): 33–45.

35 Ruth Mazo Karras, 'Knighthood, Compulsory Heterosexuality, and Sodomy,' in *The Boswell Thesis. Essays on Christianity, Social Tolerance, and Homosexuality*, ed. Mathew Kuefler (London: The University of Chicago Press, 2006), 274, 282.

36 Karras, 'Knighthood,' 278; Mathew Kuefler, 'Male Friendship and the Suspicion of Sodomy in Twelfth-Century France,' in *The Boswell Thesis. Essays on Christianity, Social Tolerance, and Homosexuality*, ed. Mathew Kuefler (London: The University of Chicago Press, 2006), 186, 194.

37 William Stubbs, ed., *Chronica magistri Rogeri de Houedene*, 4 vols. (London: Longmans, Green, Reader, and Dyer, 1868–71), iii, 288. '*Esto memor subversionis Sodomæ, et ab illicitis te abstine; sin autem, veniet super te ultio Digna Dei.*' *Hoveden*, ii, 356.

38 Ruth Mazo Karras, *Sexuality in Medieval Europe. Doing Unto Others*, 2nd ed. (Abingdon: Routledge, 2012), 170.

39 1 Genesis 19:5 (King James Version). '*Ubi sunt viri qui introierunt ad te nocte? Educ illos huc, ut cognoscamus eos.*'

40 1 Genesis 19:5 (Holman Christian Bible).

41 John Gillingham, *Richard I* (London: Yale University Press, 1999), 264.

42 Karras, *Sexuality*, 58.

43 Laurence Echard, *The History of England. From the First Entrance of Julius Caesar and the Romans to the Conclusion of the Reign of King James the Second and the Establishment of King William and Queen Mary on Upon the Throne, in the year 1688*, 3rd ed. (London: Jacob Tonson, 1720), 211, 226.

44 John H. Harvey, *The Plantagenets. 1154–1485* (London: B. T. Batsford, 1948), 33–4.

45 Gillingham, 'Berengaria,' 168–9.

46 John Gillingham, *Richard the Lionheart*, 2nd ed. (London: Weidenfeld and Nicholson, 1989), 161–2.

47 I am immensely grateful to Professor Tom Licence for his guidance and discussion on this topic. Far more nuance is needed on this topic, and analysis has been shortened here for the sake of retaining focus: further discussion of Richard and Sodom will take place in a forthcoming work by the author. William E. Burgwinkle, *Sodomy, Masculinity, and Law in Medieval Literature: France and England, 1050–1230* (Cambridge: Cambridge University Press, 2004), 4–5, 52, n. 28; G. W. Olsen, *Of Sodomites, Effeminates, Hermaphrodites, and Androgynes: Sodomy in the Age of Peter Damian* (Toronto: Pontifical Institute of Mediaeval Studies, 2011), 41.

48 For more on this trope and how sexual scandal wielded against women affected perceptions of royal masculine authority, see Henric Bagerius and Christine Ekholst, 'For Better or For Worse: Royal marital sexuality as political critique in late medieval Europe,' in *The Routledge History of Monarchy*, eds. Elena Woodacre, Lucinda H. S. Dean, Chris Jones, Russell E. Martin, and Zita Eva Rohr (London: Routledge, 2019), 636–54.

49 John Gillingham posits that Berengaria may have been barren, but that the Anglo-Navarrese alliance too valuable to dispense with: Gillingham, 'Richard I and Berengaria,' 171; Joseph Stevenson, ed., *Chronicon Ricardi Divisiensis de Rebus Gestis Ricardi Primi Regis Angliæ* (London: Sumptibus Societatis, 1838), 25. '*puella prudentiore quam pulchra.*'

50 Miriam Shadis, 'Berenguela of Castile's political motherhood: the management of sexuality, marriage, and succession,' in *Medieval Mothering*, eds. John Carmi Parsons and Bonnie Wheeler (London: Garland Publishing, 1996), 351.

51 Theresa Earenfight, 'Highly Visible, Often Obscured: The Difficulty of Seeing Queens and Noble Women,' *Medieval Feminist Forum: A Journal of Gender and Sexuality* 44.1 (2008): 86–90.

52 Kristin Geaman and Theresa Earenfight, 'Neither Heir Nor Spare. Childless queens and the practice of monarchy in pre-modern Europe,' in *The Routledge History of Monarchy*, eds. Elena Woodacre, Lucinda H. S. Dean, Chris Jones, Russell E. Martin, and Zita Eva Rohr (Abingdon: Routledge, 2019), 528.

53 Storey, 'Co-Operation,' ch. 5.

FAMILIAL AND POLITICAL RELATIONSHIPS

Berengaria's exercise of power and lordship was dependent on several factors, and access to revenues, as we have seen, was crucial. This access was dependent on Berengaria's skills as a negotiator and diplomat, and her working relationships with the many rulers and nobles in England, France, and Navarre, which was at times incredibly precarious. Berengaria's revenues outside of her dower lands were otherwise based on her collection of taxes and income from Le Mans: as the following chapter will show, this often brought her into conflict with the ecclesiastical communities of Le Mans and its environs. This chapter turns to the other side of Berengaria's rule by outlining the foundations of Berengaria's life in Le Mans, before moving to a case study examination of the dominant figures in her life: her brother Sancho VII, and sister Blanca, countess of Champagne; the French kings Philip Augustus and Louis IX; and the English king Henry III. Berengaria's relationship with John has been explored extensively and will not be the subject of further discussion here.

Of Berengaria's day to day life and court in Le Mans we know frustratingly little, although her communications with other rulers give an indication of some of the activity. Berengaria's letters and charters contain the names of male clerks and messengers from which we can garner some insight into her household. Her letter to Peter des Roches, bishop of Winchester, in 1220, is sent with the messenger Walter, a brother of the Cistercian order.[1] It has been suggested that the same Walter may have been a later abbot of Perseigne after Adam's death, but this link is tenuous.[2]

DOI: 10.4324/9781003223306-6

Regarding her household, a charter from December 1230 confirms that she employed a clerk, García, whose name suggests he was presumably of Navarrese origin. The will records García's donation to the Hôtel-Dieu, Paris, of his house in Sainte-Geneviève in return for an anniversary mass in his name and is confirmed by Berengaria at Melun.[3] The extent to which García served Berengaria is unknown, but it is interesting that Berengaria had either retained or hired a clerk of Iberian origin until she died in 1230. Documents from 1213, 1215, and 1218 reveal that a clerk named García travelled to the English court on several occasions, plausibly as an intermediary or an ambassador on Berengaria's behalf.[4] Baury and Corriol have suggested that it is likely that Blanca also employed a clerk, also named García, but without further evidence it is not clear whether the two women employed two separate men sharing the same name, or whether this was one clerk who travelled between the two households.[5] Given the long duration of Berengaria's campaign to secure her dower, one can assume she was not immensely wealthy, and thus did not have a substantial retinue to dispatch on diplomatic missions. Whether this meant that she shared servants with Blanca seems unlikely, given the distance and potential duration of diplomatic missions such a clerk would be required to undertake.

Further evidence for Berengaria's household, or at least a glimpse therein, comes from an inheritance dispute after her death over which her nephew Teobaldo presided.[6] The dispute concerned the inheritance of Raymond, bishop of Roda, whose territories had been granted in guardianship to Matthew, a canon of Tyre, several years previously. Following this grant, Matthew visited Berengaria, who was then in residence with Blanca, and granted the inheritance of Raymond to the care of a bailiff of Berengaria's named Calbet. Upon Matthew's death, the inheritance came into dispute owing to the existence of a mistress, Comparada, who had two daughters by Matthew and sought recompense for their subsistence. Comparada agreed to split the inheritance with Sancho VII, however, when Sancho died, the bishop of Illard sought to return the inheritance to the canons of Raymond in Roda. The document is undated and estimated to have been produced during Teobaldo's minority, but this gives a broad date range of between 1234 and 1253.[7] Neverthe-less, the record of the dispute indicates that Berengaria was cer-tainly present in Blanca's court at Champagne for an unspecified period – plausibly during her early dowager years, as discussed in chapter three – and that churchmen from across Europe visited her while she was there.

The role of Berengaria's natal family is especially pertinent in this case. Although we know little of Berengaria's personality, she certainly had a talent for governance, and held power in Le Mans for twenty-six years. Her natal family, predominantly her brother Sancho VII, king of Navarre, and her sister Blanca, countess of Champagne, differed in their approaches to, and relationships with, Berengaria. It was at her sister's court that Berengaria took refuge after Richard's death, and although there are suggestions that Berengaria may have visited Navarre in 1220 given Henry III's request of safe passage for her, there is little in the way of concrete proof to indicate that she ever did so.

Sancho VII, king of Navarre

Although the Anglo-Navarrese alliance was mutually beneficial whilst Richard was alive, after his death Berengaria was ignored by both her brother Sancho VII, and her brother-in-law, John. Sancho VII had inherited the Navarrese throne in 1194 upon the death of his father, Sancho VI. Like Richard, Sancho VII was a military king, engaged in warfare in the Iberian peninsula and north Africa against the Castilians, to whom he lost part of the western kingdom of Navarre between 1198 and 1200. Shortly before Richard's death, in 1198, Sancho had been chastised by Innocent III for his failure to pay Berengaria's dowry, the cas-tles of Rocabruna and San Juan de Pied de Porto. Sancho was threatened with a further mandate if the dowry was not handed over to Richard.[8] Susana Herreros Lopetegui has drawn atten-tion to the importance of Berengaria's dowry within the context of Anglo-Navarrese relations, especially the castle of Rocabruna, situated in the Ultrapuertos region between the duchy of Gascony and Navarre.[9] The Ultrapuertos region, meaning 'beyond the mountain passes [Pyrenees],' referred to the territories on the

Frankish side of the mountains and was close to Gascony. Berengaria's dowry arrangement had seen her father, Sancho VI, hand over nearly half his border territory, a substantial shift in the balance of power across northern Iberia and southern France. During Sancho VII's reign, it is apparent that he wished to retain overlordship of the region, with a series of tenancy arrangements put in place which showed the property was still firmly in the hands of the Jiménez.[10]

By 1201, John and Sancho agreed to continue their alliance, whereby they would come to each other's aid against common enemies, with the exception of the Almohad caliph, Muhammad al-Nasir, also referred to in documents composed by contemporary Christians as Miramolin.[11] The alliance between John and Sancho was confirmed in February 1202 and offered Sancho some security against Castile. However, Castile's military strength was far superior to Navarre's, and with England occupied in a war they were losing against the Capetians, John was unable to offer substantial military support should Navarre require it.[12] No correspondence survives between Berengaria and Sancho, and therefore we are unaware if she petitioned him for help with her dower or her security in her dowager period. However, it does not appear likely that Sancho intervened, given the speed with which Sancho and John negotiated a new alliance. Sancho does not appear to have been politically dominant given his lack of pressure to push for his sister's cause, and his primary concern was to maintain good relations with the Angevins rather than protesting on Berengaria's behalf. There is no other evidence to suggest that Sancho acted for Berengaria during the negotiations for the new Anglo-Navarrese alliance, merely that the alliance was arranged to maintain defence and peace.[13] Sancho continued arrangements with the Castilians, concluding a treaty with Alfonso VIII in 1207, and did not have much in the way of diplomatic leverage to push for Berengaria's cause regarding her dower dispute. John, besieged by the Capetians on the Continent and the nobility in England, did not have the political or military strength to enforce his treaty with the Navarrese or exercise authority in Gascony and along the southern borders. Once Eleanor of Aquitaine died in April 1204, the southern situation became even more dire for England.

After the alliance was confirmed, neither England nor the Angevins seem to have been a priority for Sancho, who was instead concerned with the advances of al-Nasir and conflicts with the Christian kingdoms and Islamic caliphate in the Iberian peninsula. The Christian alliance against the Almohad caliphate led to the famous Battle of Las Navas de Tolosa in July 1212. Although this battle went in the favour of the Christian rulers, they failed to capitalise on their success effectively. At some point thereafter, Sancho began to retire from public life due to illness, and plausibly ruled remotely. A letter from Sancho to Henry III in 1224 confirmed the loyalties of Henry's subjects in Bayonne, a border city between Navarre and Aquitaine where rumours abounded of a potential uprising against Henry.[14] Though Berengaria was heir presumptive as the elder sister, she does not appear to have taken any interest in ruling Navarre for her brother. The relationship between Sancho and Berengaria was never particularly close, even by the time of their deaths. Berengaria shared a greater affinity for Blanca, and it is to Blanca she continually turned for support and shelter in times of need. Sancho was far more concerned with Navarre and politics than brotherly care, and upon his death in 1231, a year after Berengaria's own, it was to his nephew by Blanca, Teobaldo, that the crown of Navarre passed, thus ending the main Jiménez line.

Blanca of Navarre, Countess of Champagne

Blanca, Berengaria's youngest sister, was born c. 1177. Much as for Berengaria and their other sister Constanza, details about Blanca's youth are scarce. Berengaria's relationship with Blanca was of great importance to her rule and power. As discussed in chapter three, it was at the court of Champagne that Berengaria plausibly chose to reside at in her early dowager years (1201–4), and it was to Blanca that Berengaria turned for support and political advice, as their letters testify. Their geographical and familial closeness undoubtedly contributed to their political alliance as well, with interactions between the pair and the French kings synchronised to ensure success and support for one another in their political dealings.[15] Once Berengaria had secured Le Mans in 1204, her correspondence with Blanca is fragmentary, but some evidence survives, nonetheless.

The county of Champagne is remarkable for its political history and rulership, but also for the range of its interactions with both the French and Navarrese kingdoms, especially during the rule of Blanca as countess of Champagne.[16] The connections between the Capetians and the Champenois had been cemented with the marriage of Adela of Champagne to Louis VII, king of France, in 1160, part of a triple alliance whereby Henry I, also known as Henry the Liberal, count of Champagne, and his brother Thibaut V, count of Blois, married Louis' two daughters by Eleanor of Aquitaine, Marie and Alix, in 1164. Philip Augustus was the heir born to Louis VII and Adela, and thus had a maternal familial connection with the Champenois.[17] Blanca married Thibaut III, count of Champagne and Philip's nephew, on 1 July 1199 at Chartres, with Berengaria present at the wedding. The marriage of Blanca and Thibaut was short-lived, since Thibaut died in May 1201 while Blanca was pregnant with his heir, the later Teobaldo IV, count of Champagne. Blanca acted as regent for Champagne until Teobaldo reached his majority in 1222. She was quick to secure Teobaldo's succession in 1201, becoming the first countess to pay homage to Philip Augustus.[18] As her charters attest, Blanca faced several conflicts during her regency, linked to the Champenois succession, but she was a strong and capable administrator and countess. Much like Berengaria, Blanca exercised full power and authority in her position as ruler. It is plausible that Berengaria's residency at the court of Champagne and her close relationship with Blanca would have provided her with a further ally in the form of her nephew, Teobaldo, had she lived longer into his reign as count of Champagne and king of Navarre.

Although Blanca was the youngest of the children of Sancho VI, she was the most politically active of the three daughters in terms of the surviving evidence. This was in part due to her elevated and enduring position as countess, but she also maintained close connections with Louis VIII, king of France, his wife and queen, Blanche of Castile, and their son, Louis IX, through Blanca's familial ties to both the Capetian and Castilian royal families. Blanca's regency initially brought her into regular contact with

Philip Augustus, who viewed Champagne as a neighbour to be neutralised in the first two decades of his reign owing to threats from the Plantagenets and Flemish across his borders.[19] Much like Berengaria, Blanca was a firm defender of her rights, and her extension of hospitality to her sister on Richard's death was not only an act of familial love and care, but also a politically astute move. By providing a residence for Berengaria in France, Blanca could ensure her sister remained in the orbit of the French monarchy, and perhaps even share guidance for Berengaria's plans as a dowager queen going forward. Blanca was an active ruler in every sense of the word, taking up military leadership and organising the resources to defend Champagne's borders where necessary.[20] Though Blanca did not command forces directly, as other royal and noblewomen could do, she otherwise acted as a count in every sense of the word.

After her time in residence at the court of Champagne until 1204, Berengaria undoubtedly had a strong ally in her sister.[21] Berengaria's time at the Champenois court may have also been instrumental in granting Berengaria confidence and knowledge on how to exercise power as a female lord by witnessing effective female statecraft firsthand. Though the letters between the pair and documentation referencing their dual presence is not substantial, it gives us an indication of the relationship between them and how they navigated the political networks and conflicts at the time. Although Berengaria and Blanca were close, they were not the only Navarrese royal family members resident in France during this period. Blanca had appointed their illegitimate nephew, Remi, as her chancellor from January 1211 to February 1220, after which he was elected bishop of Pamplona.[22] The nature of Berengaria and Blanca's relationship can also be seen through financial records and support, as between 1217 and 1218 Blanca communicated through envoys for the purchase of horses from Berengaria.[23] Champenois records also note Berengaria's expenses, with one record of funds probably for her travel and the provision of a further 24 livres tournois for various items.[24] One interesting example relates to the Battle of Las Navas de Tolosa, in which their brother Sancho VII fought alongside forces from three other Iberian kingdoms. The letter was originally believed to be from Blanche of Castile to Blanca of Champagne but has now been identified as being sent to Blanca by her sister Berengaria.[25] The letter contains an account of the battle, in which the Christian Iberian kings emerge victorious against al-Nasir and is particularly praiseworthy of Sancho's actions.[26] The survival of the letter indicates a few matters concerning the three siblings. Firstly, that despite Berengaria's reluctance to return to Navarre, and although she had little connection with Sancho according to the surviving evidence, she was very much abreast of political events and her brother's actions. Secondly, it demonstrates that Berengaria maintained some level of correspondence with her sister, and that they shared a vested interest in the fates of Sancho and Navarre.

The activities of Maurice, bishop of Le Mans, provide evidence of further connections between Champagne and Le Mans, and thus potentially between the two sisters. In October 1220, Maurice recognised that a donation of the tithes of Hambers, a town granted to the abbey of Champagne, harmed the church, and thus he restricted its financial rights.[27] Hambers was situated in Maine and came under Maurice's jurisdiction. Whether this restriction was for his own gain or an expansion of his ecclesiastical rights is unclear, but it showed the bishop's intervention in regional matters to curtail the financial benefices of another abbey. A series of charters later in the 1220s show Maurice's confirmation of donations to the abbey of Champagne from various Manceaux (originating from Le Mans) and local noble families.[28] Interconnections between clerics and regional abbeys were not uncommon, however, it seems plausible that the connection between Maurice and the abbey of Champagne came through his relationship with Berengaria and thus with Blanca, rather than simply by coincidence.

In 1226, the two sisters appear in further documents regarding the succession of the county of Perche, an area which lay between Maine and Normandy and thus close to Berengaria's interests for both political and familial reasons.[29] Berengaria and Blanca's niece, Matilda, had married Geoffrey III, count of Perche, in 1189. The Jiménez sisters' connection with the county, lying to the north-east of Maine, came through their paternal grandmother, Margaret of L'Aigle, the granddaughter of Geoffrey II, count of Perche.[30] Through Margaret, Berengaria and Blanca inherited some of the comital rights when the county fell into escheat in 1226.[31] This left the succession in the hands of Louis VIII with no direct heir to succeed William II, count of Perche. The familial links with Perche also explain the sisters' ongoing links with the abbey of Perseigne, and its abbot, Adam, who resided within Maine and Perche. From Adam's surviving correspondence we can see that he maintained a relationship with Blanca, in one letter expressing concern for her salvation.[32] One charter notes that Dreux, duke of Loches, agreed to pay the total sum of 300 marks each to Berengaria and Blanca, for the settlement of the debate surrounding Perche in April 1226.[33] This charter also contributes to our wider understanding of Berengaria's interactions with the local nobility as it features the sister of Robert d'Alençon, Ella, who was married to Hugh II, viscount of Châtellerault, as a signatory and sealer. The charter is also signed by Amaury of Craon, then seneschal of Anjou. Berengaria, Blanca, and Teobaldo received 900 marks from the viscount of Châteaudun, the lord of La Ferté-Bernard, the lady of Aumanesches, the lady of Fréteval, and the lord of Montfort as part of their agreement concerning the county.[34] Berengaria's involvement in local politics and her presence alongside her sister indicates her dedicated engagement to her role as Lord of Le Mans and her maintenance of a close working relationship with Blanca. Both women were undoubtedly aware of the complex nature of their position as ruling women without either a husband or adult man co-ruling with them, though regency and female rule, particularly at comital level, were not uncommon during this period.[35] They only had to look back to Iberia to see the reality of women ruling, with the sister queens of Portugal and Berenguela of Castile, who co-ruled with her son, as contemporary examples.[36]

Berengaria's connections with the abbey of Perseigne, and its most notable abbot, Adam, dated back to her marriage to Richard. Laurent Maillet has argued that Adam was of Champenois origin and in service to Eleanor of Aquitaine's daughter, Marie of Champagne, who was also Berengaria's sister-in-law and Blanca's comital predecessor.[37] Perseigne was the first Cistercian abbey in

Maine, founded in 1145 by William Talvas, count of Ponthieu and d'Alençon. Berengaria also had ties to the county of d'Alençon and its subsequent rulers. Berengaria's Cistercian patronage is explored in more depth in the following chapter and, given Adam's regular correspondence with Berengaria and Blanca, it is plausible that he was an ecclesiastical figure favoured by the sisters. If so, he may well have had considerable influence in encouraging their ecclesiastical patronage towards the Cistercians. Adam was certainly in favour with the papacy and the Plantagenets. At Richard's request in 1190, Adam worked to locate a site for the foundation of a new Cistercian abbey in Normandy, which became the abbey of Bonport when it was constructed later that same year.[38] Adam also undertook further missions between the Cistercians and Richard, and was chosen as a confessor by Richard, Marie, and the counts of Alençon and Perche, demonstrating the interconnectedness between the local nobility and the Cistercians. The Jiménez sisters sat within this nexus. Adam had also arranged the support of the counts of Alençon and Perche for Richard prior to his departure for the Third Crusade, with the marriage of Matilda of Saxony and Geoffrey III and the appointment of John d'Alençon as vice-chancellor cementing their positions within the Plantagenet court. Documentation from the abbey cartulary indicates that the abbey of Perseigne had a connection with Maurice, bishop of Le Mans, his predecessor Nicholas, and the neighbouring counts, as evidence of strengthening ties between both lord and bishop with the abbey.[39] The abbey likewise was the subject of charters issued by Richard I in 1198, guaranteeing the rights and privileges of the abbey, and John in 1199, confirming all the grants associated with Perseigne, a move replicated by Louis IX nearly fifty years later.[40] Therefore Adam's activity, and that of the abbey more broadly, made it an interconnecting site between the Plantagenets, Capetians, Jiménez, and nobility.

Berengaria and Blanca both grew up in a kingdom where Cistercian patronage and institutions flourished. The first Cistercian abbey in Navarre, Fitero, was founded in 1140, and more quickly followed. Across the border in Castile, similar Cistercian activity developed with the order spreading across Western Europe at a growing pace between the twelfth and fourteenth centuries.

Cistercian influence on royal women such as Berengaria and Blanca of Navarre, as well as Berenguela and Blanche of Castile, goes some way to explaining their decisions regarding their religious foundations and burial sites. Berenguela, queen consort of León from 1197 to 1204 and queen regnant of Castile and Toledo in 1217, was the daughter of Leonor of England and Alfonso VIII of Castile. Berenguela thus had familial ties with Berengaria through the Plantagenets, and Berengaria and Blanca through their mother, Sancha of Castile, who was Alfonso's aunt, making Berenguela, Blanca, and Alfonso cousins. Except for Berenguela of Castile, all these women made strong statements regarding their burial sites, choosing to be buried in Cistercian houses they had founded, at a time when in England and France it was more commonplace to be buried in familial necropolises, though Iberia had a longer established practice of queenly burial sites associated with their patronage.[41] Blanca founded Argensolles between 1220 and 1222, a female Cistercian monastery within Moulins, then a Champenois commune. It was to Argensolles she retired when her son Teobaldo took full control of Champagne in 1222.[42] If Blanca were resident in Argensolles for the rest of her life, then it is highly unlikely that she took up the regency of Navarre, since the geographical distance between the two places would have made absentee regency implausible. We have no evidence that Blanca visited or resided in Navarre in the 1220s, as is similarly the case for Berengaria.

The fragmentary records of the county of Champagne highlight other moments where Berengaria and Blanca appear together in the documentary record, as does the *Ordre de Saint-Jerusalem*, a collection of documents pertaining to the donations and grants given to the Order of Saint-Jerusalem, or Knights Hospitallers.[43] This extensive collection shows grants made by both Berengaria and Blanca to the Order. Donations to the Order were common practice amongst European royalty, and for the sisters these donations also fit within a familial tradition since their father, Sancho VI, had granted the enclosure of Estella to the Order in May 1165, followed by further grants in April 1174 and November 1189.[44] Blanca confirmed the grant of Clairembaud de Chappes to the Hospitallers in 1204 as sole countess, and a later grant was made in the name of Teobaldo IV in February 1215.[45] It was not until 1216 that Berengaria made her first and only grant to the Order, gifting the house of Thorée, which she had founded with Richard, with the grant preserved in seventeenth-century copies.[46] Berengaria and Blanca's separate donations can be viewed in the tradition of conventional piety, whereby they confirmed grants to one of the major religious orders of the time. However, the chronological proximity of their grants and the likelihood of their close communication at the time makes it plausible that their donations were in tandem. Berengaria may have wished to make a donation to the Order earlier. Given her time on crusade and Richard's donations to the Order, this may have made the Order a high priority as a religious institution deserving Berengaria's patronage.[47]

Further evidence for Berengaria and Blanca's involvement with the military orders in the Holy Land can be seen by two charters, which have previously gone unnoticed in Anglophone scholarship, that date from 1209 and 1212.[48] The documents refer to an agreement drawn up between Berengaria, Blanca, and the Knights Templar in Paris. The sisters donated a sum of 10,000 livres to the Temple in Paris. Since the gift was made in Provinoise currency it must have originated from Champagne, indicating that it was Blanca who provided the substantial sum. In return for this sizeable donation, the Templars were to use the funds to purchase lands for the support of the Order, with the revenues to go to Berengaria, granting her a considerable amount of land within the county of Champagne, without the need to be continually resident in the region.[49] The amount of money granted to the Templars was itself unusual due to its vastness. To grant money to the Templars for the purchase of land and to receive rents in return was also uncommon, but indicative of Berengaria's position as a lord, not a queen, but also that she likely did not have the administrative systems in place to manage the rent revenues directly from such a number of lands. It was far simpler to allow the Templars to deal with individual rents to then in turn pass on to Berengaria. Upon Berengaria's death she would grant 200 pounds of rent, which the Templars would pay to the benefactor. For the two years after Berengaria's death, if she willed it, the rents could be granted to whoever Berengaria desired, after which the rents would be afforded to Blanca if she outlived Berengaria. Once both Berengaria and Blanca had died, the rents would remain with the Templars.

The lands purchased are extensively listed in the charter, as are further details of the process by which payment was due to Berengaria. The 1212 charter notes that Berengaria requested the payments be increased to 800 pounds.

The arrangements recorded in these two charters are intriguing, not least because in 1209 and 1212 Berengaria was still in financial difficulties owing to a lack of restitution of her dower. Why was Blanca willing to forward such a huge sum of money to the Templars for something that was largely for Berengaria's benefit? Sisterly concern and love may of course be factors but given that the deed is a financial donation to a religious order and not explicitly for Berengaria's sustenance, we can assume this donation was part of a longer-term agreement to support the Order, perhaps with the intention that Berengaria would eventually be able to repay her sister. These two documents affirm the religious inclinations of both women and their practical support of the Templars. Both women had crusading husbands and it is plausible that the activities of the Templars and their support of the Third and Fourth Crusades encouraged Berengaria and Blanca's donations. It is plausible that given the size of the grant that Berengaria was present in Paris for the issue of both documents.

The papal support and protection Berengaria received for various ecclesiastical matters extended to Blanca as well. Papal protection for widows – and, in the case of Blanca, a regent mother – was granted to both women, and letters from Innocent III and Honorius III indicate the intervention of the papacy in Champenois affairs.[50] The protection afforded to Berengaria and Blanca may have been another aspect that brought them closer together, with both women clearly on the radar of the papacy and experiencing similar obstacles with regards to their exercise of power in Le Mans and Champagne respectively.

Philip Augustus, King of France

Berengaria's political relationship with Philip Augustus was a defining period of her time as dowager queen. King of France between 1180 and 1223, Philip was notable for his significant expansion of the royal domains, bringing an end to the Angevin

Union, and securing greater financial and political stability in the French kingdom. His rivalry with the Plantagenet kings was a defining point of twelfth- and thirteenth-century political history. Although Philip's relationship with Richard I initially started harmoniously, the English king's decision to repudiate Philip's sister Alys in favour of Berengaria caused a substantial rift between the two kings, as discussed in chapter two. Despite his rivalries with Richard and John, Philip Augustus does not appear to have extended such opposition to Berengaria, with Berengaria swearing fealty to him and exchanging her Norman dower lands for the lordship of Le Mans in the autumn of 1204.[51]

Thereafter, Berengaria and Philip Augustus established a conducive working relationship. Although Philip ultimately had differing intentions to Berengaria, namely, to work against the interests of the Plantagenets, he acted in part as a protector and intercessor for her interests at various points until his death in 1223. Berengaria's alliance with Philip ensured that she had a permanent residence in territory that was unlikely to be reclaimed by the Plantagenets due to John's increasing military failures in the wake of Capetian success. While residing in Le Mans, Berengaria had quickly established links with the local nobility and ecclesiastical officials, and maintained her relationship with Philip so she had his support in times of need. This demonstrated Berengaria's political acumen, as a harmonious relationship with the king of France would pay dividends for Berengaria's exercise of power in Le Mans.

The most frequent occasions for interactions between Berengaria and Philip Augustus were moments of ecclesiastical dispute. Philip's involvement in Le Mans typically relates to disagreements between the cathedral of Saint-Julien and the chapter (a body of clergy) of Saint Pierre-de-la-Cour, for example in 1217 when the king of France wrote to Berengaria regarding the extension of the rights of the cathedral, something that was a point of contention for her.[52] Philip Augustus was remarkably astute in his dealings with Berengaria; he intervened in situations which were beneficial to him, such as the upholding of secular authority over ecclesiastical or the early stages of Berengaria's dower dispute, but he was otherwise concerned with maintaining French royal power across his domains, and expanding it. Berengaria thus only had an occasional ally in Philip, although he treated both Berengaria and Blanca, countess of Champagne, as respected vassals and allies. He never disputed their positions as honoured rulers in their respective regions, maintaining the status quo in Le Mans and Champagne to ensure political stability. This is an indication of the normality of female lordship across France, and that Berengaria's exercise of power was part of a wider pattern. With this in mind and looking back to her reign, it is therefore a missed opportunity that Berengaria was unable to fulfil a fuller role as a queen consort.

Louis IX, King of France, and Blanche of Castile, Queen Regent

The brief reign of Louis VIII (1223–6) was primarily occupied with military expeditions such as the Albigensian Crusade, leaving the king little opportunity for negotiations with many of his nobles and vassals, including Berengaria. The accession of Louis' twelve-year-old son, Louis IX, in 1226, supported by his mother Blanche of Castile, who had married Louis VIII in 1200, changed royal policies and the nature of political negotiations with the English and the Navarrese. Connected to both families through her parents, Leonor of England and Alfonso VIII, king of Castile, Blanche's regency, extensive family networks, and patronage extended Capetian power and helped stabilise the kingdom after the military exploits of her husband.[53] The marital union between Castile and France also brought the Plantagenets more closely into French politics once again. During her political career, Blanche of Castile maintained close connections with her natal and marital families and the subsequent cousins, nieces, nephews, and great nieces and nephews who were networked across Europe.[54] Blanche grew up under the close auspices of her mother, Leonor of England, and the importance of her Plantagenet heritage was no doubt imparted upon her when her grandmother, Eleanor of Aquitaine, escorted her to France to be married (1200). It was through both Plantagenet and Capetian connections that Berengaria and Blanche became allied with one another at points during Berengaria's dowager period (1199–1230).

Blanche had familial ties to both Jiménez sisters. Berengaria's marriage to Richard made Blanche her niece. Blanche was also a first cousin once removed to Blanca of Champagne and Berengaria, as Blanche was great-granddaughter of Alfonso VII of Castile, and Blanca a granddaughter of Alfonso VII through her mother, Sancha of Castile. These familial relationships probably encouraged Blanche's son Louis to view Berengaria and Blanca favourably. Even though Louis IX was a minor king during Berengaria's lifetime, Blanche and Louis were of great support to Berengaria.

Louis IX's support is seen primarily in his grant of the lands of Espal to Berengaria, as will be discussed in the following chapter, without which she would not have been able to establish her abbey. From these grants it is apparent that he held Berengaria in high regard and wished to have a positive relationship with her, referring to her as 'our dear queen.'[55] Given the grants were made only a few years after Louis became king and during the years when his mother, Blanche of Castile, was prominent at his side, it is likely that Blanche's influence encouraged both the grant and the cordial tone of the letter. As three incredibly astute and politically active women, Berengaria, Blanca, and Blanche all realised the importance of harmonious relationships with one another and the value of partnerships with the kings of England, France, and Navarre. Through Louis, these women were able to maintain their own power and spheres of influence. Louis' support of Berengaria, through Blanche, was a significant boost to Berengaria's authority and influence in Le Mans in the final years of her life. It enabled her to continue her lordship in Le Mans without any uncertainty as to the tenuousness of her position, and Louis, like his grandfather, remained largely absent from the politics of Le Mans unless circumstances required it.

Henry III, King of England

Berengaria's relationship with her nephew, Henry III, is of interest even though he was a child ruler for most of the period from his accession to Berengaria's death (1216–30). In the early years of his minority, Henry and the regency council appeared keen to resolve Berengaria's dower issues and pay her the appropriate

FIGURE 5.1   Photograph of Berengaria's face from the effigy at L'Épau
© Sarthe Culture

revenues.[56] With ongoing internal conflict, it may have appeared sensible to ensure that Berengaria received her dues and was no longer a source of irritation to the English crown. Henry came to the throne during civil and international conflict, with William Marshal initially appointed as guardian and head of the regency council, before transferring the boy's guardianship to Peter des Roches. Henry was crowned at Gloucester Cathedral on 28 October 1216, and underwent a second coronation at Westminster Abbey on 17 May 1220. The First Barons' War and the French invasion by Prince Louis (the later Louis VIII) was resolved by September 1217 in the Treaty of Lambeth, however, the restoration of royal power took some time. Henry also acknowledged Pope Honorius III as his feudal lord shortly after his coronation and took crusading vows, enabling papal protection. The death of William Marshal in April 1219 changed the shape of the regency government, with a new government formed around the legate Pandulf Verraccio, the bishop of Winchester Peter des Roches, and the English justiciar Hubert de Burgh. Pandulf was recalled to Rome in 1221 and Hubert emerged as the head of the government after removing des Roches, his rival. Amongst this political climate, it is perhaps unsurprising that Berengaria struggled to establish a strong relationship with Henry which enabled her to maintain her dower rights.

During Henry III's reign, Berengaria finally visited England for the first time. Whether restricted by Richard or otherwise unable to travel, Berengaria had never visited this part of her domains whilst queen consort. So why did she decide to journey to England in 1220, after over twenty years of widowhood? Berengaria came to Canterbury Cathedral for the translation of Thomas Becket's bones, which were moved to the Trinity Chapel on 7 July 1220.

> From across the sea came Queen Berengaria, who was King Richard's wife and had the city of Le Mans as her dower. The archbishop of Reims came too, and so did three bishops from his province, those of Amiens, Tournai and one other. Also present were Count Robert de Dreux and Guy de Castellon, son of Walter, count of St Pol, and many other great men from the kingdom of France.[57]

The prominence of many French nobles at the translation of Becket's relics stood to benefit Berengaria through opportunities for further networking, as well as establishing her presence amongst potentially important allies. Three weeks later, on 27

July, Henry III's chancellor, Richard Marsh, sent a notice to Pope Honorius III stating that an agreement had been concluded at Westminster between Berengaria and Henry which has been outlined above.[58] In his letter to the Pope, Henry states that a solution has been reached,

> the queen herself, having recently arrived in England, we satis-fied our presence with the same queen, both on the agreement itself and on the dower she requested, combining it with this settlement.[59]

Berengaria therefore came to England to press her dower case to Henry and the regency government; she had no particular attachment to Becket or its cult, so it is unlikely that the act of piety alone motivated her. It is difficult to determine what pushed her resolve to opt for this time and place, since there had been no considerable change in arrangements or any political crisis that would increase her chances of obtaining her dower.

Aside from communications regarding her dower arrangements, there is little in the way of correspondence between aunt and nephew. In 1219, Henry III granted Berengaria safe passage to Navarre, but this stands out as unusual given that there is no evidence to support Berengaria's desire or intention to travel to her homeland at this date. Considering the lack of correspondence between Berengaria and Sancho, it is unlikely that a return to Navarre would have been purely for a familial visit. One hypothesis is that Sancho invited Berengaria to return to Navarre to act as regent, as she was theoretically heir to the Navarrese throne, but there is no other evidence to indicate the plausibility of this theory. Thus, the 1219 safe conduct letter perhaps suggests an extension of Henry's benevolence towards Berengaria and an attempt to ameliorate any disharmony between the pair, ensuring there were clear, safe lines of passage between Berengaria and the Navarrese court if required. A further letter from October 1220 saw Henry arrange safe passage for her messengers as a further extension of this good will.

Berengaria and Henry's relationship was marked by her dower dispute, much like her relationship with John. If there had been any chance of familial closeness this was underscored by Berengaria's sincere need to access the lands and revenues which she was owed as queen consort and dowager. Like John, Henry faced considerable internal political issues which affected his ability to grant Berengaria what she needed. The English crown had been left in significant debt by Richard's crusading activities and the war with France, and the First Barons' Wars only hampered this further. Personal and familial relationships aside, the immediate concerns of the regency government were politics and stability, and the factional issues also associated with the regency left Berengaria little opportunity to press her case. This made her visit to England in July 1220 for Becket's translation an ideal opportunity to remind the English government of what she was owed, and the visit was clearly a success since she negotiated a settlement that resulted in her payment, even if only in part.

Negotiator and Diplomat

It was in Berengaria's period as a dowager queen that she was able to demonstrate her ability to govern, utilising her personal connections to access and maintain her power and authority. Her success as a dowager is perhaps unexpected, since she did not possess a strong partnership with her natal or marital families that paved the way for her access to power, nor did she have children of her own who could concern themselves with securing her rights and revenues. Berengaria's dowager period ought to be viewed as one of unexpected success. Berengaria disproves the notion that women 'retire' or move away from public life, and that their power lessens, when they become a dowager or widow. She provides an example of a woman whose power and authority only increased until their death. Berengaria successfully carved a sphere of influence in Le Mans, positioning herself on the political scene. She refused to cede authority to local nobles and ecclesiastical figures, and maintained relationships with kings, popes, and other rulers to the benefit of herself and her exercise of lordship.

One of Berengaria's strengths as a dowager queen was in how she negotiated and formed alliances with other rulers and nobles in Western Europe. This was an integral part of being a royal woman, but it was a skill Berengaria had had little chance to perfect as queen consort. Developing such political skills was even more crucial in Berengaria's case because of her lack of children and other forms of familial support. Although the papacy, and to a lesser extent the French kings, showed her protection and support, they were not always able to provide Berengaria with revenues or the outcome she desired, as the papacy and monarchy needed to also maintain other balances of power in France. Berengaria was an important vassal of the king of France, a skilled and successful negotiator, and a ruler in her own right. Although she is remembered more as a local heroine and noblewoman in Le Mans than she is as a former queen of England, her position as a dowager queen was fundamental to her ability to exercise her lordship and navigate the political scene so skilfully throughout her widowhood. It is to Berengaria's rule as a lord, and her activities as an ecclesiastical patron that we now turn.

Notes

1 TNA, SC 1/1/23 (1220).
2 Ghislain Baury and Vincent Corriol, *Bérengère de Navarre (v. 1160–1230). Histoire et mémoire d'une reine d'Angleterre* (Rennes: Presses Universitaires de Rennes, 2022), 149–50.
3 Léon Briéle, ed., *Archives de l'Hôtel-Dieu de Paris (1157–1300)* (Paris: Imprimerie Nationale, 1844), no. 262.
4 Thomas Duffy Hardy, ed, *Rotuli Literrarum Patentium in turri Londinensi Asservati. Volume I* (London: Public Record Office, 1835), 106, 154; Thomas Duffy Hardy, ed., *Rotuli litterarum clausarum in Turri Londiniensi asservati*, 2 vols. (London: Public Record Office, 1833–44), i, 383.
5 Baury and Corriol, *Bérengère*, 132.
6 AGN, Codices, C.1, Cartulario 1, 264 (1234–53).
7 Printed, with notes, in Eloísa Ramírez Vaquero, Susana Herreros Lopetegui, Marcelino Beroiz Lazcano, Fermín Miranda García, and Véronique Lamazou-Duplan, eds., *El primer cartulario de los reyes de Navarra El valor de lo escrito. Le premier cartulaire des rois de Navarre. La valeur de l'écrit. Tomo II* (Pamplona: Gobierno de Navarra, 2013), no. 332.
8 Carlos Marichalar, ed., *Colección Diplomática del Rey de Sancho el Fuerte de Navarra* (Pamplona: Aramburu, 1934), 173, accessed 17 July 2022, www.euskomedia.org/PDFAnlt/cmn/1934153222.pdf; C. R. Cheney and Mary G. Cheney, eds., *The Letters of Pope Innocent III (1198–1216) concerning England and Wales. A Calendar with an*

appendix of texts (Oxford: The Clarendon Press, 1967), no. 22; J-P. Migne, ed., *Innocentii III Romani Pontificus Opera Omnia*, 4 vols. (Montrouge: 1855), ii, no. 211, 182; Étienne Baluze, ed., *Epistolarum Innocentii libri undecim. Accedunt gesta ejusdem Innocentii et prima collectio decretalium composita a Rainerio Diacono Pomposiano*, 4 vols. (Paris: Franciscum Muguet, 1682), i, 112.

9 Susana Herreros Lopetegui, 'El castillo de Rocabruna en Ultrapuertos. Una nueva teoría sobre su localización,' *Príncipe de Viana* 14 (1992): 381–6.

10 Susana Herreros Lopetegui, ed., *Las tierras navarras de Ultrapuertos (siglos XII–XVI)* (Pamplona: Departamento de Educación y Cultura, 1998), 68.

11 Marichalar, *Colección Diplomática*, 187–8.

12 Baury and Corriol, *Bérengère*, 131.

13 Thomas Rymer, ed., *Foedera, Conventiones, Literæ, Et Cujuscunque Generis Acta Publica inter Reges Angliæ et alios quosuis(?) imperatores, reges, pontifices, principes, vel communitates, ab ineunte sæculo duodecimo, viz ab anno 1101, ad nostra usque Tempora, Habita aut Tractatal ex autographis, infra secretiores archivorum regiorum thesaurarias, per multa sæcula reconditis, fideliter exscripta, Tomus I* (London: J. Tonson, 1727), 126–7; Marichalar, *Colección Diplomática*, 187–8.

14 Jacques-Joseph Champollion-Figeac, ed., *Lettres de rois, reines, et autres personnages des cours de France et d'Angleterre depuis Louis VII jusqu'a Henri IV, tirées des archives de Londres par Bréquigny. Tome I* (Paris: Imprimerie Royale, 1839), no. 26.

15 Nurith Keenan-Kedar has briefly explored the relationship between the two sisters and Blanche of Castile; see Nurith Keenan-Kedar, 'The Enigmatic Sepulchral Monument of Berengaria (ca. 1170–1230), Queen of England (1191–1199),' *Assaph - Studies in Art History* 12 (2007): 49–62.

16 The work of Theodore Evergates is crucial for any understanding of medieval Champagne; for Blanca in particular see Theodore Evergates, ed., *The Cartulary of Countess Blanche of Champagne* (Toronto: University of Toronto Press, 2010).

17 Michel Bur, 'Neveux ou cousins? Capétiens et Thibaudiens autour de 1198,' in *Art et architecture à Melun au Moyen Age. Actes du colloque d'histoire et de l'art et d'archéologie tenu à Melun les 28 et 29 novembre 1998*, ed. Yves Gallet (Paris: Picard, 2000), 29–40.

18 Theodore Evergates, 'Aristocratic Women in the County of Champagne,' in *Aristocratic Women in Medieval France*, ed. Theodore Evergates (Philadelphia: University of Pennsylvania Press, 1999), 82.

19 Michel Bur, 'Rôle et place de la Champagne dans le royaume de France au temps de Philippe Auguste,' in *La France de Philippe Auguste. Le Temps du Mutations. Actes du Colloque international organisé par le C.N.R.S. (Paris, 29 novembre – 4 octobre 1980)*, ed. Robert-Henri Bautier (Paris: C.N.R.S., 1982), 253.

20 Katrin E. Sjursen, 'Weathering Thirteenth-Century Warfare: The Case of Blanche of Navarre,' *Haskins Society Journal* 25 (2014): 205–22.

21 From one of Teobaldo IV's later charters, we can deduce Berengaria was in Champagne for longer than the brief interlude suggested by Trindade; see AGN, Comptos, Codices Real 1, Cartulario 1, 264 (1234–53).

22 Theodore Evergates, ed., Litterae Baronum. *The Earliest Cartulary of the Counts of Champagne* (Toronto: University of Toronto Press, 2003), 12.

23 Félix Bourquelot, 'Fragments de comptes du XIIIe siècle,' *Bibliothèque de l'École des chartes* (1863): 59, 64–6.

24 Auguste Longnon, ed., *Documents relatifs au comté de Champagne et de Brie, 1172–1361*, 4 vols. (Paris: Imprimerie Nationale, 1901–14), i, 2.

25 My thanks go to Nicholas Vincent for his work on the authorship and editions of this letter; a recent version is printed in Martin Alvira Cabrer, ed., *Pedro el Catolico, rey de Aragon y conde de Barcelona (1196–1213). Documentos, testimonios y memoria historica* (Saragossa: Institución Fernando el Catolico, 2010), no. 1372. For further discussion, see Anaïs Waag, 'Rethinking battle commemoration: female letters and the myth of the battle of Las Navas de Tolosa (1212),' *Journal of Medieval History* 45.4 (2019): 457–80; Theresa M. Vann, '"Our father has won a great victory": the authorship of Berenguela's account of the battle of Las Navas de Tolosa, 1212,' *Journal of Medieval Iberian Studies* 3.1 (2011): 79–92.

26 For full detailing of the various copies of this letter, see the Angevin Acta project; the copy used for this biography is Léopold Delisle and Martin Bouquet, eds., *Recueil des historiens des Gaules et de la France*, 24 vols. (Paris: Imprimerie Royale, 1840–1904), xix, 255–6.

27 Léonce Celier, ed., *Catalogue des Actes des Evêques du Mans jusqu'à la fin du XIIIᵉ siècle* (Paris: Honoré Champion, 1910), no. 447.

28 Celier, *Catalogue des Actes*, nos. 460, 475, 476, 482, 487, 507.

29 Olivier de Romanet, *Géographie du Perche et chronologie de ses comtes suives de pieces justificatives formant le Cartulaire de cette province*, 3 vols. (Mortagne: L'Écho de l'Orne, 1890–1902), ii, nos. 15 and 16; Kathleen Thompson, *Power and Border Lordship in Medieval France: The County of the Perche, 1000–1226* (Woodbridge: The Boydell Press, 2002), 162.

30 Michel-Jean-Joseph Brial, ed., *Recueil des Historiens des Gaules et de la France. Tome Dix-Huitième. Contenant la Seconde Livraison des Monumens des Règnes de Philippe-Auguste et de Louis VIII, depuis l'an MCLXXX jusqu'en MCCXXVI* (Paris: Imprimerie Royale, 1822), 796.

31 Baury and Corriol, *Bérengère*, 134.

32 Placide Deseille, ed., *Adam de Perseigne. Lettres II (Lettres XVI-XXXII)*, trans. Jean Bouvet and Placide Deseille (Paris: Éditions du Cerf, 2015), no. 30. The letter has not been conclusively dated: Bouvet notes that it was after 1201, and Adam died in 1221.

33 My thanks to Nicholas Vincent for communicating this otherwise unknown charter to me in the early stages of my research: BNF, Latin 2454, fols. 479v–480r (April 1226); see also Romanet, *Perche*, no.

13. '*Ego Droco dominus Locarum, notum facio omnibus presents litteras inspecturis, quod ego me obligavi plegium et debitorem dominæ Berengariæ reginæ Angliæ et dominæ Blanchæ comitissæ Campaniæ, de trecentist marcis argenti, quod Jacobus de Castrogonteri, cum venerit ad ætatem legitimam, quem Jacobum Amauricus dominus de Craon habet in baillio, ratam habebit et sigillo suo sigillabit et integre observabit compositionem illam et pacem quæ facta fuit, de comitatu Pertici et ejus pertinenciis, sicut scripta est et sigillata sigillo ejusdem Amaurici et dominæ Berengariæ, reginæ Angliæ, et dominæ Blanchæ, comitissæ Campaniæ, et vicecomitis Bellimontis, et vicecomitis Castriduni, et dominæ Ele, sororis Roberti comitis de Alençon et quorumdam aliorum.*'

34 Romanet, *Perche*, no. 15; see also nos. 7–25 for full exploration of the Perche succession and the sisters' involvement. '*Nobili viro A[maurico] de Credone senescallo Andegavensi, G[aufridus] vicecomes Castroduni, Hugo de Feritate-Bernardi, Ela de Aumanesches, A[alis] domina de Fractavalle, R[otroldus] de Monteforti, salute et dilectionem. Unanimiter et concorditer vobis mandamus requirentes ut illos plegios quos nobis debebatis dare de nogentis marcis argenti, super conventionibus quas super comitatu Pertici ad invicem habemus, sicut in nostris communibus litteris plenius continetur detis illustribus Berengariæ reginæ et B[lanchæ] comitissæ Trecen[sis] et Theobaldo comiti Campaniæ, et nos ratum et gratum habemus, et nos tenemus pro pagatis de hoc quod super dicta plegiatione per vos factum fuerit cum supradictis regina et comitissa et comite vel cum altero ex ipsis nominee eorumdem.*' Romanet's transcription.

35 See Heather J. Tanner, ed., *Medieval Elite Women and the Exercise of Power, 1100–1400. Moving Beyond the Exceptionalist Debate* (Cham: Palgrave Macmillan, 2020).

36 Extensive work has been undertaken on Berenguela of Castile; see Miriam Shadis, *Berenguela of Castile (1180–1246) and Political Women in the High Middle Ages* (Basingstoke: Palgrave Macmillan, 2010); Janna Bianchini, *The Queen's Hand. Power and Authority in the Reign of Berenguela of Castile* (Philadelphia: University of Pennsylvania Press, 2012); H. Salvador Martínez, *Berenguela the Great and Her Times (1180–1246)*, trans. Odile Cisneros (Leiden: Brill, 2021). For the sister queens of Portugal see Miriam Shadis, 'The First Queens of Portugal and the Building of the Realm,' in *Reassessing the Roles of Women as 'Makers' of Medieval Art and Architecture*, ed. Therese Martin, 2 vols. (Leiden: Brill, 2012), ii, 671–702.

37 Laurent Maillet, 'Les missions d'Adam de Perseigne, émissaire de Rome et de Cîteaux (1190–1221),' *Annales de Bretagne et des Pays de l'Ouest* 120.3 (2013): 99.

38 Maillet, 'Les missions,' 102. For more on Bonport see Annick Gosse-Kischinewski, 'La fondation de l'abbaye de Bonport: de la légende à la réalité politique,' in *1204. La Normandie entre Plantagenêts et Capétiens*, eds. Anne-Marie Flambard Héricher and Véronique Gazeau (Caen: CRAHM, 2007), 61–74.

39 Gabriel Fleury, ed., *Cartulaire de l'abbaye cistercienne de Perseigne* (Mamers: Fleury Dangin, 1880), nos. 341–52.

40 Fleury, *Cartulaire*, nos. 37, 41, 45.

41 Lucy Pick, *Her Father's Daughter. Gender, Power, and Religion in the Early Spanish Kingdoms* (Ithaca: Cornell University Press, 2017), 175–80.

42 Theodore Evergates, 'Countess Blanche, Philip Augustus, and the War of Succession in Champagne, 1201–1222,' in *Political Ritual and Practice in Capetian France*, eds. M. Cecilia Gaposchkin and Jay Rubenstein (Turnhout: Brepols, 2021), 77.

43 The major collection of grants to the Order is J. Delaville le Roux, ed., *Cartulaire Général de L'Ordre des Hospitaliers de Saint Jean de Jérusalem (1100–1310)*, 4 vols. (Paris: Ernest Leroux, 1844–1906), with some grants pertaining to those with a Navarrese connection listed separately in Santos A. García Larragueta, ed., *El gran priorado de Navarra de la ordren de San Juan de Jerusalen*, 2 vols. (Pamplona: Institución Príncipe de Viana/Editorial Gomez, 1957).

44 García Larragueta, *El gran priorado*, i, nos. 346, 462, 880.

45 García Larragueta, *El gran priorado*, ii, nos. 1183, 1434.

46 Bibliothèque Sainte-Geneviève, ms. 701, f. 78, copy presented in Bibliothèque Sainte-Geneviève, ms. 675; Delaville le Roux, *Cartulaire Général*, ii, no. 1451.

47 Léopold Delisle, ed., *Cartulaire Normand de Philippe-Augusute, Louis VIII, Saint-Louis, et Philippe-le-Hardi* (Geneva: Mégariotis Reprints, 1978), no. 27.

48 My deepest thanks go to Nicholas Vincent for his communication of the references for these documents, which will appear with full discussion and notes in the Angevin Acta project; otherwise, for further discussion see also Baury and Corriol, *Bérengère*, 133–4.

49 My thanks to Nicholas Vincent for his further elaboration on the material here, which has aided my own analysis of the documents under discussion.

50 Raymond Foreville, *Le Pape Innocent III et la France* (Stuttgart: Anton Hiersemann, 1992), 281–2.

51 John W. Baldwin, François Gasparri, Michel Nortier, and Elisabeth Lalou, eds., *Recueil des historiens de la France. Documents financiers et administratifs. Tome VII. Les Registres de Philippe Auguste. Volume I: Texte* (Paris: Imprimerie Nationale, 1992), no. 47; Henri-François Delaborde, Charles Petit-Dutaillis, and J. Monicat, eds., *Recueil des Actes de Philippe Auguste Roi de France. Tome II Années du Règne XVI à XXVII (1 Novembre 1194–31 Octobre 1206)* (Paris: Imprimerie Nationale, 1943), nos. 837, 840.

52 René-Jean-François Lottin, *Chartularium insignis ecclesiae Cenomanensis quod dicitur liber albus capitula* (Le Mans: Monnoyer, 1869), nos. 10 and 12.

53 See Lindy Grant, *Blanche of Castile* (London: Yale University Press, 2016), for more on her career.

54 Grant, *Blanche of Castile*, 164–8.

55 BNF, Latin 17124, fol. 6, fol. 29 (1229–30). '*carissima domina nostra Berengariana quondam regina Anglorum.*'

56 For Henry's reign, see David A. Carpenter, *The Minority of Henry III* (London: Methuen, 1990); David Carpenter, *Henry III. The Rise to Power and Personal Rule. 1207–1258* (London: Yale University Press, 2020); David Carpenter, *Henry III. Reform, Rebellion, Civil War, Settlement. 1258–1272* (London: Yale University Press, 2023).

57 TNA, E 368/3/2 (1220); Carpenter, *Henry III. The Rise to Power*, 179; Paul Webster, ed., and Janet Shirley, trans., *The History of the Dukes of Normandy and the Kings of England by the Anonymous of Béthune* (Abingdon: Routledge, 2021), 191–2. Shirley's translation.

58 TNA, SC 1/4/67 for John Marshal's letter concerning Berengaria's dower payment (July 1220); TNA, C 66/23, m. 1–3d (1220), for Henry's agreements. Marshal's letter has been edited and translated in David Crouch, ed., *The Acts and Letters of the Marshal Family: Marshals of England and Earls of Pembroke, 1145–1248* (Cambridge: Cambridge: University Press, 2015), no. 151. See also H. C. Maxwell-Lyte, ed., *Patent Rolls of the Reign of Henry III, preserved in the Public Record Office, A. D. 1216–1225* (London: His Majesty's Stationery Office, 1901), 245.

59 TNA, C 66/23, m. 3 (1220). '*Eidem regine presentiam nostram in Anglia nuper adeunti, tam super ipsa conventione quam super dote sua quam petit satisfecimus, componendo cum ea in hac forma.*'

LORD OF LE MANS

Rulership and Religion[1]

Once Berengaria had exchanged her Norman dower lands with Philip Augustus and became lord of Le Mans, her position soon changed as she established herself as a ruler. Although Berengaria was occasionally titled *domina Cenomannis*, 'Lady of Le Mans', the title of lord is far more appropriate in encompassing the full range of her powers and activities, and a more grammatically accurate translation of the Latin term *domina* is 'female lord.' Lordship, like power and agency, can have many meanings but, for our purposes, it is dependent upon the possession of property to provision oneself with resources – material, financial, and personal – alongside other activities.[2] The exercise of lordship also depended on interpersonal relationships and maintaining authority over one's vassals, particularly in an area such as Maine where lands and titles were not always documented in writing – as seen with the series of eyewitness testimonies that appear in the 1246 *enquête*, discussed below. It is in Le Mans, free of her unsupportive marital family and without any husband, that Berengaria was able to establish her role in the political arena and exercise genuine power. Chapter three touched on the initial issues surrounding Berengaria's dower, but her dower rights continued to be an issue for the rest of her life and her campaign to secure her dower merits further attention here. The remainder of the chapter then considers her religious relationships and networks, namely that with the papacy and Maurice, bishop of Le Mans, and then her ecclesiastical patronage, with a particular focus on two institutions dear to her heart, her chapter of Saint Pierre-de-la-Cour and L'Abbaye de L'Épau.

DOI: 10.4324/9781003223306-7

Dower

Berengaria's agency and determination to obtain her dower rights can be seen most clearly in the period 1204–30, as this section demonstrates. Berengaria had hypothetically been granted the duchy of Gascony to provide her with income until Eleanor of Aquitaine's death, whereby Berengaria would inherit the lands that formed part of the queenly demesne, although this was by no means fixed in the twelfth century. However, Gascony had allegedly been granted to Berengaria's sister-in-law, Leonor, as part of her dowry for her marriage (1170) to Alfonso VIII, king of Castile.[3] Neither Berengaria nor Leonor were able to access the revenues for Gascony initially. When Eleanor died in April 1204, Berengaria ought to have had rights to all the dower lands that belonged to the English queen, with the expectation that Gascony would pass to Leonor and Alfonso. However, there is no evidence that indicates Berengaria received any income from her dower lands as consort, and particularly not from Gascony as consort or dowager. The dower dispute was complicated: dower was for life unless stated otherwise, and as Eleanor continued to live until 1204, and John married Isabella of Angoulême and took her as queen in 1200, all three women needed to have financial provisions through dower. The dower campaign is an integral part of Berengaria's dowager period, and far more evidence survives from these years, including several letters to her from kings and popes.[4]

As noted in chapter three, Berengaria successfully wielded power in Le Mans from 1204 until her death in 1230 and she clearly received revenues from the city itself. However, revenues from her Plantagenet dower lands outside of Normandy continued to be problematic.[5] Surviving letters between Berengaria and first John, king of England, then his son and successor, Henry III, show the determination with which she pursued her dower rights, and her persistence in exacting what she was owed from the English crown. John certainly had other concerns, and assuaging the rights of his former sister-in-law was not one of them, particularly in the first decade of the thirteenth century.

Pope Innocent III issued a letter concerning Berengaria's situation and dower to Hubert Walter, archbishop of Canterbury,

Eustace, bishop of Ely, and Mauger, bishop of Worcester, on 16 December 1204.[6] Innocent informed the ecclesiastical officials of his admonishment of John for failing to provide Berengaria with sufficient income and her dower, thus forcing her to leave her residence to seek refuge with her sister Blanca in Champagne. The pope expressed his displeasure with John for the precarity in which he had placed Berengaria and reminded the bishops of the Church's responsibility to protect widows and orphans. The bishops received orders to investigate Berengaria's appeal and to return their judgement to Innocent.

This initial request from the papacy does not appear to have galvanised John into action. He did not respond until March 1206, when he was preparing for an expedition to France, at which point he officially invited Berengaria to England to discuss matters. Following a consultation with the queen's messengers and the arrangement of a truce with Philip Augustus regarding Plantagenet-Capetian hostilities, John renewed his invitation to Berengaria in November the same year.[7] The precise nature of the interventions taken by Innocent III and Honorius III receive greater attention below, however, it is clear that John was caught between a rock and a hard place, as he so often was during Berengaria's dower campaign. John had ample reason not to hurry in making provision for Berengaria, however, including ongoing conflict with the Capetians, excommunication, domestic disputes concerning prelates and nobles, such as the contestation over the election of the archbishop of Canterbury, as well as the need to make provision for his own queen consort, Isabella of Angoulême. Based on the limited surviving evidence, it is clear Berengaria was persistent. Whether she continued to make her claim personally between 1206 and 1213 is unknown, although the papacy certainly petitioned John on her behalf during these years.

Berengaria was in regular contact with the papacy from the beginning of her widowhood through to her death in 1230. In September 1207, Innocent III had sent a further mandate to the Eustace, bishop of Ely, and Mauger, bishop of Worcester, to summon John to appear by proctor before the papacy to answer to Berengaria or her representative regarding the payment of her dower, since it was still unpaid.[8] John dispatched a letter in November 1207 to Berengaria acknowledging that he had received her messengers, and letter, and returned the messengers with said letter, but otherwise the details of Berengaria's payments are oblique.[9] This mandate from Innocent does not appear to have sparked any immediate reaction, since he followed up in the spring of 1208 and in February 1209 with further exhortations that if John did not make satisfaction to Berengaria within six months all the English lands that constituted her dower would be placed under interdict.[10] This would not be the first, nor the last, time that interdict was to affect England, as seen in the Langton dispute between 1207 and 1213. Innocent's efforts were to little avail however. A year later, in May 1210, Innocent sent a mandate to Gilbert, bishop of Rochester, and Herbert, bishop of Salisbury, to publish the sentence of interdict resulting from John's failure to pay Berengaria her dower and other sums.[11] Another letter dated 14 May 1210 showed Innocent's proclamation the interdict would be enforced as John had not appeared regarding Berengaria's dower. [12] However, an ecclesiastical dispute regarding the appointment of the archbishop of Canterbury, with John attempting to install John de Gray, the monks of Canterbury their candidate, Reginald their subprior, and Innocent III opting for Stephen Langton, had caused serious disharmony between John and Innocent as well.

Although the interdict and excommunication were resolved by the 1213 agreement between John and Innocent, Berengaria's dower was not. An initial letter regarding Segré, one of Berengaria's dower castles in Anjou, was sent by Innocent's papal successor, Honorius III, on 15 November 1216 to the archbishop, deacon, and archdeacon of Tours, mandating their support to enable Berengaria to receive the castle.[13] Several months later, a further letter dated February 1217 once again requested that the archbishop and dean of Tours support Berengaria in her acquisition of the castle of Segré.[14] A further letter in August 1217 to the abbot of Josaphat and the dean and chancellor of Chartres requested them to arrange the restitution of Segré.[15] The matter of Segré spread far further than Berengaria and the surrounding ecclesiastics. Clergy in Le Mans were later involved with the land too, as evidenced by Maurice, bishop of Le Mans' confirmation of the acquisition of territory in Segré for the cathedral chapter in 1228.[16] Further mandates and confirmations of the agreement between Berengaria and Henry III were issued in 1221 and 1228.[17] The final letter attests that, despite the initial payments received by Berengaria and detailed in an earlier section of this chapter, by 1228 she was still owed dower which she should have received over thirty years before. The commitment shown by the papacy and its interventions concerning Berengaria's dower were not entirely extraordinary – surviving letters indicate papal involvement in a range of disputes involving women – however, it is clear that papal authority was not absolute in resolving these issues, particularly in the face of weakening royal authority during John's reign and a struggling economy.

The Patent Rolls are the most forthcoming source for exchanges between John and Berengaria, at least from an English perspective, as they contain copies of the royal letters patent. In December 1213, John arranged for the safe conduct of two messengers from Berengaria and gave them an audience at court.[18] Negotiations must have continued as John again issued a passage of safe conduct for her messengers in March 1214 to allow negotiations with Peter des Roches, John's chief justiciar.[19] Peter was related to William, the seneschal of Anjou and sometime ally of Berengaria, although the definitive nature of the relationship between Peter and William is unclear.[20] William appears several times in connection with Berengaria and her negotiations, and it is plausible that he was part of the Manceaux (Le Mans) negotiating party, namely the messengers who had been dispatched on Berengaria's behalf.[21] In September 1215, John made contact with Berengaria outlining a new dower agreement, at a time of crisis when England was in the midst of the First Barons' War and John had requested papal support against the threat of French invasion.[22] The agreement would certainly have been beneficial to John if he could attain it: he proposed a situation in which he would confirm Berengaria's possession of Le Mans and the surrounding environs, known as Quinte, return her dower castles of Segré and Mervent if he obtained them, and provide her with an annuity.[23] These arrangements were to Berengaria's liking, and she confirmed the arrangement in October 1215. John made his formal pledge to her the following month and agreed to pay Berengaria 2000 marks to constitute the arrears, as well as a payment of 1000 marks annually.[24] This settlement was confirmed by Innocent III in January 1216.[25] However, the agreement was far from being resolved. Less than a year later, John petitioned Berengaria with a request to delay his payment due to the rebellion taking place in England.[26] Whether Berengaria agreed to this postponement is unclear, but she was quick to follow up her petitions with her nephew, Henry III, who, as a minor king, succeeded John after his death in October 1216.

The exchanges between aunt and nephew are documented in Henry III's Close Rolls, which contain transcripts of royal letters of an executive nature which conveyed orders and instructions. In 1220, Henry – or at the very least, his regency government – agreed to make payments to Berengaria. The English king attested that he would arrange for the settlement to be made in full, with further payments to clear the arrears for the twenty-one years that Berengaria had been lacking her dower revenues.[27] Berengaria requested 4500 pounds sterling to be paid to her to remedy the arrears. Henry agreed to pay Berengaria 1000 pounds immediately to clear some of the arrears, with 2000 pounds to be paid annually to clear the arrears of the remaining 3500 pounds. The charter attests that she would then receive 1000 pounds annually after the arrears were cleared to honour the original settlement, in two separate payments of 500 pounds at Ascension and All Saints' Day. Additionally, Berengaria would receive the 1000 marks originally agreed with John from tin mine revenues in Devon and Cornwall, to be supplemented from the London treasury if the mine income was not sufficient. All seemed well. The Patent Rolls document minor payments for Berengaria's expenses between 1219 and 1221, with a larger payment of 500 pounds owed in debt to be paid in 1221.[28] These financial arrangements did not last.

In October 1225, a letter from Berengaria requested a payment of 1000 pounds, indicating that Henry had fallen behind with what he owed her. The Close Rolls record that Henry made a payment of 1000 pounds in May, and therefore was likely failing to honour the agreement with the arrears payments.[29] This was quickly remedied, with notice of a second payment of 1000 pounds made in December 1225.[30] Berengaria was also the recipient of other smaller payments, likely to cover household expenses rather than as part of her dower arrangements. She received another payment of 1000 pounds in May 1226, but this was to be the last, and she had only received 3000 pounds in total, thus falling short of the 4500 pounds that she had agreed with Henry.[31] Whether Henry, upon gaining his majority as king in 1227, decided that his aunt's dower was no longer a priority is unclear. She was never to be fully recompensed for her dower arrangements, even though surviving papal letters show that she had the backing of popes Innocent III, Honorius III, and Gregory IX who acted as her spiritual protectors, often intervening in disputes on her behalf. Throughout the negotiations to receive recompense for her dower, Berengaria was a successful and persistent negotiator and diplomat.

Religious Relationships and Patronage

Dower disputes were not the only focus of Berengaria's activities as lord of Le Mans. She was actively involved in religious patronage and relationships with the Church on both a local and international level. While she was queen consort, we have little evidence to support the notion of Berengaria as a religious patron, however, her dowager period provides plentiful evidence of her connections with different institutions and religious orders. By gaining Le Mans, Berengaria had an area under her rulership, even if she still needed to swear fealty to Philip Augustus as her overlord. Through the revenues she accrued as lord of Le Mans, Berengaria became a financially empowered noblewoman. This section will consider two dominant areas of Berengaria's religious activities: firstly, by expanding on her relationship with the and the ecclesiastical officials of Le Mans, and secondly by focusing on her patronage in Le Mans, particularly in relation to Saint Pierre-de-la-Cour and her establishment of L'Abbaye de L'Épau.

Papal Relations and the Church

Berengaria's relationship with the papacy during the early thirteenth century was crucial to her dower campaign. The papacy was expected to act as spiritual protector of the vulnerable, and as a widow, Berengaria fulfilled this category. By acting on behalf of Berengaria, the papacy was able to legitimise her actions and put pressure on others, whether kings, nobles, or ecclesiastics, who obstructed the queen's rights. Berengaria's relationship with Pope Honorius was of particularly great benefit in her disputes with local churchmen in Le Mans.

Berengaria was not naïve; she would have realised the significance of papal protection and the piety she needed to demonstrate to keep this ecclesiastical support, providing security to her as a widow. Though papal protection and support was not always guaranteed, Berengaria was aware of the advantages of having the papacy on her side against determined bishops and other ecclesiastical officials in Le Mans.

The following years were by no means plain sailing for Berengaria when it came to local ecclesiastical relationships, but the papacy does not appear to have been involved again in local affairs in Le Mans until 1223. Early in this year, Honorius issued a mandate extending protection to Berengaria's officials, Peter, Alfric, and William, all of whom were under threat from the bishop of Le Mans.[32] At the same time, Honorius wrote to the abbots of Saint Vincent and Saint Pierre-de-la-Couture regarding misbehaving clerics, setting out the appropriate punishments for them, and demonstrating Honorius's interest in protecting Berengaria and her lordly rights.[33] Berengaria's relationship with the abbey of La Couture was complicated and poorly documented. The abbey was situated on the outskirts of Le Mans and had previously maintained a connection with the counts of Maine, who had incorporated the Benedictine abbey into their sphere of authority.[34] However, since the death of Elias, count of Maine, in 1110, the abbey had obtained its long argued for autonomy from the comital and ecclesiastical authority of both Maine and Le Mans respectively.

Berengaria's business with La Couture relates primarily to her acquisition of a vineyard, within the fief of La Couture, from a Jew named Copinus. She then granted the vineyard to the abbey in 1209 in return for 15 livres manceaux, to be paid to her knight Martin.[35] The same Martin appeared in an undated charter (estimated to date from between 1204 and 1230) whereby Berengaria confirmed Martin's sale to the abbey of Saint Vincent of the property and vineyards which had belonged to another Jew, Desirée, for 15 livres manceaux.[36] The provenance and authenticity of several of the Manceaux charters, including those of Saint Vincent, have been discussed by Robert Latouche, however, the donation by Berengaria is believed to be genuine.[37] Similar to La Couture, the vineyards granted to Saint Vincent were already located within its fief. In the same charter Berengaria agreed for the establishment of an anniversary mass for her 'most revered husband Richard, king of England,' a description which lacked especially affectionate language but undoubtedly acknowledged the importance of their prior relationship.[38] The abbey appeared again in 1216 during a dispute between Berengaria and Maurice, bishop of Le Mans, which is described in more detail below, with La Couture acting as one of the arbiters, alongside Robert d'Alençon and William des Roches.[39]

Further evidence of Berengaria's relationship with Jews in areas under her authority has been documented in a charter of unknown origins, presented by Eugène Hucher. The charter, dating from 1206, records the conversion of a Jew, previously named Dexlebeneie Cornutus, and his family, who had sold their holdings in La Barillerie to Geoffrey the clerk for 4 1/2 libris manceaux, and 5 solidis manceaux to their children, for granting the sale.[40] This record demonstrates further the presence of a Jewish community in Le Mans: given there is no notable expulsion or migration of Jews from Le Mans in Berengaria's time as lord, it is plausible that her rule was not as dangerous as her former husband's. However, the presence of converted Jews in this charter raises questions: did Berengaria push a policy of conversion during her tenure? Did Dexlebeneie and his family convert prior to Berengaria's lordship in 1204? The Dominican order, who were particularly fervent in their mission to convert Jews, did not settle in Le Mans until c. 1230. The area where Dexlebeneie's lodgings were was adjacent to the road which today holds the name of Rue de la Juiverie and is located near the court of the Jewry. This charter also provides further evidence for the presence of a knight, or servant, of Berengaria's, named Paulin Boutier, as La

Barillerie was situated within his fief. Paulin appears elsewhere in the *enquête* where he was eventually exonerated by Saint-Julien for taking measures of wine from La Chapelle-Saint-Aubin, and refusing to return them, between 1216 and 1226.[41] Paulin lived in the faubourg Saint-Nicolas with his family, owned a meadow near Gue Bernisson, and died in July 1230.[42] Paulin likely exercised his seigneurial rights over the Jews in his fief, including taxation, which in turn would have been paid to Berengaria. However, given that the authenticity of the document cannot be traced to an original we can only hypothesise about the further extent of Berengaria's relationship with and control of the Jewish community in Le Mans.

The appearance of William des Roches in this dispute is also of interest.[43] After Berengaria exchanged her Norman dower with Philip Augustus in 1204, she also agreed to grant her dower property of Château-du-Loir, a Manceaux property to the south of Le Mans, to William des Roches in September the same year.[44] In return, William surrendered his rights as seneschal of Le Mans, but retained his control of wider Maine. In May 1206, William had been granted the position of seneschal of Anjou, with William holding some rights in Touraine as well, although Philip claimed the majority of the comital rights for himself.[45] A further agreement in January 1207 saw Philip Augustus extend his own rights further across Touraine and Anjou, restricting William's position as seneschal.[46] Despite this and the seneschal's previous history of wavering allegiances between the Plantagenets and Capetians, William remained loyal to Philip.

William's presence in the region, his control of Château-du-Loir, and his position as seneschal meant that he had frequent interactions with Berengaria, many of which can be attested by their joint presence in charters. It can only be speculated as to whether the relationship was harmonious. It may have been with some disgruntlement that William surrendered his rights to control Le Mans in return for the lesser prize of Château-du-Loir, however, he does appear to have ruled in Berengaria's favour on certain occasions. William's presence in Maine can be seen through his religious patronage and establishment of a female Cistercian house, Bonlieu, near Château-du-Loir in 1219.[47] William and Berengaria shared an affinity for the Cistercian order. They both created personal foundations – Berengaria at L'Épau and William at Bonlieu – with William perhaps intending to transform Bonlieu into a dynastic mausolea.[48] Whilst Berengaria and William's religious foundations were only linked by the order they housed, William's establishment of Bonlieu added to the growing Cistercian presence in Maine and its environs. William's foundation was unique at this time in that it was the first female Cistercian order established in Maine; when Berengaria founded her own Cistercian community at L'Épau a decade later, she opted for a male monastery.

Berengaria was by no means isolated as a female lord in this period. Aside from Blanca in Champagne, other contemporary female lords include Eleanor, countess of Vermandois (d. 1213), and Joan, countess of Flanders (d. 1244), who both ruled their respective regions in their own right. However, like any lord, she had to navigate maintaining harmonious, or at least cordial, relationships with other rulers on her doorstep, such as William des Roches and the counts of Perche. Due to William's displacement from Le Mans, their relationship had the potential to be hostile. However, William's affinity with Philip Augustus seems to have made him unwilling to upset the balance of power across Maine, operating around the city but not directly interfering in the region unless requested to do so by the French king, as in the case of the judicial proceedings mentioned above.

According to Bliss's papal registers, which need to be treated with some caution owing to their inaccuracies and lack of substantive evidence, Honorius issued two mandates – the originals are no longer extant – to the neighbouring deans of Orléans and Mehun, asking them to intervene and restrain the ecclesiastical officials of Le Mans who would not acknowledge the papal indults granted to Berengaria, in February 1223, several years after the majority of Berengaria's ecclesiastical disputes, which brings further doubt to their veracity and authenticity. These indults had forbidden anyone to issue sentences of excommunication against her or place her or her chapel under interdict, discussed in more detail in the following section.[49]

This was by no means the end of Berengaria's interactions with the local church, however. The *Enquête de 1245 relative aux droits*

du Chapitre Saint-Julien du Mans, actually published in 1246, records several disputes between Berengaria and ecclesiastical officials, largely centred around the dissension between the cathedral
of Saint-Julien and Berengaria's chapel of Saint Pierre-de-la-Cour.
The *enquête* is a collection of eyewitness and testimonial accounts,
however, not all those who provided testimony had first-hand
knowledge of the matter under discussion. The *enquête* not only
demonstrates the handling of ecclesiastical disputes in the thirteenth century, but also the extent of ecclesiastical and lordly
power during this period.[50] Berengaria, determined as she was to
collect revenues and exercise rights, came under fire from the cathedral when her agents imprisoned André and Foulques Benoît
after failing to pay a tax, from which they believed they were ex-
empt.[51] In retaliation, the cathedral chapter of Saint-Julien placed
Berengaria and Saint Pierre under interdict.[52] This prompted one
of Honorius's proclamations of papal protection.

Though Honorius undoubtedly intervened (often by request)
in Berengaria's affairs, he was not always able to act in her
interests – ultimately Honorius's role was as a mediator and defender of the interests of the Church. He did protect Berengaria's
interests at times, as seen with his actions against John and Maurice. The spate of letters in the spring of 1218 is evidence of such
protection. Since this was a time when the regency government
in England was failing to keep control of wardships and fiefs and
was particularly vulnerable, as David Carpenter has shown, it is
unsurprising that Honorius continued to intervene with a sense
of urgency at this date.[53] He did so to ensure Berengaria's rights
were upheld despite the continuous political upheaval in England,
which pushed her dower campaign to the sidelines.

As is often the case with correspondence involving royal
women, we do not have both sides of the story. Therefore, it is difficult to gauge Berengaria's requests explicitly, or fully understand
their timing and persistence, unless these are topics specifically
noted in the papal letters. Nevertheless, Berengaria determinedly
pushed for the return of her dower lands, or failing that, suitable
compensation for their loss. Her doggedness and tenacity indicate
the confidence she held in her position and her rights, as well as
her ability to request ongoing intercession on her behalf to ensure

these were upheld. Berengaria's dower was threatened from many angles: the dower rights of Eleanor of Aquitaine and Isabella of Angoulême, the dowry rights of Leonor of Castile, the political instability of England, a weakened treasury, and the reluctance of both her natal and marital family to completely address her need for her dower income.

There were many factors shaping Berengaria's relationship with the Church, including her ability to exercise power and collect revenues, the restrictions or opposition she faced from local ecclesiastical officials in both these arenas, and her ability to intervene in disputes and resolve cases involving disorderly monks. In all the instances discussed above, papal intervention became necessary, both because of the religious nature of the disputes but also because of Honorius's role as a spiritual protector for Berengaria. Although the threat of excommunication or interdict was not unusual in this period – the papacy used it against monarchs for misbehaviour, and other ecclesiastical officials could also use it – the enforcement of this was still a disturbance to society and lordly power.[54]

Maurice, Bishop of Le Mans

As the previous discussion has illuminated, Berengaria's relationship with local officials was not always plain sailing. The relationship between Berengaria and Maurice, bishop of Le Mans (1216–31), is of interest for several reasons: it provides a case study for interactions between (female) lords and the higher clergy, and indicates the activities of Berengaria in Le Mans and the extent of her power at certain points.[55] Pope Honorius's mediation between Berengaria and Maurice, in particular, showed the balance of power, and its fragility, between secular and ecclesiastical rulers.[56] In the April 1218 dispute, Honorius actually overruled Berengaria and Maurice, proclaiming that he would make the final decision regarding clerical misbehaviour. This was despite the request from Berengaria for aid, as noted in the letter from Honorius in April 1218, where he states that 'on your part it was put forth to us.'[57]

There may have been instances where Berengaria and Maurice worked more harmoniously, outside the disputes between the cathedral chapter and the chapel of Saint Pierre, but any evidence for more co-operative action has been largely speculative.[58] The surviving records detail many occasions where Berengaria was in disagreement with Maurice. Maurice was bishop of Le Mans from 1216 to 1231, until he took up the archbishopric of Rouen. His origins are uncertain, though Jörg Peltzer has argued that it was unlikely that Maurice came from outside the Angevin lands.[59] Regardless of his background and any associated loyalties, Maurice was vociferous in his defence of the cathedral and his own episcopal rights. Under his directorate, the cathedral chapter of Saint-Julien clashed with Berengaria's chapel of Saint Pierre-de-la-Cour, and their disagreements over rights and revenues became evident early on in their relationship. One such dispute, already briefly mentioned above, concerned Maurice's claim to revenues from La Chapelle-Saint-Aubin, which lay within the sphere of Berengaria's lordship. Berengaria attempted to secure the revenues she was entitled to as its lord. However, La Chapelle-Saint-Aubin was a villa of Maurice's cathedral chapter and claimed its exemption from Berengaria's lordly dues. Although Berengaria succeeded in her claim with the support of her royal allies, the resolution did little to improve the relationship between Berengaria and Maurice, and it is not clear whether she successfully obtained the tax from La Chapelle-Saint-Aubin.

Berengaria's rightful claims to the taxes she was owed as lord of Le Mans, as noted in her 1204 exchange charter with Philip Augustus, often brought her into dispute with both the cathedral chapter and the populace. The 1246 *enquête* details several of these disputes, from which we can deduce that Berengaria had rights to certain taxes and customs, including payments in kind on some products.[60] However, the population of Le Mans often used the protection of the cathedral chapter to excuse themselves from paying the appropriate taxes.[61]

One such dispute was to have significant implications for Berengaria's power and the extent of her authority. Relations between the chapter of Saint-Julien and Berengaria had been rocky until 1212, however, the elevation of the former dean of Saint-Julien, Nicolas, to the position of bishop of Le Mans (1214–6) and the promotion of Hugh de la Ferté as head of the cathedral

chapter in 1214 allowed Berengaria's opponents to gain the up-
per hand in their opposition to the dowager queen.[62] This power
play comes to light with the attempt by Hubert Riboul, a knight
residing in Quinte, to evade a tax imposed by Berengaria due to
ecclesiastical exemption. The case was escalated to Philip Augustus for arbitration and received the attention of a judicial court
comprised of Robert, count of Alençon, William des Roches, and
the abbot and prior of La Couture.[63]

Further conflict arose during the period of interdict in Le Mans
in 1217–8. The levying of a tax on Julian Laurent for the sale of
animals, which took place in La Chapelle-Saint-Aubin, under the
jurisdiction of Saint-Julien, was done under Berengaria's auspices.
The canons of Saint-Julien excommunicated the bailiff who had
levied the tax and summoned Berengaria to restore to them the
tax of 5 livres tournois. Berengaria refused to pay, and the dean
and Maurice placed the city of Le Mans under interdict. This was
a calculated move and unfortunate error on Maurice's part. Maurice likely believed he would have the backing of the pope for his
ecclesiastical sanctions. Berengaria, however, petitioned Honorius for assistance, who in turn reproached the bishop of Tours
and Maurice for passing sentences of interdict and excommunication without reasonable cause.[64] Hugh and Maurice were not
deterred, however, and continued with the ban, closing the doors
of the cathedral and ordering all churches and abbeys within the
city's jurisdiction to stop their offices.

On 10 January 1217, Honorius wrote to the archbishop of
Tours to permit Berengaria to exercise her power over misbehaving clerics.[65] A few days later, Honorius issued a mandate to the
archbishop of Tours, and the bishop and chapter of Le Mans, to
prevent their impending excommunication of Berengaria.[66] This
mandate came at a time of tension in Le Mans. Berengaria was
determined to exercise her rights and power in the region, but the
local churchmen were adamant they would retain control of ecclesiastical matters in the region.

By April 1218, the major dispute between Berengaria and ecclesiastical officials in Le Mans had developed even further. Honorius granted Berengaria permission to punish literates (those
who wrote Latin) under her rule who were acting interchangeably

as ecclesiastical and secular men in order to escape punishment, namely as they had chosen to marry, and to avoid payments.[67] Other letters from April 1218 indicate that Berengaria had not resolved her ongoing quarrels with the dean, archdeacon, and chapter of Le Mans. The first of these letters from Honorius, dated 4 April 1218, granted Berengaria an appeal to the apostolic see against the Le Mans bishop, dean, archdeacon, and chapter because they had asserted customs of the Church against her and had issued a sentence of excommunication against her.[68] Honorius further publicised his support for Berengaria in managing local ecclesiastical officials in Le Mans, offering her a licence to exact services from former clerks who had married and then taken up ecclesiastical duties again. The clerks had been encouraged in such behaviour (cohabitation) by the leading ecclesiastics of Le Mans, namely Maurice, bishop of Le Mans, and the cathedral chapter of Saint-Julien, as will be detailed further below.[69] In the 4 April letter, Honorius had also extended a broader grant of protection for Berengaria against anyone who was to issue a sentence of excommunication or interdict against her or her chapel without papal mandate, an indication both of the ecclesiastical strife that Berengaria faced but also the strength of papal support behind her.[70] This was not the first time that Berengaria had faced a sentence of interdict, as one had been issued by Saint-Julien between 1204 and 1205 owing to tax levies issued by Berengaria, which they viewed as overstepping her boundaries as lord.

This particularly swift dispatch of letters and the extension of protection to Berengaria is indicative of the seriousness of the threat she encountered from local ecclesiastics in Le Mans. Frustratingly, her own letters and proclamations concerning these events do not survive, so we cannot know if Berengaria was equally speedy in pressuring Honorius for support, or what statements she made in her correspondence with local officials. This event does demonstrate two of the continual themes of Berengaria's rule: firstly, that she was adamant that she would exercise power as a lord in the region, and not be viewed merely as an administrator or temporary placeholder; and secondly, that the support of the papacy was politically useful and bolstered her strength in her dispute in Le Mans. The language used in the letters is full of promises of protection and concern for Berengaria in her position as a vulnerable person. For example, Honorius stated in one of the April 1218 letters that 'we are compelled to offer care and solicitude to widows showing special grace.'[71] This 'special grace' is no doubt indicative of Berengaria's vulnerability and the piety she exacted in Le Mans.

The continuing interdict resulted in Berengaria's chapel, Saint Pierre-de-la-Cour, celebrating mass behind closed doors with only Berengaria having access to religious services. This soon became untenable and she was eventually forced to leave Le Mans because of her inability to take religious services, choosing to seek refuge in Thorée in Anjou, as two of the witnesses from the 1246 *enquête* attest.[72] Her residence in Thorée made geographical and political sense as Richard and Berengaria had acquired the site during their reigns, and it was slightly over the border between Maine and Anjou, thus allowing her to be removed from the authority of Saint-Julien but still within travelling distance. It is plausible that Berengaria sought the benevolence of the bishop of Angers, William II de Beaumont, who was related to her through the lineage of the lords of Aigle, to which they both had a maternal link.[73] Berengaria's relationship with Thorée was explored in more detail in the previous chapter, however, prior to her grant of property, she remained resident there, receiving word in November 1217 that Philip Augustus had agreed that the canons of Saint-Julien could enlarge the cathedral choir, and with this plausibly reinforce their sense of superiority and authority.[74]

From papal letters to Berengaria, we can ascertain that she had again petitioned Honorius for assistance in the spring of 1218. His replies have been discussed above, but they permitted her to receive services and removed her from the threat of excommunication. Honorius issued two further letters in April 1218 to Jean de la Faye, bishop of Tours, and the abbot of Josaphat to grant justice to Berengaria.[75] In these letters Honorius is particularly scathing of the ecclesiastics of Le Mans and their injustice towards Berengaria, emphasising the power and authority of the pope to decide on matters of interdict and excommunication. Mediation took place between Berengaria and the chapter under the auspices of William d'Auvergne, archdeacon Cantorius, and a knight, Pierre

Sauvary, with the abbot of Josaphat and the prior of Saint-Père de Chartres acting effectively as mediators.[76] The matter appears to have been initially resolved in August 1218 when Berengaria returned to Le Mans, the canons lifted the ban in the chapter, and she agreed to pay the 5 deniers owed. Baury and Corriol have argued that Berengaria did not willingly pay the 5 deniers. It was only after repeated requests by the abbot of Josaphat and the prior that Berengaria agreed to pay, and even then, her clerk passed the money to the pontifical judges, who then passed the money to the canons, with the entire affair taking place in private in the comital palace.[77] The longstanding nature of the conflict and Berengaria's exile to Thorée show the weakness of her position as lord of Le Mans at the end of the 1210s, with the cathedral chapter of Saint-Julien and the associated clerics in ascendancy. It was only with the support of Honorius that the conflict was extinguished, although its embers remained and tempered relationships between Berengaria and the clergy of Le Mans, particularly Maurice.

Evidence from *L'Histoire de l'Eglise du Le Mans* does indicate that Berengaria and Maurice were able to settle and negotiate in peace at least sometimes during their tenures. *L'Histoire* is a nineteenth-century compendium outlining Le Mans' religious history through a pastiche of charters, not all of which are verifiable, and several originals are now lost. The agreement reached between Maurice and Saint Pierre-de-la-Cour shows a level of friendliness between Berengaria and Maurice, or at least their desire to reach an agreement with one another. The 1230 charter includes the phrase '*amicabiliter initam,*' 'beginning in a friendly manner.'[78] This is a substantial shift in their relationship given the disagreement and conflict between the pair in the previous two decades. Berengaria continued to draw on her diplomatic and political skills, particularly in her interactions with Maurice, showing her acumen and keen judgement as she worked with the ecclesiastical networks in Le Mans. She was able to agree upon a solution that worked well for both parties. By 1230, the conflict between Berengaria and Maurice had waned significantly, as Maurice confirmed two grants in 1229 and 1230 respectively which resolved the sales of soldiers that had previously been confirmed by Berengaria.[79]

Towards the end of Berengaria's tenure of Le Mans, Maurice appears to confirm and approve the ratification of a number of charters concerning Berengaria. One, dated 1230, sees Maurice confirm the ratification by Marguerite, wife of William de Riveillon, of a sale made by William to Berengaria.[80] Two further charters, originals located in Bibliothèque Nationale de France Latin 17124 and Archives Départementales de la Sarthe 111 AC 833, are concerned with L'Épau, and are discussed below. A final record shows that Maurice, in January 1231, the month after Berengaria's death, confirmed the alms of Thibaut Beaumont and his wife, Agnes, to L'Épau, perhaps an indication that he had taken an immediate interest in the abbey following Berengaria's death.[81]

Much like other churchmen of the time, Maurice was strong-willed and determined to defend the rights of the Church, and his own position, against secular interference. As the financial disputes outlined above have displayed, the collection of revenues was crucial for both parties, and the involvement of Philip Augustus and Louis IX as overlords and Honorius III and Gregory IX as papal protectors and intercessors shows the importance and interest in the rights of the Church in contested areas. After Berengaria's death in 1230, Maurice was soon appointed as archbishop of Rouen, leaving the bishopric of Le Mans to be filled by Geoffroi de Laval, another ecclesiastical official with whom Berengaria had many dealings, as detailed in the *enquête*. Conflict between secular and ecclesiastical rulership was nothing new – indeed, Berengaria only had to look back throughout the recent history of her marital family to see the conflicts between ruler and Church. However, Berengaria appears to have been firm but diplomatic with regards to her negotiations with the officials of Le Mans, ensuring her prerogatives were upheld without abusing the rights of the Church.

Saint Pierre-de-la-Cour

Berengaria's interactions with her chapter of Saint Pierre-de-la-Cour, and her defence of it, are one of the few opportunities where we get glimmers of Berengaria's personality and attitude to rulership. Her exercise of power, defiance, and steadfastness in adversity show that Berengaria was a lord with agency and authority. One of the religious institutions in Le Mans that Berengaria had several dealings with, some of which have been detailed above, is the chapter of Saint Pierre-de-la-Cour. This was the chapel of the counts of Maine and was thought to have been founded at the end of the tenth century. The first recorded donation to the community is from Hugh I, count of Maine, between 974 and 997, though its authenticity is doubtful.[82] Berengaria's dealings with the chapter are detailed within the house's own cartulary, the *Cartulaire du Chapitre Royal de Saint-Pierre-de-la-Cour*, an edited pastiche from 1907 which contains the earlier cartulary in the possession of Menjot D'Elbenne, alongside the further documents collected by Savare, and included documents relating to the community's history. It is in the cartulary, for example, that we hear of Berengaria's appointment of Pierre, a member of her household, to the chapel, as discussed below.[83] Not all of the charters recorded in the Elbenne collection can be verified, with many (including the numbers 44 and 45 which demonstrate Berengaria's ties to the chapel most strongly) unable to be traced back to the now lost original cartulary of Saint Pierre-de-la-Cour. The original cartulary was a thirteenth-century composition, with fourteenth-century additions, and was lost during the French Revolution in 1789. Two folios survived from this original and are held in the Archives Départementales de la Sarthe. On 13 February 1754 the chapter of Saint Pierre instructed Guillaume Savare to compile a history of the chapter and rights whilst in a dispute with the bishop of Le Mans.[84] A copy of the most important charters from Savare's work was made, but D'Elbenne notes, by incompetent copyists.[85] Thus the 1907 edition is utilised here, alongside some of the surviving originals from Archives Départementales de la Sarthe G 479, with the acknowledgement that many of the charters need to be treated with caution.

The earliest recorded incident between Berengaria and Saint Pierre was in August 1210, when Berengaria presided over a duel between Raoul Flory and Josset le Febvre.[86] Other than her presence, no further detail is recorded about this duel, but it is an indication of Berengaria's authority and participation in the judicial and daily life of Le Mans, something which was painfully absent during her tenure as queen consort of England. Her activity within the community of Saint Pierre can be seen by her appointment of her cleric, Pierre, as the new cantor at the chapel in 1219.[87] Berengaria arguably overextended her jurisdiction here, not through her appointment of the cleric but by removing his obligation to reside within the Church. Such actions could only serve to intensify tensions between the lord and the Church; although Berengaria held certain ecclesiastical rights as lord of Le Mans, it was not in line with Church doctrine to encourage absenteeism.

Another charter related to the rights of Saint Pierre is evidence of Berengaria's continued relationship with the king of France, Philip Augustus. In March 1220, at Philip's instigation, Honorius III transferred rights from the dean of Tours to the abbot of Saint-Père and the dean of Saint-Maurice of Angers, making the latter two men responsible for investigating the freedoms and customs of Saint Pierre, for removing any episcopal censures against the canons of Saint Pierre, and for ensuring that the offices of Saint Pierre were upheld.[88] Such a move by Philip, to act to restore the rights of Saint Pierre, was presumably at Berengaria's instigation. Berengaria and the French king had an amicable working relationship, and she was well aware of the advantages of maintaining a strong alliance with Philip Augustus, particularly when so little support from her male natal and marital families was forthcoming.

One final example of Berengaria's ardent defence and involvement in the rights of Saint Pierre comes in 1226, when she judged a dispute between the chapter and the knight Gervaise de Cogners.[89] Gervaise and his heirs were ordered to pay a suspended fine of 60 livres tournois to the chapter if they further acted against the chapter, implying that Gervaise had already been in dispute with Saint Pierre. Berengaria arbitrated due to the growing tension between Gervaise and the chapter. It is highly plausible given Berengaria's previous interest and defence of Saint Pierre that she would have ruled in their favour. Such localised disputes were often overseen by the local lord or nobility, in this case Berengaria, and as such she fulfilled the role as expected. Meeting such expectations should not be seen as anything out of the ordinary, since many women acted as lords in the thirteenth century and proved highly capable administrators. However, Berengaria's previous lack of experience in lordship until she began ruling Le Mans meant that she had had few opportunities to demonstrate her capabilities and skills to act as a lord throughout much of her life. Saint Pierre suffered from intervention from various parties. For example, a charter from August 1229 demonstrates that Maurice sought to determine the extent of his rights and jurisdiction over the chapter.[90] Despite Berengaria's continued intervention, the chapel continued to be much contested between ecclesiastical and lordly demands. Maurice appears, for the most part, an ambitious and determined bishop, who certainly met his match in Berengaria. Though Saint Pierre was but one area of dissension, both lord and bishop continued to vie for power until Berengaria's death in December 1230.

Saint Pierre also brought Berengaria back into contact with one of her noble companions, William des Roches, seneschal of Anjou. Two documents from 1209–10 and 1216–7 attest to William's presence in the area. The first charter concerns William abandoning to the canons of Saint Pierre the tithes situated in his fiefs and his seat as seneschal.[91] To abandon fiscal rights may be seen as a weakness in power. In this instance, William's grant was made under the advice of Geoffrey, archbishop of Tours, the implication notwithstanding that granting the tithes to the chapter was the ecclesiastically benevolent option. The second charter sees William judge a dispute between the chapter and William de Cormenant, a local noble who had disputed the rights of the abbey in the Riboul woods. However, having then confirmed the rights of the canons to use the woods, William de Cormenant took back his previous contention and granted that the canons of Parennes should have the sequestered woods and pastures for their use, as the chapter desired.[92] William des Roches' presence in the area, particularly as an arbiter in disputes, demonstrates his power as seneschal, and his judgements were usually in favour of Berengaria's interests, as seen with Saint Pierre here. As noted earlier, this was indicative of a continuous and harmonious working relationship between the pair which often brought great benefit to Berengaria's own authority in the region.

As the patron and protectoress of the chapter, Saint Pierre was close to Berengaria's heart and affinities. The chapter remembered

Berengaria's protection for centuries, with a recorded dispute between Saint Pierre and Saint-Julien from 13 February 1754 recalling Berengaria's defence of their rights and privileges.[93] This in part explains her defence of the chapter against the cathedral chapter of Saint-Julien, as well as the close continued interactions she had with the chapter of Saint Pierre. The most prominent event involving the chapter of Saint Pierre was the dispute between the chapter and Saint-Julien, which I have discussed above. Due to Berengaria's arrest of André and Foulques, Saint-Julien placed all other churches under interdict, including Saint Pierre. The interdict was only resolved with the intervention of the papacy as Saint Pierre continued to defy the cathedral and allowed religious services to continue. The abbey's defiance was due to a combination of factors – having secured the protection of both Berengaria and the papacy and asserting its own rights against that of the cathedral's. The relationship between Berengaria and the chapter is a demonstration of her growth in authority and power in the region, and an indication of her confidence as she continually intervened and asserted the rights of herself and the abbey on several occasions. Berengaria's interactions with local

FIGURE 6.1   Photograph of the exterior of L'Abbaye de L'Épau
© Sarthe Culture

churches like Saint Pierre show that she remained as committed to protecting and defending her rights as lord of Le Mans as she was to pursuing her dower rights as former queen of England.

L'Abbaye de L'Épau

The most famous religious site associated with Berengaria is her foundation, L'Abbaye de L'Épau, in Le Mans. She commissioned its construction in 1229, although her death in December 1230 meant she did not live to see its completion. Its foundation was slightly complex. The land the abbey was built on had been granted to her by Louis IX, grandson of Philip Augustus, in 1228, another Capetian king with whom she had a strong working relationship.[94] However, the brothers of a local hospital, Coëffort, claimed in 1230 that they had been granted the lands by Berengaria's nephew, Arthur I, duke of Brittany (d. 1203), leading to a dispute between the two parties regarding the ownership of the land. This dispute was resolved later in 1230 as Berengaria paid for the deeds to the lands.[95] The Coëffort dispute had the potential for wider political ramifications; allegations had abounded since Arthur's death that he had been murdered on the orders of John, king of England, due to the succession dispute for the throne of England. By paying for the deeds, Berengaria was in part acknowledging the ownership of the land by Arthur and involving herself further in Plantagenet politics, which in turn could lead to disfavour with her other nephew, Henry III, because of the allegations surrounding Arthur's death.[96] John's imprisonment of Arthur's sister, Eleanor of Brittany, negated the risk that Eleanor posed to the control of Brittany by the Plantagenets and her wider claim to the English throne which she inherited from Arthur.[97] Whether, with time, this payment for lands would have led to disharmony with Henry III will never be known – given the ongoing dower dispute, Berengaria was by no means on loving terms with her nephew. However, Berengaria achieved what she wanted, securing complete confirmation that she owned the lands of L'Espal, where she would found her abbey.

A series of documents held in the Archives Départementales de la Sarthe detail Berengaria's donations, purchases, and grants associated with the abbey between 1229 and 1230.[98] One document concerns the purchase for 100 livres of a farm which would be for the benefit of the abbey.[99] Other documents concern the sale by Fontevraud Abbey of vineyards and rents as well as donations and exchanges by surrounding families and nobility, often between the sum of 50 to 100 livres.[100] Several of the charters are confirmed or granted by local nobility, namely knights, or ecclesiastical officials such as Maurice, bishop of Le Mans.[101] The rapid collection of lands, rents, and money towards the abbey's foundation, as well as Berengaria's determination to resolve the ownership question regarding L'Espal, demonstrate not only its personal importance to her but also perhaps a growing awareness of her legacy and memory. By 1229, Berengaria was feasibly approaching her eighth decade and matters of her memorialisation and salvation may have prayed more closely on her mind.

The Cistercian order, founded in the mid-twelfth century, already had some support in France, not least from Berengaria's niece, Blanche of Castile, the mother of Louis IX, king of France.[102] Berengaria granted the abbey and revenues to the Cistercians in the spring of 1230.[103] Berengaria then moved to appoint and move representatives to the abbey, with her appointment of Thibaut Beaumont, a local knight with connections to L'Épau, in 1230 taking place under the auspices of Louis IX, perhaps an indication that she had travelled to the French court to engineer support for her venture.[104] Le Mans was home to a number of different religious orders including the Franciscans and Dominicans, and the addition of another Cistercian order to the region showed the benevolence and extent of Berengaria's piety. The choice of a Cistercian order was not altogether surprising, since there were both natal and marital connections with the order, and discussions between Berengaria and the Cistercians regarding a new site had been ongoing whilst she was in the process of acquiring L'Espal. Evidence of the order's connection with both Berengaria and her younger sister Blanca can be found in the surviving Cistercian statutes. An initial record from 1223 notes that Berengaria will be remembered by the entire order as evidence of her patronage and affinity to the Cistercians.[105] A further entry,

FIGURE 6.2 Photograph of Berengaria's effigy, full length © Sarthe Culture

five years later, notes that on the day that Berengaria will be commemorated, her sister Blanca, countess of Champagne will also be remembered.[106] The further commitment of the two sisters to the order can be seen after Blanca's death on 13 March 1229. The order was to say a prayer for Blanca's soul on the anniversary of her death until Berengaria also died, whenceforth their anniversaries would be joined. The joint commemoration of both women was instigated on 10 January 1231.[107]

The foundation of L'Épau was not for religious reasons alone however: it held a personal and dynastic significance too. It is hardly surprising that Berengaria did not wish to be associated with the Plantagenet mausoleum of Fontevraud Abbey, where her husband and mother-in-law Eleanor were buried, alongside Henry II. Moreover, given the distance between Berengaria and her marital family, it is appropriate that Berengaria chose a mausoleum of her own as her final resting place. The foundation of dynastic mausolea and religious institutions was nothing unusual for women within the wider Plantagenet family. Eleanor had a long association with Fontevraud prior to her death, her daughter-in-law Constance of Brittany was buried at Villeneuve Abbey, Nantes, in 1201, and Eleanor's daughter and Berengaria's sister-in-law, Leonor, similarly founded El Monasterio de Santa María la Real de las Huelgas alongside her husband, Alfonso, where she was later buried.[108]

As founder of L'Épau, Berengaria ensured that her memory would be preserved in Le Mans for generations to come. The Cistercian monks who resided in the abbey would be responsible for her commemoration and the preservation of her memory over the centuries, and her tomb would serve as an ever-present reminder of her position as the community's founder. Berengaria's legacy was to endure beyond the abbey as well. Her patronage and longevity as the lord of Le Mans preserved her in local memory for generations to come, and with the survival of the abbey future generations would also continue to connect Berengaria to Le Mans as one of its local heroines.

Berengaria's establishment of L'Épau not only indicates her piety, but also her desire to have a legacy in the city which had been her home for twenty-four years. Her foundation is a testament to her independence from her family, both natal and marital, as well as her devotion to Le Mans. L'Épau is the site of her tomb and a splendid effigy.[109] Her effigy holds a small book depicting, in my opinion uniquely for the period, a miniature of Berengaria on the front cover.[110] Effigies often featured the figure holding a book of some description, often a Book of Hours or another indication of their culture, literary interest, or piety. The effigy of Berengaria's mother-in-law Eleanor similarly depicts the queen holding a book. Berengaria's depiction of herself on the book's front may have been influenced by her Navarrese female ancestors Estefania de Foix and Felicia de Roucy, two eleventh-century queens of Navarre who commissioned their own self-portraits during their lifetimes.[111] Other striking features of the effigy are the sculptures of a lion and a dog at the base of her effigy. The lion is particularly interesting because of its implicit connection with her marital family, as the lion one was one of the earliest royal emblems to decorate the shields of the kings of England. The dog, associated with married women, is indicative of loyalty to one's spouse. Berengaria's effigy has trace remnants of paintwork: it was temporarily repainted in a similar manner for the exhibition connected with the launch of the French biography of her in 2022. Not all of the paintwork can be dated, but some can be tentatively to a repainting effort that took place in the fourteenth century.[112] Berengaria's image and tomb otherwise survive in the later drawings by Louis Boudan for Roger de Gaignières, which depict the tomb with further decorations than have survived to the present day. The abbey retains a strong connection to local history and Berengaria, as its founder, has taken the place of local heroine in Le Mans.[113] Had Berengaria lived beyond the abbey's confirmation and construction, it is entirely plausible it would have developed even further as a centre for Cistercian learning and exchange, benefiting from her continued patronage.

Though the construction and foundation of the abbey was by no means slow, it was only confirmed in January 1231, a month after Berengaria's death, by her protector and erstwhile ally Pope Gregory IX.[114] As desired, she was buried at the abbey shortly after her death, though no details of her funeral survive. Her burial is, as noted above, a continuation of a pattern of Angevin

FIGURE 6.3   Photograph of the base of Berengaria's effigy © Sarthe Culture

royal women choosing to be buried at a religious institution they had patronised, rather than a familial necropolis that was not of their making. Berengaria's decision not to be buried within her natal or marital mausolea is noteworthy, and perhaps explains her decision to found L'Épau. Holding no great connection with either her natal or marital families, and during a period where the foundation of royal mausolea by women was a steady occurrence, there was no reason why Berengaria could not choose and found her own abbey and mausoleum. A smaller foundation was appropriate as she had no heirs and allowed her to maintain her independence and freedom.

Berengaria's reluctance to be interred at Fontevraud is understandable given her poor relationships with the Plantagenets, although it is intriguing to compare this with her sister-in-law, Isabella of Angoulême, who did choose Fontevraud as her burial place and had a close association with the abbey by the time of her death in 1246.[115] The cathedral of Pamplona had become the resting place of the Navarrese royals since the time of Berengaria's grandfather, king García Ramírez. However, uncertainty around the Navarrese succession upon the death of Sancho VII in Tudela led to his eventual burial at Roncesvalles, not Pamplona, with Sancho's burial site an issue unresolved at the time of Berengaria's death.[116] Given Berengaria's distance from her natal family in Navarre, it was unlikely that she would be interred in Pamplona or Tudela, the key cities associated with the Jiménez dynasty. Her death on 23 December 1230 passed without much comment in the chronicles, and of her will we know only traces of it from later sources. A reference to William of Fougères, the seneschal of Anjou, Poitou, and Touraine, receiving payment in 1234 for the executors of the 'queen of Le Mans' indicates that Berengaria did leave a testament.[117] Other than this note in the royal records there is no indication of a pre-existing relationship between Berengaria and William, but given his position as a local magnate and with a connection to the royal court, it is perhaps unsurprising that he was trusted with the funds to be paid to the executors, a total of 80 pounds and 7 sous. The other trace of the will can be found in connection with the cathedral chapter of Saint-Julien, which was granted 30 livres manceaux from her property, to supplement an annuity for the canons to celebrate the anniversary of the date of her death, with the money only being paid to the canons who participated in the commemoration.[118]

Several centuries after her death, in 1602, a commemorative plaque was placed by Cardinal de Gondi, abbot of L'Épau and bishop of Paris. The inscription was recorded on behalf of Gaignières by Louis Boudan in 1695, and this faithful copy is preserved in the Bodleian Library, Oxford.[119] The plaque reads:

In the year 1229, while Gregory IX administered the apostolic See, reigned in Germany Frederick II, blessed Louis IX in Gaul, Henry III in England, Berengaria, daughter of Sancho, king of Aragon and Navarre and count of Barcelona, who had been united in marriage to the late King Richard, first of his name (nicknamed Coeur-de-Lion), childless, founded this convent of L'Épau, also called Piété-Dieu, dedicated to the Virgin and Saint John the Baptist by lord Geoffrey de Laval, bishop of Le Mans. One hundred and thirty years later, that is to say in the year 1365, faced with the urgent danger and so that it could not serve as a refuge for the English surrounding the city of Le Mans, it was set on fire and largely destroyed. Funeral honours have been paid to Berengaria according to royal custom, her body was buried in this site.[120]

Evidently there are errors on the plaque. However, it is indicative that the tomb and abbey were subject to the consequences of local warfare and thus explains why the original plaque does not survive. This also explains the uncertainty around the position of Berengaria's burial site, as this was not the only time the tomb and remains were to be moved. Further evidence of this can be seen with another slate plate, placed in a lead box with what may be Berengaria's bones, dating from 1672. This plaque, placed with the box inside the tomb, reads:

This mausoleum of the serene Berengaria, queen of the English, illustrious founder of this monastery, was restored and moved to his more honourable place; and there were enclosed the bones which were found with the old tomb.[121]

Based on this inscription alone we can only hypothesise that this was the period when the tomb was moved and reinstalled in the choir of the abbey, where it was attested to be in 1695 and where it was found during the French Revolution. The slate was found at the same location where it was interred, during the restoration of the tomb in 1817. However, this is the only piece of evidence and there may have yet been other movements of the tomb. The rediscovery of Berengaria's tomb, by Charles Stothard in 1816, saw plans to relocate the tomb to the cathedral of Saint-Julien, at a huge expense as detailed in the surviving institutional records.[122] The tomb was moved to Saint-Julien on 2 December 1821, in the north transept, before being moved to the south transept in 1861 due to a funerary monument being constructed for the bishop, Jean-Baptiste Bouvier, who had died in 1854. The tomb then moved again to the north transept in 1921 to make space for a First World War commemorative monument. Amidst these relocations the base upon which Berengaria's tomb rested disappears, although further care is taken to preserve the box containing the skeleton.[123] In 1920, an inscription on the box lid notes their presence.

Berengaria's agency and authority can clearly be seen in the last two decades of her life. As lord of Le Mans, she had the revenues, power, and networks to establish her own foundation successfully, invest further resources into the abbey, and act as a capable patron and intercessor. By choosing Le Mans, her home, as the site for the abbey and her burial, she showed her independence and strength of character. Her rule as lord of Le Mans is indicative that she was not only a woman with substantial political and diplomatic skills, but also that her power was not dependent on harmonious familial connections. As chapters five and six have shown, Berengaria was able to exercise power, intercede, and act as a negotiator and diplomat across the courts of Western Europe, and it is from this we can only hypothesise of the activities she may have undertaken during her reign as queen consort had she been afforded the opportunity to do so. For all her obscurity as queen of England, it is as a lord of Le Mans, a former queen, and a successful negotiator that we should remember Berengaria.

Notes

1 Dates are included in the footnotes for several letters where the dating has been disputed, particularly between Bliss, Horoy, Migne, and Cheney's collections.

2 Richard Barton, *Lordship and the County of Maine, c. 890–1160* (Woodbridge: Boydell Press, 2004), ch. 6.

3 Ivan Cloulas, 'Le douaire de Bérengère de Navarre, veuve de Richard Cœur de Lion, et sa retraite au Mans,' in *La Cour Plantagenêt (1154–1204). Actes du colloque tenu à Thouars du 30 avril au 2 mai 1999*, ed. Martin Aurell (Poitiers: Université de Poitiers, Centre d'Études Supérieures de Civilisation Médiévale, 2004), 90.

4 AN, J 628, no. 4 (1205); Thomas Rymer, ed., *Foedera, Conventiones, Literæ, Et Cujuscunque Generis Acta Publica inter Reges Angliæ et alios quosuis(?) imperatores, reges, pontifices, principes, vel communitates, ab ineunte sæculo duodecimo, viz ab anno 1101, ad nostra usque Tempora, Habita aut Tractatal ex autographis, infra secretiores archivorum regiorum thesaurarias, per multa sæcula reconditis, fideliter exscripta, Tomus I* (London: J. Tonson, 1727), 208–9; TNA, SC 1/1/23 (1220); Walter Waddington Shirley, ed., *Royal and other Historical Letters Illustrative of the Reign of Henry*

III. Volume I. 1216–1235 (London: Longman, Green, Longman, and Roberts, 1862), 273–4.

5 See appendix for the full list of Berengaria's dower lands.

6 Othmar Hagender, Andrea Sommerlechner, Herwig Weigl, Christoph Egger, and Rainer Murauer, eds., *Die Register Innocenz' III. 7. Band, 7 Pontifikatsjahr, 1204–1205 Texte und Indices* (Wien: Verlag der Österreichischen Akademie der Wissenschaften, 1997), no. 168.

7 TNA, C 66/5 (1205–6); TNA, C 66/6 (1206–7).

8 Original lost, calendared in C. R. Cheney and Mary G. Cheney, eds., *The Letters of Pope Innocent III (1198–1216) concerning England and Wales. A Calendar with an appendix of texts* (Oxford: Clarendon Press, 1967), nos. 765 and 766 [incorrectly recorded as dowry]; J.-P. Migne, ed., *Innocentii III Romani Pontificus Opera Omnia* (Montrouge: 1855), ii, cols. 1218–9; Etienne Baluze, ed., *Epistolarum Innocentii libri undecim. Accedunt gesta ejusdem Innocentii et prima collectio decretalium composita a Rainerio Diacono Pomposiano*, 4 vols. (Paris: 1682), ii, 69.

9 Thomas Hardy Duffy, ed., *Rotuli Literrarum Patentium in turri Londinensi Asservati. Volume I* (London: Public Record Office, 1835), 68.

10 Migne, *Innocentii III*, ii, cols. 1537–9; Cheney and Cheney, *Letters*, nos. 789 and 836.

11 Andrea Sommerlechner, ed., *Die Register Innocenz III. 13. Pontifikatsjahr, 1210/1211, Texte und Indices* (Wien: Austrian Academy of Sciences Press, 2015), no. 74; Migne, *Innocentii III*, iii, cols. 268–70.

12 Cheney and Cheney, *Letters*, no. 868; Migne, *Innocentii III*, ccxvi, 268–70.

13 César Auguste Horoy, ed., *Honorii III Romani Pontificis Opera Omnia*, 4 vols. (Paris: Imprimerie de la Bibliothèque Ecclésiastique, 1879–1880), ii, cols. 56–7.

14 Horoy, *Honori III*, ii, cols. 179–81.

15 Horoy, *Honori III*, ii, cols. 701–2.

16 Léonce Celier, ed., *Catalogue des Actes des Évêques du Mans jusqu'a la fin du XIIIᵉ siècle* (Paris: Honoré Champion, 1910), no. 527.

17 Horoy, *Honori III*, iii, cols. 672–5 (14 February 1221); Horoy, *Honori III*, iv, cols. 819–20 (10 June 1221); W. H. Bliss, ed., *Calendar of Entries in the Papal Registers Relating to Great Britain and Ireland. Papal Letters Vol. I. A. D. 1198–1304* (London: Eyre and Spottiswoode, 1893), XIV, 120 (1228); Lucien Auvray, ed., *Les Registres de Grégoire IX*, 4 vols. (Paris: Albert Fontemoing, 1896–1955), i, no. 280.

18 TNA, C 66/10 (1213–4).

19 TNA, C 66/10 (1213–4).

20 Nicholas Vincent posits that they 'may have been brothers, but more likely cousins or uncle and nephew' in his work on Peter: Nicholas Vincent, *Peter des Roches: An Alien in English Politics, 1205–1238* (Cambridge: Cambridge University Press, 1996), 25.

21 Ghislain Baury and Vincent Corriol, *Bérengère de Navarre (v. 1160–1230)*. *Histoire et mémoire d'une reine d'Angleterre* (Rennes: Presses Universitaires de Rennes), 119.

22 TNA, C 66/14 (1215); BL, Cotton Charter VIII, 24, outlines John's original agreement to place England under the overlordship of Rome (1214).

23 Rymer, *Foedera*, 70.

24 Rymer, *Foedera*, 208–9; Thomas Duffy Hardy, ed. *Rotuli litterarum clausarum in Turri Londiniensi asservati*. 2 vols. (London: Public Record Office, 1833–44), i, 202.

25 Bliss dates the letter as February 1217; W. H. Bliss, ed., *Calendar of Entries in the Papal Registers Relating to Great Britain and Ireland. Papal Letters Vol. I. A. D. 1198–1304* (London: Eyre and Spottiswoode, 1893), 40; Augustino Theiner, ed., *Vetera Monumenta Slavorum Meridionalium. Historiam Illustrantia Maximam Partem Nondum Edita Ex Tabularis Vaticanis Deprompta Collecta ac serie chronologica disposita. Tomus Primus. Ab Innocentio PP. III. Usque Ad Paulum PP. III. 1198–1549* (Osnabrück: Otto Zeller, 1968), no. 29; Cheney dates the letter as between December 1215 and January 1216: Cheney and Cheney, *Letters*, no. 1051.

26 TNA, C 66/15, m.7 (1216).

27 TNA, C 66/23, m.4 (1220).

28 Hardy, *Rotuli litterarum clausarum*, i, 462.

29 Hardy, *Rotuli litterarum clausarum*, ii, 38.

30 Hardy, *Rotuli litterarum clausarum*, ii, 85.

31 Hardy, *Rotuli litterarum clausarum*, ii, 115.

32 Horoy, *Honori III*, iv, cols. 285–6; dated 11 February 1223.

33 Horoy, *Honori III*, ii, cols. 279–80. For more on the history of Saint Vincent and its donations, see Bruno Lemesle, *La société aristocratique dans le Haut-Maine (XIᵉ–XIIᵉ siècles)* (Rennes: Presses Universitaires de Rennes, 1999), ch. 2.

34 Baury and Corriol, *Bérengère*, 154.

35 P. D'Albert, ed., *Cartulaire des abbayes de Saint-Pierre de la Couture et de Saint-Pierre de Solesmes* (Le Mans: Monnoyer, 1881), 153–4, no. 195.

36 André Chédville, ed., *Liber Controversiarum Sancti Vincentii Cenomannensis ou Second Cartulaire de l'Abbaye de Saint-Vincent Du Mans. Texte édité avec introduction, notes et index par A. Chédville* (Paris: Institut de Recherches Historiques de Rennes, 1968), no. 97.

37 Latouche argues that several of the documents had no legal value and were of fictitious origin: Robert Latouche, *Histoire du Comté du Maine pendant le Xᵉ et le XIᵉ siècle* (Paris: Honoré Champion, 1910), appendix 1.

38 *Cartulaire des abbayes*, 154, no. 195. '*reverentissimi viri Ricardi quondam regis Anglorum.*'

39 AN, J 126, no. 143 (1216); *Cartulaire des abbayes*, 186–7, no. 252; Michel Nortier and Charles Samaran, eds., *Recueil des Actes de*

Philippe Auguste, roi de France. Tome 4, Années du règne XXXVII à XLIV (1ᵉʳ nov. 1215–14 juillet 1223) (Paris: Imprimerie Nationale, 1976), no. 1456; Alexandre Teulet, ed., *Layettes du Trésor des Chartes*, 2 vols. (Paris: Henri Plon, 1863–6), i, no. 1272.

40 Eugène Hucher, 'Charte de Bérengère concernant des Juifs,' *Revue des sociétés savants de la France et de l'étranger* 10 (1869): 465. '*Universis fidelibus ad quos presens scriptum pervenerit, salute in actore salutis. Notum sit omnibus presentem cartulam inspecturis, quod Patricius et uxor ejus Johanna, de Judaismo ad Christianitatem conversi, qui ante conversionem suam, ille Judeus, Dexlebeneie Cornutus, et illa, Leota, publice vocabantur, herbegamentum suum de Barilleria, situm in feodo Poolini Boter, quod de proprio catallo suo comparaverant, Gaufrido cleric quatuor libris et dimidio cenomanesibus vendiderunt, concedentibus filiis suis Willelmo, Simone, Michaele, Jamelo, et filia sua Agnete, qui, cum essent Judei, his nominibus vocabantur: Vinardus, Vaslinus, Salemius, Mordahai, Joion; qui quinque cenomanenses habuerunt pro concedenda venditione predicta; de qua siquidem venditione per rectum defendenda, Poolinus Boter, dominus feodi, se in plegium obligavit.*' There are evidently issues here with the currency transcription as well: either *livres manceaux* or *libris*.

41 Julian Chappée, A. Ledru, and Louis J. Denis, eds., *Enquête de 1245 relative aux droits du Chapitre Saint-Julien du Mans* (Paris: Honoré Champion, 1922), 117, 125, 127–8, 130.

42 AD Sarthe, 111 AC 940, no. 925.

43 For more on William des Roches, see Ghislain Baury, 'Le sénéchal d'Anjou, les Plantagenêts et le Maine: le cas de Guillaume des Roches (1199–1222),' in *Les Plantagenêts et le Maine. Territoires, relais et représentations du pouvoir*, eds. Martin Aurell, Ghislain Baury, Vincent Corriol, and Laurent Maillet (Rennes: Universitaires Presses de Rennes, 2022), 128–51.

44 Henri-François Delaborde, Charles Petit-Dutaillis, and J. Monicat, eds., *Recueil des Actes de Philippe Auguste Roi de France. Tome II Années du Règne XVI à XXVII (1 Novembre 1194–31 Octobre 1206* (Paris: Imprimerie Nationale, 1943), 419–20.

45 *Recueil des Actes de Philippe Auguste*, ii, 948. The position of seneschal of Anjou changed several times in the twelfth and thirteenth centuries, sometimes referring to 'Grand Anjou,' meaning Anjou, Maine, and Touraine, and other times referring solely to the county of Anjou.

46 Baury, 'Le sénéchal,' 141–2.

47 Ghislain Baury, 'Les moniales cisterciennes dans le Maine médiéval. Bonlieu Abbey: Cistercian Nuns in Medieval Maine,' *Annales de Bretagne et des Pays de l'Ouest* 120.3 (2013): 52.

48 Baury, 'Les moniales cisterciennes,' 61.

49 Bliss, *Papal Registers*, XII, 89.

50 Richard Barton, 'Experiencing Power in Western France, c. 1190–1245,' *Anglo-Norman Studies* 43 (2021): 177–96.

51 Date unclear but likely before 1214 owing to the presence of Hamelin, bishop of Le Mans (d. 1214), most plausibly between 1204 and 1206; *Enquête de 1245*, 32–34, 56. Note that despite the name, the enquiry dates from 1246.
52 *Enquête de 1245*, 77–8.
53 David Carpenter, *The Minority of Henry III* (London: Meuthen, 1990), 78–81.
54 Most notably, John, king of England, was excommunicated in 1209 and the kingdom placed under interdict in 1208 after a dispute over the appointment of the archbishop of Canterbury, referred to in the text above.
55 For a short biography of Maurice, see Matz, *Diocèse*, 181–7.
56 Horoy, *Honori III*, ii, 698–9.
57 Horoy, *Honori III*, ii, 698–9. '*Ex parte tua fuit propositum coram nobis.*'
58 Trindade, *Berengaria*, 164.
59 Jörg Peltzer, *Canon Law, Careers and Conquest. Episcopal Elections in Normandy and Greater Anjou, c.1140-c.1230* (Cambridge: Cambridge University Press, 2008), 192–3.
60 *Enquête de 1245*, 32–3, 35–6, 39–42, 57–61.
61 Baury and Corriol, *Bérengère*, 144.
62 Baury and Corriol, *Bérengère*, 162.
63 *Enquête de 1245*, 107.
64 Horoy, *Honori III*, ii, cols. 187–8.
65 Horoy, *Honori III*, ii, cols. 149–50.
66 Letter dated 17 January 1217. Horoy, *Honori III*, ii, cols. 182–183; Bliss records the date as February 1217 in Bliss, *Papal Registers*, IX, 43.
67 Horoy, *Honori III*, i, cols. 269–70; Horoy, ii, cols. 699–700.
68 Horoy, *Honori III*, ii, cols. 698–9.
69 Horoy, *Honori III*, i, cols. 362–5; dated 5 April 1218. For more on the history of the cathedral and the diocese of Le Mans itself, see Jean-Michel Matz, *Diocèse du Mans* (Turnhout: Brepols, 2018).
70 Horoy, *Honori III*, ii, cols. 698–9.
71 Horoy, *Honori III*, ii, cols. 696–7. '*quo curam et sollicitudinem gerere cognimur viduarum specialem gratiam exhibendo.*'
72 *Enquête de 1245*, 41, 60–1, 86, 132; for more detail see Baury and Corriol, *Bérengère*, 162–9.
73 Baury and Corriol, *Bérengère*, 166.
74 John W. Baldwin, François Gasparri, Michel Nortier, and Elisabeth Lalou, eds., *Recueil des historiens de la France. Documents financiers et administratifs. Tome VII. Les Registres de Philippe Auguste. Volume I: Texte* (Paris: Imprimerie Nationale, 1992), no. 1505; *Recueil des actes de Philippe-Auguste*, iv, 130–1.
75 Horoy, *Honorii III*, ii, cols. 700–2.
76 *Enquête de 1245*, 60.
77 Baury and Corriol, *Bérengère*, 168.
78 Paul Piolin, ed., *Histoire de l'Eglise Du Mans*, 10 vols. (Paris: Imprimerie Libraires au Mans, 1851–71), iv, no. 70.

79 BNF, Latin 17124 (1229–30), 27–28, 28.
80 AD Sarthe, 111 AC 939, no. 915 (1230); Celier, *Catalogues des actes*, no. 539. Note that in AD Sarthe two charters of William's are numbered 915 but are separate documents.
81 Celier, *Catalogue des actes*, no. 551.
82 Samuel Menjot D'Elbenne and Louis J. Denis, eds., *Cartulaire du Chapitre Royal de Saint-Pierre-de-la-Cour, du Mans* (Le Mans: Siège de la Société, 1907), no. 1. See Robert Latouche for doubts on the authenticity of the founding charters; Latouche, *Histoire du Comté du Maine*, appendix 2, 105–7.
83 *Saint-Pierre-de-la-Cour*, nos. 44 and 45.
84 Samuel Menjot D'Elbenne and Louis J. Denis, *Le chapitre royal de l'église collégiale de Saint-Pierre-de-la-Cour, Sainte-Chapelle-du-Mans* (Le Mans: Siège de la Société, 1909), 147
85 D'Elbenne, *La chapitre royal*, 149.
86 *Saint-Pierre-de-la-Cour*, no. 39.
87 AD Sarthe, G 479 (1219).
88 *Saint-Pierre-de-la-Cour*, nos. 46, 47.
89 AD Sarthe, 1 J 1281 (1226); *Saint-Pierre-de-la-Cour*, no. 49.
90 Celier, *Catalogue des actes*, no. 533.
91 *Saint-Pierre-de-la-Cour*, no. 38.
92 *Saint-Pierre-de-la-Cour*, no. 40.
93 AD Sarthe, G 479.
94 BNF, Latin 17124, 29 (1228); see also AD Sarthe, 111 AC 941.
95 Piolin, *Histoire*, iv, 583–5; BNF, Latin 17124, 28–9.
96 Carpenter, *Minority*, 138, 251.
97 The threat of Eleanor's claim persisted into the reign of Henry III, who kept her imprisoned until her death in 1241.
98 The most extensive of these is AD Sarthe, 111 AC 939 (1229–30); with a further series of documents in H 859 (1229–30).
99 AD Sarthe, 111 AC 939 (1229–30).
100 AD Sarthe, 111 AC 941 (January 1230).
101 AD Sarthe, 111 AC 939, nos. 915–921 (1229–30).
102 Jean Barrère, *La Piété-Dieu de L'Épau. Construction et Aménagement d'une Abbaye Cistercienne (1230–1365)* (PhD Thesis, Le Mans, 1968), 5. For more on Blanche and her religious foundations, see Lindy Grant, *Blanche of Castile* (London: Yale University Press, 2016).
103 BL, Additional Charter 46402 (1230); also see AD Sarthe, H 833, no. 7 (1230).
104 AD Sarthe, 111 AC 939, no. 20 (1230); Baury and Corriol, *Bérengère*, 188.
105 Joseph-Marie Canivez, ed., *Statuta capitulorum generalium ordinis cisterciensis ab anno 1116 ad annum 1786*, 8 vols. (Louvain: Bibliothèque de la Revue d'histoire ecclesiastique, 1933–41), i, 24.
106 Canivez, *Statuta*, i, 66.
107 Canivez, *Statuta*, i, 77, 94.
108 Joëlle Quaghebeur, *La Cornouaille du IXème au XIIème siècles: mémoire, pouvoirs, noblesse* (Rennes and Quimper: Presses Universitaires

de Rennes, Société archéologique du Finistère, 2002), 367; Colette Bowie, *The Daughters of Henry II and Eleanor of Aquitaine* (Turnhout: Brepols, 2014), ch. 5.

109 My thanks go to Kathleen Nolan for sharing her chapter and thoughts on Berengaria and her tomb with me. Kathleen Nolan, 'Symbolic Geography in the Tomb and Seal of Berengaria of Navarre, Queen of England,' in *Moving Women, Moving Objects (400–1500)*, eds. Tracy Chapman-Hamilton and Mariah Proctor-Tiffany (Leiden: Brill, 2019), 59–85.

110 Nolan, 'Symbolic Geography,' 75. Nolan argues for the influence of Eleanor of Aquitaine's tomb, where Eleanor holds an open book, on Berengaria's tomb.

111 Verónica Abenza, 'In the Name of the Queen: Female patron portraits and inscriptions in 11th Century Navarre,' in *Zeichentragende Artefakte im sakralen Raum. Zwischen Präsenz und UnSichtbarkeit*, eds. Wilfried E. Keil, Sarah Kiyanrad, Christoffer Theis, and Laura Willer (Berlin: De Grutyer, 2018), 285–307.

112 Baury and Corriol, *Bérengère*, 250–1.

113 Baury and Corriol, *Bérengère*, 243–92.

114 Greater discussion of the construction of the abbey and tomb appear in Baury and Corriol, *Bérengère*, 244–56, based on their interpretation and discussions of material from cultural and governmental resources that I have not been permitted access to.

115 Nicholas Vincent, 'Isabella of Angoulême: John's Jezebel,' in *King John: New Interpretations*, ed. Stephen D. Church (Woodbridge: Boydell Press, 1999), 165–219.

116 Xavier Dectot, *Les tombeaux des familles royales de la péninsule ibérique au Moyen Age* (Turnhout: Brepols, 2009), 36–7.

117 Léopold Delisle and Natalis de Wailly, eds. *Recueil des historiens des Gaules et de la France. Tome Vingt-Deuxième contenant la troisième livraison des monuments des règnes de Saint Louis, de Philippe le Hardi, de Philippe le Bel, de Louis X, de Philippe V, et de Charles IV, depuis MCCXXVI jusqu'en MCCCXXVIII* (Paris: Imprimerie Royale, 1855), 577. *'reginae Cenomanis.'*

118 G. Busson and A. Ledru, eds., *Nécrologe-obituaire de la Cathédrale du Mans* (Le Mans: Siège de la Société, 1906), 336–7. My thanks go to Ghislain Baury and Vincent Corriol for this reference.

119 Bodleian Library, Oxford, MS. Gough drawings-Gaignières 15.

120 Bodleian Library, Oxford, MS. Gough drawings-Gaignières 15. Transcription, translation, and editing my own.

121 Baury and Corriol, *Bérengère*, 253.

122 AD Sarthe, 3 V 10.

123 Baury and Corriol, *Bérengère*, 267.

LEGACY

Berengaria is one of the most forgotten queens of England, but there is much to say about her representation, memory, and legacy. She may have received scant attention as a queen of England, but her participation in the Third Crusade has made her an occasional side character in modern films and novels. Furthermore, both her position as lord of Le Mans for twenty-six years and her burial in the city has encouraged significant local attention to be paid to Berengaria over the centuries. This concluding chapter addresses two questions concerning Berengaria's later legacy: firstly, how has she been remembered and represented as a queen of England in modern scholarship, cultural memory, and popular media? Secondly, how has Berengaria been memorialised and remembered as the lord of Le Mans?

Queen

Although Berengaria has not been completely neglected in the historiography on medieval rulership, she has certainly lacked more focussed and detailed surveys of her entire political career. French historiography has largely, and sometimes single-mindedly, devoted attention to her tenure of Le Mans. The extent of the evidence for her actions in Le Mans make this an obvious choice, but her time as the city's ruler needs to be placed within the wider context of her entire life, including Navarrese influences on her approach to lordship, and greater understanding of the neglect she experienced as queen of England. Conversely, Anglophone

DOI: 10.4324/9781003223306-8

historiography has primarily viewed Berengaria in terms of one 'significant' event – her marriage to Richard I – and there have been a few short and speculative biographical studies.

The Spanish historiography has adopted a similar approach, although greater attention has been given to her birth and position as an infanta of Navarre, alongside her marriage to Richard.[1] Despite the long history of queenship in England, it is only relatively recently that modern scholarship has turned more fully to consider women's lives and aspects of gender. Berengaria's lack of prominence, longevity as queen consort, and lack of heir have all contributed to her partial erasure from the historical record of English queens. Both her marriage and coronation occurred outside of the territories of the kings of England, a rare event, and she undertook the remarkable, though unusual, venture of accompanying her husband on the Third Crusade after her coronation as queen of England. Whether Berengaria's decision to accompany Richard was one of genuine choice and personal commitment to the Crusade, or whether it was by Richard's orders is uncertain. Whereas contemporary chroniclers commented on her presence alongside Richard on crusade, later historians have paid little attention to Berengaria from this perspective. Berengaria's time as queen outside the Anglophone sphere and her perceived lack of political activity are major contributors to her status as a forgotten queen of England. Historical writers in the medieval period and beyond were far more concerned with the deeds of kings, military and foreign events, and activities that drew scandal or attention.

Berengaria's legacy as queen has also suffered within Anglophone scholarship because she and Richard did not produce an heir. At a time when succession passed through the paternal line to a male heir (as the unsuccessful succession of the Empress Matilda not sixty years before had shown), bearing a son remained an essential task for a queen consort. Although Berengaria was not unique in her position as a childless queen, as Edith of Wessex, Sybilla of Normandy, and Anne of Bohemia show, Berengaria's absence from her kingdom meant that she lacked the opportunity to patronise, network, and otherwise establish herself as queen of England so that such concerns over a lack of heir did not destabilise her.[2] With no heir, Berengaria's line ended with her. She was removed from the historical record, rendered into obscurity, and had no further dynastic successors to trace. Had she remarried – and the reasoning behind why she did not have already been discussed – she may have merited more attention as a former queen of England. As such, her lack of heir marked another reason why her time as queen has received so little attention in the longer historical record.

Lastly, as noted, Berengaria's time as queen is marked by a lack of evidence. This was driven in part by her absence from England, but also by the dominance of her mother-in-law, Eleanor of Aquitaine, during Berengaria's reign. It would be unwise to speculate at this juncture on the personal relationship between the two women, as personal feelings are usually lost in the historical record. However, the notion of hostility on Eleanor's part towards Berengaria is likely unfounded. What can be seen from the surviving evidence is continued proof of Eleanor's political activity as dowager queen of England and ruler within the Angevin domains. She does not appear to have ceded any lands or authority to Berengaria, and as a ruler of immense experience and competency, Eleanor was a suitable choice to not only rule in Richard's stead alongside a regency council whilst he was on the Third Crusade, but also to maintain order and authority across the Angevin domains whilst Richard was engaged in military campaigns in France. Eleanor was a tried and tested ruler; Berengaria was not. Richard's decision not to co-rule with Berengaria and instead to keep Eleanor in a position of prominence made political sense, but it pushed Berengaria to the sidelines. Richard's choice not to associate Berengaria with his rule, even upon his return from the Third Crusade, only contributed to her further diplomatic and political isolation, and made her time as queen of England appear even more unremarkable.

All these factors – the agendas of different historiographical traditions, Berengaria's childlessness, and the dominance of her mother-in-law – contributed to obscuring details of her life and her position as queen within the historical record. These are all reasons why her modern legacy is minimal. Berengaria had little opportunity to rule and act as a true queen with the power that ought to have been afforded to her. She did not have any scandalous moments from her reign worthy of contemporary commentary either.

Berengaria's legacy further suffered from being a chaste, unremarkable queen of England, positioned between two royal women – Eleanor of Aquitaine and Isabella of Angoulême – who received significantly more chronicle attention as a result of political and sexual scandal. Placed alongside the somewhat politically explosive legacies of Eleanor and Isabella, Berengaria stood little chance of being remembered or memorialised.

Queens on Screen and in Popular Culture

The surge in medievalism as a field of study over recent decades has encouraged analyses of gender and power in depictions of the Middle Ages in various media.[3] The representation of queens in popular media undoubtedly leaves a mark on its audience, and can introduce new perspectives on historical figures, whether unknown or infamous. Popular media primarily intends to entertain, and it is this aim that has often been the focus of scrutiny and ire from historians, especially when this objective can lead to (occasionally wild) deviations from historical accuracy. Even when historians have acted as research consultants for televisual media, or when novelists and writers have drawn upon historical scholarship, history remains only a basis for popular culture, not the dominant resource or primary output.

Given the plethora of media that has been produced over the last century, it is somewhat of a surprise that the crusades and the early Plantagenets have received such little attention from the creative industry. Other forms of warfare and the Tudors remain dominant choices for creatives, though some queens, especially in Anglophone media, have merited significant attention: Eleanor of Aquitaine has been the subject of several novels, and the reigns of Mary I, queen of Scotland, and Elizabeth I of England have also received cinematic representations. The Angevins and early Plantagenets are a family ripe for creative depictions, especially considering their rivalry with France. Since representations of the early Plantagenets in popular culture have often focussed on the figures of Richard I and Eleanor of Aquitaine, Berengaria has not been depicted as a main character and instead has been juxtaposed between these two figures.

Where can we first see Berengaria in film? The Italian silent movie *Il talismano [The Talisman]* (1911), based on Walter Scott's 1825 novel *Richard the Lion-hearted*, includes the character of Berengaria as queen consort, though to little note. An American adaptation released twelve years later, where Kathleen Clifford played Berengaria, received greater acclaim, although does little to provide Berengaria with any particular plot or character development. Loretta Young depicted Berengaria in the 1935 film *The Crusades*, once again based on Scott's novel. This retelling dramatically differs from the earlier two – and from the novel – since it propels Berengaria to centre stage, making her an essential figure in the actions of the Third Crusade. I am inclined to agree with Baury and Corriol that this script change is due to Young's popularity and position.[4] Whilst one credits the imagination of the scriptwriters in highlighting Berengaria rather than isolating her, as many women often are in historical dramas, Berengaria's role on the Third Crusade is otherwise unknown and, consequently, the 1935 film takes several historical liberties.[5] The film shows Berengaria at the centre of a love triangle between Richard I and Saladin after she sacrifices herself by crossing enemy lines in the hopes of resolving the tensions between the English and French forces.[6]

The Crusades is a film that engages several typical tropes to engage its audience: a historical adventure, a clash of civilisations between West and East, and a love triangle. It does draw upon aspects of historical fact: Richard and Berengaria did go on crusade together, and there was indeed tension between Richard and Philip Augustus after the former's repudiation of the latter's sister Alys (also depicted in the film). Berengaria's religious fervour and conviction are also highlighted. As discussed in chapter five, it is highly plausible that piety was important to Berengaria, evidenced by her religious patronage and establishment of L'Abbaye de L'Épau. However, we do not know anything about her personal belief in the religious motivations underpinning the Third Crusade. Berengaria's involvement in the Crusade was circumstantial; it was a political necessity that she marry Richard to secure the Anglo-Navarrese alliance at this time, and it was for this reason she journeyed across Western Europe to join him. We have no evidence to prove that she was particularly devout, or that she ever came close to meeting Saladin.

A fourth filmic incarnation of Scott's novel, *King Richard and the Crusaders*, appeared in 1954. This historical adventure followed some of the same avenues as the 1935 version, and Berengaria is represented in this movie by Paula Raymond. Unlike the earlier 1935 edition, this adaptation expressed anti-war sentiments, caricaturised Saladin, and offered less of a prominent role for Berengaria, instead centring on Edith Plantagenet, a fictional character who may have been partially based on Joanna Plantagenet, Richard's sister. Edith's central role was as part of a marital alliance with the Muslim forces.[7]

Representations of Berengaria were not solely limited to Western cinema. The Egyptian director Youssef Chahine created the 1963 drama *Al Nasser Salah Ad-Din*, which refocussed depictions of the Third Crusade from an Islamic perspective. This film pushed Saladin to the fore, with the historical epic depicting him as an educated liberator and saviour of Jerusalem. Its purpose was in part propaganda to draw comparisons with the pan-Arabic movement occurring in Egypt at the time, led by Gamal Abdel Nasser, the Egyptian president.[8] For this reason, Berengaria is again moved to the sidelines of the action, and her portrayal by Laila Taher serves only as a juxtaposition against the power-hungry Virginia, widow of Renaud de Châtillon, who is the other primary female historical protagonist.

Berengaria was also depicted in two further adaptations of *The Talisman* which appeared in Russian cinema directed by Evgeniy Gerasimov: *Richard Lvinoe Serdtse* (1992) and its sequel *Rytsar Kennet* (1993). Both these films were driven by an anti-Western agenda, with Richard emerging in a decidedly negative light. Berengaria's depiction also suffers in these films. Played by Svetlana Amanova, Berengaria appears a cold, impassionate, and somewhat dull queen consort, drawing no sympathies or attention from the audience.

In all these crusading films, Berengaria remains a cipher and an object, primarily as a device to further a male plotline, occasionally to draw attention away from military matters, but with no real attempt at giving Berengaria her own legacy or reputation. The brief appearances of Berengaria in crusading films demonstrates that she has usually been relegated to being a side character with little development, mirroring her representations in the medieval record. On the one occasion where her character is fleshed out more fully (1935, *The Crusades*), extreme historical liberties are taken in order to provide her with a more dramatic and fuller portrayal. Other films depicting dramatizations of the events leading up to Third Crusade focus on the politics of the kingdom of Jerusalem – most recently and notably, Ridley Scott's 2005 epic *Kingdom of Heaven*, with the film ending with Richard I's journey to the Holy Land: thus, it would be inaccurate for Berengaria to have appeared at this stage. Instead, the film's primary female protagonist is Sibylla, the queen of Jerusalem, as portrayed by Eva Green.

Televisual portrayals of Berengaria offer further insight into her legacy and historical memory. From 1962 to 1963, the British Broadcasting Corporation produced a series of episodes on Richard's reign entitled *Richard the Lionheart*. Berengaria features as a central character, depicted by Sheila Whittingham, and appears in twelve episodes. Berengaria first appears in episode 12, 'The Bride,' as an indicator of Richard's desire to abandon the Anglo-French alliance in return for the new Anglo-Navarrese one. In episode 14, 'The Great Enterprise,' Richard and Berengaria's honeymoon is interrupted as treachery abounds at the English court; later in the episode, Berengaria is accused of treason. Episode 22, 'Queen in Danger,' sees Richard dispatch Berengaria to England in fear of her safety on the Third Crusade, however, she is captured by Richard's supposed ally, Conrad of Montferrat. In episode 29, 'A King's Ransom,' we see Berengaria active in raising the ransom for Richard's release when he is captured on his return from crusade. Berengaria also makes an appearance in the final instalment, episode 39,' The People's King,' when Richard has been safely returned to England and is crowned as king of England in the country for the second time. What *Richard the Lionheart* shows is an interesting portrayal of a politically active queen – indeed, the many roles and activities Berengaria ought to have fulfilled as queen consort. Much is fabrication: Berengaria never came to England during Richard's lifetime, and as far as the evidence demonstrates, did not have a part to play in raising Richard's ransom. The television series, featuring Berengaria and Richard's relationship as a central focus of the series, presents a level of amiability and friendliness between the couple for which there is little evidence in the historical record. Given the lack of co-ruling between Richard and Berengaria that can be deduced from the historical record, one could interpret that Richard and Berengaria's relationship lacked a certain level of harmony and trust and this has been mirrored on screen.

After the 1962–3 series, Berengaria makes a further appearance in the 1978 drama, *The Devil's Crown*, which moves away from the praiseworthy depictions of Richard towards one more critical. Zoë Wanamaker is cast as Berengaria, represented alongside a dominant Eleanor who has chosen Berengaria as her son's bride. *The Devil's Crown* presents a new take on Berengaria, portraying her as everything a conventional bride was not: ugly, dim, and lacking in character. *The Devil's Crown* was one of the more popular Plantagenet adaptations, bringing the royal family to a new audience in an entertaining and somewhat comedic style, however, it did little to remedy Berengaria's legacy in terms of popularity or accuracy.

Two years later, another BBC adaptation appeared, again taking its inspiration from Scott's novel and thus aptly named *The Talisman*. Joanne Pearce took up the mantle of Berengaria in this series, although her depiction was nothing of note to a British audience. Berengaria was pretty but lacking in personality, provoking the view that the historical Berengaria was of no great interest or knowledge. Pretty, or 'fair,' and lacking any personality worthy of comment is perhaps the impression that could be derived from the historical record if one focussed only on chronicle or literary material from Berengaria's years as queen consort. Without examining any other arenas of Berengaria's life, filmmakers have largely presented a one-dimensional and uninteresting queen, aiding her path into obscurity rather than shedding further light on her actions and legacy.

Berengaria in Literature

Berengaria does not fare much better in literature, whether romantic historical novels, or adventure stories and dramatic accounts. As mentioned above, Walter Scott's novel, *The Talisman* (1825), inspired many visual depictions and enabled Berengaria to appear on screen. In the novel, Berengaria is presented as a louder than life character. She is commanding, according to Scott, 'thoughtless,' and a leading figure at court; a far stretch from any historical record that mentions Berengaria.[9] In chapter sixteen, Scott elaborates further on Berengaria's appearance and personality:

The high-born Berengaria, daughter of Sanchez, King of Navarre, and the Queen-Consort of the heroic Richard, was accounted one of the most beautiful women of the period. Her form was slight, though exquisitely moulded. She was graced with a complexion not common in her country, a profusion of fair hair, and features so extremely juvenile as to make her look several years younger than she really was, though in reality she was not above one-and-twenty. Perhaps it was under the consciousness of this extremely juvenile appearance that she affected, or at least practised, a little childish petulance and wilfulness of manner, not unbefitting, she might suppose, a youthful bride, whose rank and age gave her a right to have her fantasies indulged and attended to. She was by nature perfectly good-humoured, and if her due share of admiration and homage (in her opinion a very large one) was duly resigned to her, no one could possess better temper or a more friendly disposition; but then, like all despots, the more power that was voluntarily yielded to her, the more she desired to extend her sway. Sometimes, even when all her ambition was gratified, she chose to be a little out of health, and a little out of spirits; and physicians had to toil their wits to invent names for imaginary maladies, while her ladies racked their imagination for new games, new head-gear, and new court-scandal, to pass away those unpleasant hours, during which their own situation was scarce to be greatly envied. She was confident in her husband's favour, in her high rank, and in her supposed power to make good whatever such pranks might cost others. In a word, she gambolled with the freedom of a young lioness, who is unconscious of the weight of her own paws when laid on those whom she sports with.[10]

With such a detailed description – far surpassing that of medieval chronicles – one could imagine Berengaria to be an active and spritely queen. Scott also refers to Berengaria holding power. Although, for the most part, medieval queens did indeed access and hold some form of power whilst they were consort, in Berengaria's case (and likewise for her successor, Isabella of Angoulême) we can see that this was not always the case.

Scott's novel understandably drew much attention from contemporaries and future filmmakers, as seen by the numerous depictions of *The Talisman*. Scott was one of few novelists to pay much attention to Berengaria, giving her fuller and more detailed character development than many others. Placing Berengaria within a crusading context was always a hook for readers interested in medieval military campaigns and the heroics of Richard the Lionheart. However, Scott's depictions did little to draw any lasting attention to Berengaria from the general public. Like many of her filmic depictions, Berengaria remained a fleeting figure, on the periphery, and did not inspire further attention.

Scott was not the only novelist to represent Berengaria. Rachel Bard, a historian and novelist of Navarre, penned *Queen Without A Country*, one of the few novels to place Berengaria centre-stage.[11] As Berengaria was left largely unaided by her natal and marital family, Navarre and England were unlikely to be places of refuge, hence the name of the novel. In it, Bard casts Berengaria as a protagonist surviving all adversity: a domineering mother-in-law, a childless marriage, and travels across Europe. A romantic drama, Berengaria is portrayed as beautiful and captivating Richard's attention, yet also a pious woman as founder of L'Épau.

Bard was not the only author to give Berengaria the romantic heroine treatment. Victoria Sauers, author of *Lionhearted Queen: Berengaria of Navarre*, emphasises, like Bard, how Richard and Berengaria met and developed affection for one another after a tournament in Pamplona, as well as the involvement of Eleanor in their marriage arrangements. However, Sauers discusses the matter of Richard's homosexuality in more detail than other novelists and presents certain historical debates as facts without due consideration The prerogative of the novelist, like the filmmaker, is to entertain, not necessarily to maintain historical accuracy in creative works. Both Sauers and Bard managed to bring Berengaria to a new audience, as the early 2000s saw a rise in popularity of historical romance fiction, particularly centred on queens.

Many other historical novels focussing on either the Plantagenet world or the Third Crusade feature Berengaria to varying degrees of importance, including Jean Plaidy's *The Heart Of The Lion* (1977); *Propinquity* by John Macgregor (1986); *Willow Maid* by Maureen Peters (1974); *My Lord Brother the Lionheart* by Molly Costain Haycraft (1968); Norah Lofts' *The Lute Player* (1951); *Standard of Honour* by Jack Whyte (2007); G. A. Henty's *Winning His Spurs* (1882) and *The Boy Knight* (1882); Fern Michaels' *Valentina* (1978); *The Queen's Witch* by Cecelia Holland (2011); Sharon Kay Penman's *Lionheart* (2012) and *A King's Ransom* (2014); in two of Pamela Kaufman's Alix of Wainthwaite trilogy, *Shield of Three Lions* (1983) and *Banners of Gold* (1986); Margaret Campbell Barnes's *The Passionate Brood* (1945); and Elizabeth Chadwick's *The Autumn Throne* (2016). The novels also vary in their treatment and depictions of Berengaria: *Propinquity* for example, depicts Berengaria as a follower of the Indian mystic Kabir, and focusses on the attempts by a group to revive Berengaria, located under the Chapel of Henry VII in Westminster Abbey, from a trancelike state in the 1970s. She features as a secondary character in much of the historical fiction based in the twelfth and thirteenth centuries, such as *The Lute Player* which focuses on Blondel, the lute player who accompanies Richard's court on the Third Crusade, or *Standard of Honour* which is a story of the Knights Templar. Berengaria gets more centrality in *Lionheart* and appears as a strong and likeable figure, who adjusts well to life on the Third Crusade, as well as delving into the more personal aspects of Berengaria and Richard's relationship. *Valentina* presents an altogether different Berengaria: one who is jealous, stubborn, and an adulterer, having sex with Christian and Muslim alike. Two divergent themes appear when considering Berengaria's depictions: either she remains a secondary figure, though she can be either a timid shadow or a more outspoken individual, but nevertheless not central. Or she becomes a more dominant figure, but in connection with something shocking, such as following an Indian mystic or engaging in infidelity. It is perhaps *A King's Ransom* in which one can garner more sympathy for Berengaria's lot, mirroring the reality that she was neglected by Richard.

The world of historical fiction and novella being as diverse as it is, one would expect some variances in portrayals of Berengaria. However, much like the films and television series, in novels where Berengaria is not the protagonist, she suffers from malignment on one end of the spectrum to gross exaggeration of character traits on the other. Although novels are by no means meant to be realistic, the continuance of falling intro tropes when presenting medieval queens – either that of swooning heroine, scandalous Jezebel, or quiet and pious shadow – means that the fictional world has some way to go before a more balanced and enjoyable representation of Berengaria appears on the page of a novel. Interestingly, unlike her mother-in-law Eleanor, a protofeminist Berengaria has never emerged in media, when her story offers many opportunities for a feminist retelling to be created.

Berengaria and L'Épau

Berengaria's memory and reputation has also endured and survived through her local legacy in Le Mans. This has been the focal point of the studies of Le Mans and Berengaria, and since this is an aspect which receives particular attention in Baury and Corriol's biography the topic will only be treated briefly here.[12] Throughout archaeological and architectural studies of Le Mans, in particular those focusing on the L'Abbaye de L'Épau, Berengaria's tomb and foundation have remained a prominent starting point.

In the centuries after Berengaria's death, and once the Plantagenets had been far removed from local memory and rulership of the region, interest in Berengaria would stem from scholars with either an ecclesiastical or architectural background and knowledge of the region. As explored in chapter five, through the work of Roger de Gagnières and Charles Alfred Stothard we have an idea of what the tomb looked like in the early modern period, and how Berengaria's effigy has changed over the last two

FIGURE 7.1 Photograph of the side view of Berengaria's effigy ©
Sarthe Culture

centuries. Robert Triger discussed the hypothesis of Berengaria's
residence in Le Mans, sparking a thirty-year debate regarding the
site of Berengaria's residence and what to do with the properties
that may have been her residence.[13] Ultimately the three houses
at the centre of the debate were purchased by Le Mans in February 1914, with two of the (adjoining) houses turned into a mu-
seum dedicated to popular arts and local history, which opened
in 1924, and the Société historiques et archéologique du Maine
resident in the third house on cour de la Pôte.

Local interest in Berengaria has also spiked over the last century following the discovery of a skeleton in the abbey in 1960,
which is presumed to be Berengaria. The excavation work undertaken by an amateur archaeologist, Pierre Terouanne, saw the
unearthing of eight tombs in the chapter house, one of which con-
tained a small skeleton, attributed to a woman who was around
sixty years old when she died. Intensive archaeological debate has
followed, but thus far archaeological examination has not conclusively proved that the skeleton is her. The president of the Société
d'agriculture, sciences et arts, André Bouton, first argued in 1963

that the bones were not Berengaria's, then stated in 1964 that neither the bones in the box or those found in the chapter house were
Berengaria's, and that the queen's remains are lost, before changing his argument again in 1969 that the bones found in the 1960s
were hers.[14] As the decades have progressed the debate around
the skeleton has been of interest, but become more muted with
less proclamations that the bones found in the chapter house are
definitively hers. Nevertheless, the discovery sparked a revival of
scholarly and popular interest in the former queen and lord of Le
Mans. The effigy was first reinstalled to the transept in 1974, after
this intensive debate. The effigy, alongside the box containing the
bones that had previously been interred with it, and the bones
from the chapter room, were kept together in a singular monument and relocated to the chapter room. The abbey and tomb receive a consistent and steady flow of local visitors, as well as other
regional, national, and international tourists who have a knowledge of Plantagenet and local history. As Le Mans was the capital
of Maine, the former Plantagenet country, the city draws in visitors from further afield and the abbey receives these accordingly.
A revival programme launched with the Sarthe Culture centre in
2016 has concentrated focus on the abbey and Berengaria, with a
series of research papers by Bénédicte Fillion-Brauget providing a
new interpretation of Berengaria's tomb, and justification for its
relocation to the abbey church.[15] The cultural programme's intentions to popularise Berengaria and the abbey can be seen with its
Berengaria-branded merchandise available at L'Épau. Berengaria
is one of the primary connections to Plantagenet history within
the city and it is for this that she continues to be remembered and
utilised as point of commemoration.

Berengaria's position as lord of Le Mans, founder of L'Épau, and
her residence and patronage of Le Mans drew a closer connection
between her and the city than any of her predecessors or successors. The endurance of her tomb and effigy – particularly when so
many were damaged during the French Revolution – have enabled
her memory and legacy to survive. Berengaria's prominence in the
history of Le Mans was exemplified by a local exhibition held in
conjunction with the launch of the French biography by Ghislain
Baury and Vincent Corriol, and the release of a comic book by

Bruno Rocco, Olivier Renault, Bénédicte Fillion-Brauget, Ghislain Baury, and Vincent Corriol.[16] The exhibition drew a significant number of visitors on the opening day (20 November 2022), and it ran until 13 March 2023. Through promotion of ties with the local community, the exhibition provided a biographical overview of Berengaria's life and informed visitors about other aspects of life and society during the Middle Ages.[17] It emphasised her connections and role as patron of Le Mans, as well as the wider context of her marriage to Richard. The exhibition demonstrated the many roles royal and noble women played in medieval society as well. This renewed interest has encouraged more visitors to the abbey and engagement with local citizens of all ages, aided by the participation of re-enactment groups on the opening day. By emphasising Berengaria's place in Le Mans – as a local founder and ruler – the exhibition and abbey continue to promote Berengaria's legacy and memory, to ensure it endures for future generations.

In future, continued analyses of Berengaria's tomb and the abbey, and further examination of her depictions in novels and films, alongside other popular culture, will help provide even greater understanding of how Berengaria's reputation has been distorted and maligned in popular media. We can highlight how, not only as a queen of England, but also as lord of Le Mans, Berengaria needs to and ought to be remembered.

Notes

1 Mariano González-Arnao Conde-Luque, 'Berenguela de Navarra y Ricardo Corazón de León,' *History 16* 111 (1985): 67–75. Note this is a popular history piece, such is the scant discussion of Berengaria in Spanish historiography. The most encompassing Spanish work is the new edition and translation of Ann Trindade's biography; Ann Trinidade, *Berenguela de Navarra. Reina de Inglaterra. Buscando a la consorte de Ricardo Corazón de León*, trans. Manuel Sagastibelza, 2nd ed. (Pamplona: Editorial Mintzoa S. L., 2022).

2 My thanks to Emma J. Trivett for her notes and discussions about childless queens and (in)fertility in the medieval period.

3 See Gabrielle Storey, ed., *Memorialising Premodern Monarchs. Medias of Commemoration and Remembrance* (Cham: Palgrave Macmillan, 2020); Janice North, Karl Christian Alvestad, and Elena Woodacre, eds., *Premodern Rulers and Postmodern Viewers. Gender, Sex, and Power in Popular Culture* (Cham: Palgrave Macmillan, 2018);

Michael R. Evans, *Inventing Eleanor. The Post-Medieval Image of Eleanor of Aquitaine* (London: Bloomsbury, 2014); Zita Eva Rohr and Lisa Benz, eds., *Queenship and the Women of Westeros: Female Agency and Advice in* Game of Thrones *and* A Song of Ice and Fire (Cham: Palgrave Macmillan, 2020).

4 Ghislain Baury and Vincent Corriol, *Bérengère de Navarre (v. 1160–1230). Histoire et mémoire d'une reine d'Angleterre* (Rennes: Presses Universitaires de Rennes, 2022), 219.

5 Lorraine K. Stock, 'Now Starring in the Third Crusade: Depictions of Richard I and Saladin in Films and Television Series,' in *Hollywood in the Holy Land: Essays on Film Depictions of the Crusades and Christian-Muslim Clashes*, eds. Nickolas Haydock and Edward L. Risden (Jefferson, NC: McFarland, 2009), 93–122.

6 *The Crusades*, directed by Cecil B. DeMille (New York: Paramount Pictures, 1935).

7 For the proposed marriage between Joanna Plantagenet and al-'Âdil, Saladin's brother, see Martin Aurell, 'Joan of England and al-'Âdil's Harem: The Impossible Marriage between Christians and Muslims (Eleventh-Twelfth Centuries),' *Anglo-Norman Studies* 43 (2021): 1–14.

8 Fawaz A. Gerges, *Making the Arab World: Nasser, Qutb, and the Clash That Shaped the Middle East* (Princeton: Princeton University Press, 2018).

9 Walter Scott, *The Talisman* (1825, reprint 1998), ch. 13, accessed 23 January 2023, https://gutenberg.org/cache/epub/1377/pg1377-images.html.

10 Scott, *The Talisman*, ch. 16.

11 Rachel Bard, *Queen Without A Country* (London: Minerva Press, 2000).

12 Baury and Corriol, *Bérengère*, 243–92.

13 Robert Triger, 'La maison dite de la Reine Bérengère au Mans,' *Bulletin Monumental* 58 (1893): 4–26.

14 André Bouton, 'Quelle est cette dame de l'Épau? À la recherche de la reine Bérengère,' *La vie mancelle et sarthoise* 41 (1963): 8–10; André Bouton, 'La reine perdue,' *La vie mancelle et sarthoise* 43 (1964): 6–7; André Bouton, 'La reine Bérengère perdue et retrouvée,' *Bulletin de la Société d'agriculture, sciences et arts de la Sarthe* 439 (1969): 15–26, all quoted from Baury and Corriol, *Bérengère*, 283.

15 Several of the papers are only available internally; my thanks to Bénédicte Fillion-Brauget for sharing her recent paper with me: Pauline Ducom and Bénédicte Fillion-Brauget, 'Le Mans. Abbaye de l'Épau: le tombeau à gisant de la reine Bérengère de Navarre,' *Bulletin Monumental société française d'archéologie* 181.1 (2023): 77–82.

16 Bruno Rocco, Olivier Renault, Bénédicte Fillion-Braguet, Ghislain Baury, and Vincent Corriol, *Bérengère de Navarre, du trône de l'Angleterre à l'abbaye de l'Épau* (Nantes: Petit à Petit, 2022).

17 Exhibition. *Bérengère, à la rencontre d'une Reine*. L'Abbaye de L'Épau, 19/11/2022–13/03/2023.

CONCLUSION

Exploring Berengaria's story has brought further into the light more information about not only her political career, but also Berengaria's place within the rulership of the Angevin Union and as a female lord in thirteenth-century France. Overshadowed as queen consort by a warrior king husband and a powerful and successful mother-in-law, Berengaria's life has been consigned to obscurity. This biography has shown that there is much more to Berengaria's life than previously thought.

A fuller exploration of her Navarrese origins and the experience of female rulers in the Iberian peninsula has shown the precedents for strong female rulership that had a formative influence on Berengaria as she grew up. Though much further work needs to be undertaken on the royal women of Navarre and the surrounding kingdoms, the grant of Monreal in 1185 held significance as part of a wider trend of royal women being utilised to administrate family lands. As with so many medieval women, details of her childhood, education, and life before marriage are unfortunately scarce, and as such establishing her date of birth is also complicated. Berengaria's agency – her ability to make decisions and influence those around her – and power – exercising authority and control over subjects and territory – did not come into full force until her dowager period. On her journey to Cyprus, we see a moment of agency as she and Joanna, dowager queen of Sicily, prevaricated to avoid being captured by Isaac Comnenus, but otherwise we know frustratingly little. Her time on the Third Crusade was spent in the companionship of two

DOI: 10.4324/9781003223306-9

other noblewomen in an unfamiliar situation – Joanna, and the unnamed Byzantine princess. Other than the 1193 charter, Berengaria's queenship is notably absent for her lack of presence, with contemporary chroniclers unable to provide her residence for the later part of her reign.

It is the turning point of 1199 where we see Berengaria act and make decisions around her future. No more was she to be the pawn of a disinterested marital family and a seemingly neglectful royal brother. It was to her sister Blanca, with whom she held a strong and close relationship with throughout her thirty-one years as a dowager, who she turned in this moment of crisis. Berengaria emerged from the edges of the political arena more firmly in 1204 as she negotiated with Philip Augustus to barter her dower lands for the lordship of Le Mans, an apt choice which was away from any lingering Plantagenet-Capetian conflict. From 1204 onwards we have a much richer picture of Berengaria and her activities.

Although frustratingly little survives in her own words, the letters and charters that do exist give us an indication of the strength and steadfastness of Berengaria's charter. She was a woman who was determined to rule and to exercise her rights and authority in Le Mans. She did not shirk from conflict with the local nobility or ecclesiastical figures, and she continued to utilise her position as a widow, in need of protection, with intent when it came to invoking the support of the kings of France and the papacy. Berengaria was a skilled negotiator and diplomat and this can be seen most clearly with her relationships with the French rulers and nobility. When it came to her dower campaign, her strength of character and tenacity shines through: although this was less successful in terms of the longevity of the campaign and Berengaria never received her full dues, she continued to push forward her cause for over four decades. The success of Berengaria's petition for her dower lands was dependent on several factors, and ultimately the financial and political turmoil of thirteenth-century England won out.

Given the lack of evidence it would be beyond my remit to make too many assumptions about Berengaria's personality, especially with so little in her own words, but from that does survive I believe we can see courage, steadfastness, and tenacity. She did not give up, or run hot-headedly into conflict. Instead, with a political astuteness that we can only wish to have seen during her time as queen consort, she assessed the options open to her and opted for the one that would grant her the most independence but without being at the heart of conflict. Roundly abandoned or neglected by the majority of her natal and marital family, Berengaria persevered and worked to obtain lands, revenues, and the right to both exercise power and accrue it.

Similar to other thirteenth-century queens and female lords, genuine power and agency can be attested to from the surviving documents, and in Berengaria's case it is those from Le Mans. Such power was not unusual: as noted, there were a plethora of female lords wielding authority across Western Europe in the high Middle Ages. Evidence of Berengaria's day-to-day administration of her lordly territories is sadly lacking in places, however, what does survive gives an indication of her ability to exercise power and the disputes in which she was drawn, including her exile to Thorée in 1217. Berengaria is part of a wider pattern of female lordship; however, her interest and exceptionalism derives from the fact that not many were former queens, and fewer had to campaign so intensely and with such dedication for revenues to ensure their survival. This lack of revenues goes some way to explaining why we know so little of Berengaria's household and daily life.

Berengaria's position as a childless queen was not uncommon, but nevertheless remarkable as it closed off another avenue to power for her in her dowager period. Without resources, a supportive family, or a child through which to influence and intercede, her options in 1199 appear limited. However, Berengaria chose an alternative path: she could exercise agency at this juncture, and it became apparent that John was not going to easily provide her with her rightful revenues. Berengaria acted and negotiated with Philip Augustus, king of France, realising that the current state of affairs would not quickly lead to financial satisfaction and personal comfort. Berengaria's activities as a dowager are further proof of an established theory that women became much more powerful as they aged, and certainly as widows. Although the previously established notion was that a woman as a queen consort was in her apex, the restrictions of marriage, visibility, and poor partnerships often resulted in a woman being able to exercise far more power and authority without a man by her side. Undoubtedly the visibility of evidence gives us a better picture of Berengaria's dowager period than her consortship, but it can be stated with certainty that she was more active and politically astute in the years 1204 to 1230.

Berengaria's story has often been left on the sidelines in a time of significant events, with the collapse of the Angevin Union and the Third Crusade, and during a period of some of the most dominant figures in medieval history such as Richard the Lionheart, John, and Louis IX. It is perhaps extraordinary that we do not know more about her given her interactions with these rulers. Perhaps, if anything, the misnomer of the only queen never to set foot in England, placed along the epithets of a 'forgotten' and 'shadow' queen have perpetuated this misremembrance and misrepresentation, labelling her as a figure of whom we know and have little surviving evidence for. As noted, the only charter referencing Berengaria during her tenure is the 1193 loan which she witnessed in Rome. Such a dearth of evidence gives us only opportunities to hypothesise about what her queenship may have been like had she been granted more power. What is clear throughout is that a combination of childlessness, poor personal partnership with Richard, and a lack of visibility with her subjects negated Berengaria's access to royal power. Her marriage to Richard was politically important for several reasons: it provided Richard with security on his southern borders whilst he was on the Third Crusade, and Sancho rose to the terms of the agreement when needed. For better or worse, the marriage also decisively fractured the relationship between Richard and Philip Augustus, with the status of Alys as Richard's intended bride no longer in any doubt.

What has emerged from this study is that the exercise of the office of queenship in twelfth- and thirteenth-century England was not clearly defined or embodied by all queens consort: it was very much dependent on the models of co-rulership and power-sharing that the king chose to invoke. Richard's decision to utilise his mother, Eleanor of Aquitaine, as a co-ruler was pragmatic: however, it did little to grant Berengaria any genuine power. Greater understanding of the office is garnered over a comparative study which I have previously undertaken, and through this, a greater appreciation of the complex situation both kings and queens of England in the twelfth and thirteenth centuries were in, not least owing to the growing strength of the Capetian kings which reached an apex under Philip Augustus.

Berengaria's negotiating and diplomatic skills also ought to be paid testament to here. It is through the deployment of these that she maintained a regular connection with the papacy, who in turn continued to act on her behalf during her dower campaign until the last years of her life. Her ability to intercede, influence, and work with the kings of France and the nobility, both local and further afield, in the French domains was often to her benefit in times of ecclesiastical dispute. To view these interactions in the context of her lordship, Berengaria can be seen as a successful member of the nobility who maintained her authority for the majority of her tenure. Emboldened, determined, and resolute: these are the definitions of Berengaria's lordship.

Berengaria's foundation of L'Abbaye de L'Épau has arguably had the most impact on her memory and legacy. Without L'Épau, it is plausible that she would have been buried in the cathedral of Saint-Julien, as was the case when her tomb was moved in the nineteenth century. Her legacy would have been far less impactful set alongside other famous lords across the centuries. Berengaria shaped her legacy both with the foundation and the construction of her effigy, which is a testament to her agency and to her commitment to Le Mans as a burial site. The unique depiction, for the period, of her miniature on the book she holds may have had influences from both Navarre and Fontevraud, but it was herself that she chose to present on the front, emphasising her own agency and commemoration. Both the abbey itself and Berengaria's tomb are irrevocably tied together, and so they should remain. L'Épau is essentially Berengaria: it would not be there without her, and its survival has allowed Berengaria's memory and reputation to endure until the present day. Berengaria's decision to found her own abbey and choose it as her burial site, and one of a Cistercian order, which was close to her heart, demonstrates further how her agency increased during her widowhood. Le Mans was *her* place, not her family's, and not her husband's.

As a queen of England, it has often been posited why more has not been known of Berengaria and her reign. The frank answer is the lack of surviving evidence; the more nuanced one is that Berengaria sat amongst a complex network of co-ruling partnerships, and that Richard made the decision to not involve Berengaria as co-ruler and thus remitted her to the background of the Plantagenet political sphere. Without a child, and without resources during her reign, Berengaria had little leverage to push herself to the front of the scene and become more visible. Therefore, it may have been very easy for Berengaria to have disappeared into obscurity completely. Other than being a biographical work, it has been the intention of this biography to dispels the epithet that Berengaria is a 'queen in the shadows' or a forgotten queen. Married to one of the most famous kings in English history, Berengaria deserves to be more well known. As lord of Le Mans, Berengaria should be known for her independent exercise of power and success as a lord. Berengaria's story is no longer in the shadows, but now in the open, for all to read, and for all to see.

APPENDIX

The dower lands of Berengaria of Navarre have been the subject of some debate throughout the years. Taken from the research undertaken for my doctorate and to highlight, for the first time, the discrepancies between the dower properties of the three Angevin queens, the tables below list the dower holdings of Eleanor of Aquitaine, Berengaria of Navarre, and Isabella of Angoulême, as documented in their dower charters or copies thereof. In the table **a** denotes properties issued in Isabella's 1200 dower charter (Rotuli Chartarum 74–5), **b** denotes properties granted in her 1204 charter (Rot. Chart. 128).

Table A.1 Table of the dower lands of Berengaria of Navarre, Eleanor of Aquitaine, and Isabella of Angoulême

Eleanor of Aquitaine[1]	Berengaria of Navarre[2]	Isabella of Angoulême
Lillebonne (Normandy)[3]		
Falaise (Normandy)	Falaise (Normandy)	Falaise (Normandy)[b4]
Domfront (Normandy)	Domfront (Normandy)	Domfront (Normandy)[b]
Bonneville-sur-Tocques (Normandy)	Bonneville-sur-Tocques (Normandy)	Bonneville-sur-Tocques (Normandy)[b]
		Saintes (Poitou)[a5]
		Niort (Poitou)[a]
Loches (Touraine)	Loches (Touraine)	Saumur (Anjou)[a]
Montbazon (Touraine)	Montbazon (Touraine)	La Flèche (Anjou)[a]

(Continued)

Table A.1 (Continued)

Eleanor of Aquitaine[1]	*Berengaria of Navarre*[2]	*Isabella of Angoulême*
Mervent (Poitou)	Mervent (Poitou)	Beaufort-en-Vallée (Anjou)[a]
Jaunay (Poitou)	Jaunay (Poitou)	Bauge (Anjou)[a]
Château-du-Loir (Anjou)	Château-du-Loir (Anjou)	Château-du-Loir (Anjou)[a]
Oléron (Poitou)	Oléron (Poitou)	
Ilchester (Somerset)	Ilchester (Somerset)	Ilchester (Somerset)[b]
Monkton (Somerset)	Monkton (Somerset)	
Recene (Rutland)	Recene (Rutland)	Recene (Rutland)[b]
Bradecost (Rutland)	Bradecost (Rutland)	Bradecost (Rutland)[b]
North Luffenham (Rutland)	North Luffenham (Rutland)	North Luffenham (Rutland)[b]
Lambourne (Berkshire)	Lambourne (Berkshire)	
Wilton (Wiltshire)	Wilton (Wiltshire)	Wilton (Wiltshire)[b]
Malmesbury (Wiltshire)	Malmesbury (Wiltshire)	Malmesbury (Wiltshire)[b]
		Biddesden (Wiltshire)[b]
Arundel (Sussex)	Arundel (Sussex)	
Chichester (Sussex)	Chichester (Sussex)	Chichester (Sussex)[b]
Stanton (Oxfordshire)	Stanton (Oxfordshire)	
Rockingham (Northamptonshire)	Rockingham (Northamptonshire)	Rockingham (Northamptonshire)[b]
Northampton (Northamptonshire)	Northampton (Northamptonshire)	
Kenton (Devonshire)	Kenton (Devonshire)	Kenton (Devonshire)[b]
Linton (Devonshire)	Linton (Devonshire)	Linton (Devonshire)[b]
Addiscott (Devonshire)	Addiscott (Devonshire)	Addiscott (Devonshire)[b]

Notes

1 Lands listed based on the Edmond Martène and Ursin Durand, eds., *Veterum Scriptorum et Monumentorum, Historicorum, Dogmaticorum, Moralium Amplissima Collectio*, 9 vols. (Paris: 1724–33), cols. 995–7, accessed 18 July 2022, https://archive.org/veterum_scriptorum, wherein Berengaria was to hold all the lands listed, that belonged to Eleanor.

2 *Veterum Scriptorum*, cols. 995–7: note that all lands granted to Eleanor by Henry II are to pass to Berengaria.

3 AD Seine Maritime, FRAD076_018HP0007_10 (1189–91).

4 Thomas Duffus Hardy, ed., *Rotuli Chartarum in Turri Londinensi asservati. Volume I Part I* (London: His Majesty's Stationery Office, 1837), 128; Thomas Rymer, ed., *Foedera, Conventiones, Literæ, Et Cujuscunque Generis Acta Publica inter Reges Angliæ et alios quosuis(?) imperatores, reges, pontifices, principes, vel communitates, ab ineunte sæculo duodecimo, viz ab anno 1101, ad nostra usque Tempora, Habita aut Tractatal ex autographis, infra secretiores archivorum regiorum thesaurarias, per multa sæcula reconditis, fideliter exscripta, Tomus I* (London: J. Tonson, 1727), 132–5.
5 Hardy, *Rotuli Chartarum*, 74b–75; *Veterum Scriptorum*, col. 1032; John W. Baldwin, François Gasparri, Michel Nortier and Elisabeth Lalou, eds., *Recueil des historiens de la France. Documents financiers et administratifs. Tome VII. Les Registres de Philippe Auguste. Volume I: Texte* (Paris: Imprimerie Nationale, 1992), no. 39.

BIBLIOGRAPHY

Primary Sources

Unpublished Primary Sources

Archives Départementales de la Sarthe, France
1 J1281
111 AC 939
111 AC 940
111 AC 941
3 V 10
G 479
H 17
H 833
H 859
H 926
H 1371

Archives Départementales de Seine-Maritime, France
7 H57
FRAD076_018HP0007_10

Archivos Eclesiásticos, Tudela, Spain
C 233

Archivo General de Navarra, Spain
Comptos, Codices Real 1, Cartulario 1.

Archives Nationales, France
JJ 1
J 198

J 626
J 628
J 427
J 460

Bibliothèque Muncipale de Le Mans, France
MS 259

Bibliothèque Sainte-Genevieve, France
MS 675
MS 701

Bibliothèque Nationale de France, France
Baluze 45
Latin 2454
Latin 17124
Touraine-Anjou 5

Bodleian Library, UK
MS. Gough drawings-Gaignières 15.

British Library, UK
Additional MS 46402
Cotton Charter VIII

The National Archives, UK
C 66/14
C 66/15
C66/20
C 66/23
C 66/24
C 66/25
E 368/3/2.
E 372/45
E 372/46
E 372/47
E 372/48
E 372/49
E 401/2
E 401/3A
E 401/1564
E 401/1771
SC 1/1/23

SC 1/2/5
SC 1/2/156
SC 1/3/81

Published Primary Sources

Adam of Eynsham. *Magna Vita Sancti Hugonis. The Life of St Hugh of Lincoln.* Translated and edited by Decima L. Douie and David Hugh Farmer. 2 volumes. Oxford: Clarendon Press, 1985.

Adam of Perseigne. *The Letters of Adam of Perseigne. Volume I.* Translated by Grace Perigo, introduction by Thomas Merton. Kalamazoo: Cistercian Publications, 1976.

Ailes, Marianne, and Malcolm Barber, eds. and trans. *The History of the Holy War. Ambroise's Estoire de la Guerre Sainte.* 2 volumes. Woodbridge: The Boydell Press, 2002.

D'Albert, Pierre, ed. *Cartulaire des abbayes de Saint-Pierre de la Couture et de Saint-Pierre de Solesmes.* Le Mans: Monnoyer, 1881.

Alvira Cabrer, Martin, ed. *Pedro el Catolico, rey de Aragon y conde de Barcelona (1196–1213). Documentos, testimonios y memoria historica.* Saragossa: Institución Fernando el Catolico, 2010.

Alvira Cabrer, Martin. *Las Navas de Tolosa, 1212. Idea, Liturgia y Memoria de la Bataila.* Madrid: Sílex Ediciones, 2012.

Appleby, John. T., ed. and trans. *The Chronicle of Richard of Devizes of the Time of King Richard the First.* London: Thomas Nelson and Sons, 1963.

Argita Y Lasa, D. Mariana. *Colección de Documentos Inéditos para la Historia de Navarra. Tomo Primero.* Pamplona: Imprenta Provincial, á cargo de J. Ezquerro, 1900.

D'Arbois de Jubainville, Henri, ed. *Histoire des Ducs et des Comtes de Champagne. Tome IV. 1181–1285. Deuxième Parte.* Paris: Aug. Durand, 1564.

Auvray, Louis, ed. *Les Registres de Grégoire IX.* 4 volumes. Paris: Albert Fontemoing, 1896–1955.

Baldwin, John W., François Gasparri, Michel Nortier, and Elisabeth Lalou, eds. *Recueil des historiens de la France. Documents financiers et administratifs. Tome VII. Les Registres de Philippe Auguste. Volume I: Texte.* Paris: Imprimerie Nationale, 1992.

Baleztena, Javier, ed. *Documentos Navarros en Los Archivos Nacionales Franceses Paris.* Pamplona: Institución Príncipe de Viana, 1978.

Baluze, Étienne, ed. *Epistolarum Innocentii libri undecim. Accedunt gesta ejusdem Innocentii et prima collectio decretalium composita a Rainerio Diacono Pomposiano.* 4 volumes. Paris: Franciscum Muguet, 1682.

Bliss, W. H., ed. *Calendar of Entries in the Papal Registers Relating to Great Britain and Ireland. Papal Letters Vol. I. A. D. 1198–1304.* London: Eyre and Spottiswoode, 1893.

Bond, Edward A., ed. *Chronica Monasterii de Melsa, A Fundatione Usque Ad Annum 1396, Auctore Thoma de Burton, Abbate. Accedit Continuatio Ad Annum 1406 A Monacho Quodam Ipsius Domus. Volume I.* London: Longmans, Green, Reader, and Dyer, 1866.

Bourquelot, Félix. 'Fragments de comptes du XIIIe siècle.' In *Bibliothèque de l'École des Chartes, Volume IV*, edited by René de Lespinasse, 51–79. Paris: Alb. L. Herold, 1863.

Brial, Michel-Jean-Joseph, ed. *Recueil des Historiens des Gaules et de la France. Tome Dix-Huitième. Contenant la Seconde Livraison des Monumens des Règnes de Philippe-Auguste et de Louis VIII, depuis l'an MCLXXX jusqu'en MCCXXVI.* Paris: Imprimerie Royale, 1822.

Briéle, Léon, ed. *Archives de l'Hôtel-Dieu de Paris (1157–1300).* Paris: Imprimerie Nationale, 1844.

Broussillon, Bertrand de, and Eugène Vallée, eds. *Cartulaire de l'évêché du Mans (965–1786).* Le Mans: Siège de la Société, 1908.

Brutails, J.-A., ed. *Documents des archives de la chambre des comptes de Navarre (1196–1384).* Paris: 1890.

Bryant, Nigel, ed. and trans. *The History of William Marshal.* Woodbridge: Boydell and Brewer, 2016.

Busson, G., and A. Ledru, eds. *Actus Pontificum. Cenomannis in Urbe Degentium.* Le Mans: Siège de la Société, 1902.

Busson, G., and A. Ledru, eds. *Nécrologe-obituaire de la Cathédrale du Mans.* Le Mans: Siège de la Société, 1906.

Bustron, Florio. *Historia overo commentarii de Cipro.* Paris: 1886.

Canivez, Joseph-Marie, ed. *Statuta capitulorum generalium ordinis cisterciensis ab anno 1116 ad annum 1786.* 8 volumes. Louvain: Bibliothèque de la Revue d'histoire ecclesiastique, 1933–1941.

Carte, Thomas, ed. *Catalogue de Rolles Gascons, Normans et Francois dans les archives de la Tour de Londres. Tome Premier.* Paris: Jacques Barois, 1743.

Castro, José Ramón, Florencio Idoate, and Javier Baleztena, eds. *Catálogo del Archivo General de Navarra, Sección de Comptos: documentos.* 2 volumes. Pamplona: Gobierno de Navarra, Departamento de Educación y Cultura, Institución Príncipe de Viana, 1988–1993.

Cauvin, Thomas, and Eugène Hucher. *Institut des provinces de France. Mémoires – 2ᵉ série. Tome Premier. Géographie ancienne du diocese du Mans, par M. Th. Cauvin, suivie d'un essai d'un essai sur les monnaies du Maine, par M. E. Hucher.* Paris and Le Mans: Derache Libraire and Imprimeur-Libraire, 1845.

Champollion-Figeac, Jacques-Joseph, ed. *Lettres de rois, reines, et autres personnages des cours de France et d'Angleterre depuis Louis VII jusqu'a Henri IV, tirées des archives de Londres par Bréquigny. Tome I.* Paris: Imprimerie Royale, 1839.

Chaplais, Pierre, ed. *Diplomatic Documents preserved in the Public Record Office. Volume I. 1101–1271.* London: Her Majesty's Stationery Office, 1964.

Chappée, Julien, A. Ledru, and Louis J. Denis, eds. *Enquête de 1245 relative aux droits du Chapitre Saint-Julien du Mans.* Paris: Honoré Champion, 1922.

Chédville, André, ed. *Liber Controversiarum Sancti Vincentii Cenomannensis ou Second Cartulaire de l'Abbaye de Saint-Vincent Du Mans. Texte édité avec introduction, notes et index par A. Chédville.* Paris: Institut de Recherches Historiques de Rennes, 1968.

Cheney, C. R., and Mary G. Cheney, eds. *The Letters of Pope Innocent III (1198–1216) concerning England and Wales. A Calendar with an appendix of texts.* Oxford: Clarendon Press, 1967.

Celier, Léonce, ed. *Catalogue des Actes des Évêques du Mans jusqu'a la fin du XIIIᵉ siècle.* Paris: Honoré Champion, 1910.

Cooper, Louis, ed. *El Liber Regum. Estudio Linguistico.* Zaragoza: Institución 'Fernando el Católico,' 1960.

Cooper, Louis, ed. *La Gran Conquista de Ultramar. Edición Crítica con Introducción, Notas y Glosario.* 4 volumes. Bogotá: Imprenta Patriótica del Instituto Caro y Cuervo, 1979.

Corvasier, Antoine le. *Histoire des evesques du Mans, et de ce qui s'est passe de plus memorable dans le Diocese pendant leur Pontificat.* Paris: Sebastien Cramoisy and Gabriel Cramoisy, 1648.

Croizy-Naquet, Catherine, ed. *L'estoire de la guerre sainte.* Paris: Honoré Champion, 2014.

Crouch, David, ed. *The acts and letters of the Marshal family: Marshals of England and Earls of Pembroke, 1145–1248.* Cambridge: Cambridge University Press, 2015.

D'Elbenne, Menjot, and Louis J. Denis, eds. *Cartulaire du Chapitre Royal de Saint-Pierre-de-la-Cour, du Mans.* Le Mans: Siège de la Société, 1907.

Delaborde, Henri-François, ed. *Œuvres de Rigord et de Guillaume le Breton. Historiens de Philippe-Auguste.* 2 volumes. Paris: Librairie Renouard/Société de l'Histoire de France, 1882–1885.

Delaborde, Henri-François, ed. *Recueil des Actes de Philippe Auguste Roi de France. Tome I Années du Règne I à XV (1 Novembre 1179–31 Octobre 1194).* Paris: Imprimerie Nationale, 1916.

Delaborde, Henri-François, Charles Petit-Dutaillis, and J. Monicat, eds. *Recueil des Actes de Philippe Auguste Roi de France. Tome II Années du Règne XVI à XXVII (1 Novembre 1194–31 Octobre 1206).* Paris: Imprimerie Nationale, 1943.

Delaville le Roux, J., ed. *Cartulaire Général de L'Ordre des Hospitaliers de Saint Jean de Jérusalem (1100–1310)*. 4 volumes. Paris: Ernest Leroux, 1844–1906.

Delisle, Léopold, and Martin Bouquet, eds. *Recueil des historiens des Gaules et de la France*. 24 volumes. Paris: Imprimerie Royale, 1840–1904.

Delisle, Léopold, and Natalis de Wailly, eds. *Recueil des historiens des Gaules et de la France. Tome Vingt-Deuxième contenant la troisième livraison des monuments des règnes de Saint Louis, de Philippe le Hardi, de Philippe le Bel, de Louis X, de Philippe V, et de Charles IV, depuis MCCXXVI jusqu'en MCCCXXVIII*. Paris: Imprimerie Royale, 1855.

Delisle, Léopold, ed. *Catalogues des actes de Philippe-Auguste, avec une introduction sur les sources les caractères et l'importance historiques de ces documents*. Paris: A. Durand, 1856.

Delisle, Léopold. 'Notes sur quelques manuscrits de la bibliothèque de Tours.' *Comptes rendus des séances de l'Académie des Inscriptions et Belles-Lettres* 12 (1868): 392–408.

Delisle, Léopold. 'Notice sur vingt manuscrits du Vatican.' *Bibliothèque de l'École des chartes* 37 (1876): 471–527.

Delisle, Léopold, ed. *Cartulaire Normand de Philippe-Augusute, Louis VIII, Saint-Louis, et Philippe-le-Hardi*. Geneva: Mégarotis Reprints, 1978.

Deseille, Placide, ed. *Adam de Perseigne. Lettres II (Lettres XVI–XXXII)*. Translated by Jean Bouvet and Placide Deseille. Paris: Les Éditions du Cerf, 2015.

Hagender, Othmar, Andrea Sommerlechner, Herwig Weigl, Christoph Egger, and Rainer Murauer, eds. *Die Register Innocenz' III. 7. Band, 7 Pontifikatsjahr, 1204–1205 Texte und Indices* Wien: Verlag der Österreichischen Akademie der Wissenschaften, 1997.

Duggan, Anne J., ed. *The Correspondence of Thomas Becket. Archbishop of Canterbury, 1162–1170*. 2 volumes. Oxford: Clarendon Press, 2000.

Edbury, Peter W., ed. *The Conquest of Jerusalem and the Third Crusade. Sources in Translation*. Abingdon: Routledge, 1999.

Edbury, Peter W. 'The Old French Continuation of William of Tyr.' In *The Conquest of Jerusalem and the Third Crusade. Sources in Translation*, edited by Peter W. Edbury, 11–145. Abingdon: Routledge, 1999.

Evergates, Theodore, ed. and trans. *Feudal society in Medieval France. Documents from the County of Champagne*. Philadelphia: University of Pennsylvania Press, 1993.

Evergates, Theodore, ed. Litterae Baronum. *The Earliest Cartulary of the Counts of Champagne*. Toronto: University of Toronto Press, 2003.

Evergates, Theodore, ed. *The Cartulary of Countess Blanche of Champagne*. Toronto: University of Toronto Press, 2010.

Fleury, Gabriel, ed. *Cartulaire de l'abbaye cistercienne de Perseigne*. Mamers: Fleury Dangin, 1880.

Fuentes Pascual, Francisco, ed. *Catálogo de los archivos ecclesiásticos de Tudela*. Tudela: Institución Príncipe de Viana, 1944.

Fuentes Pascual, Francisco, ed. *Catálogo del Archivo Municipal de Tudela*. Tudela: Imprenta Oroz y Martínez, 1947.

García Larragueta, Santos A., ed. *El gran priorado de Navarra de la ordren de San Juan de Jerusalén*. 2 volumes. Pamplona: Institución Príncipe de Viana/Editorial Gomez, 1957.

Giles, John Allen, ed. and trans. *Roger of Wendover's Flowers of History Comprising The History of England From the Descent of the Saxons to A. D. 1235, Formerly Ascribed to Matthew Paris*. 2 volumes. London: George Bell & Sons, 1892.

Hageneder, Othmar, Werner Maleczek, and Alfred A. Strnad, eds. *Die Register Innocenz' III. 2. Pontifikatsjahr, 1199/1200. Texte*. Wien: Verlag der Österreichischen Akademie, 1979.

Hardy, Thomas Duffy, ed. *Rotuli litterarum clausarum in Turri Londiniensi asservati*. 2 volumes. London: Public Record Office, 1833–1844.

Hardy, Thomas Duffy, ed. *Rotuli Literrarum Patentium in turri Londinensi Asservati. Volume I*. London: Public Record Office, 1835.

Hardy, Thomas Duffus, ed. *Rotuli Chartarum in Turri Londinensi asservati. Volume I Part I*. London: His Majesty's Stationery Office, 1837.

Herreros Lopetegui, Susana, ed. *Anales del reino de Navarra / José de Moret; edición anotada e índices dirigida*. Pamplona: Institución Príncipe de Viana, 1987.

Herreros Lopetegui, Susana, 'El castillo de Rocabruna en Ultrapuertos. Una nueva teoría sobre su localización.' *Príncipe de Viana* 14 (1992): 381–6.

Herreros Lopetegui, Susana, ed. *Las tierras navarras de Ultrapuertos (siglos XII–XVI)*. Pamplona: Departamento de Educación y Cultura, 1998.

Holman Christian Bible.

Horoy, César Auguste, ed. *Honorii III Romani Pontificis Opera Omnia*. 4 volumes. Paris: Imprimerie de la Bibliothéque Ecclésiastique, 1879–1880.

Howlett, Roger, ed. *Chronicles of the Reigns of Stephen, Henry II., and Richard I. Volume I Containing the First Four Books of the Historia Rerum Anglicarum of William of Newburgh*. London: Longman & Co., 1884.

Howlett, Roger, ed. *Chronicles of the Reigns of Stephen, Henry II., and Richard I. Volume II Containing the Fifth Book of the Historia Rerum Anglicarum of William of Newburgh, The Continued Chronicle of William of Newburgh to AD 1298 and the Draco Normannicus*. London: Longman & Co., 1885.

Hucher, Eugène. 'Charte de Bérengère concernant des juifs.' *Revue des sociétés savants des départements* 10 (1869): 464–8.

Idoate, Florencio, ed. *Catálogo de los cartularios reales del Archivo General de Navarra: años 1007–1384*. Pamplona: Gómez, 1974.

Janauschek, P. Leopoldus, ed. *Originum Cisterciensum. Tomus I. In quo praemissis congregationum domiciliis adjectisque tabulis chronologico-genealogicis veterm abbatiarum a monachis habitarum fundationes ad fidem antiquissimorum fontium primus descripsit*. Vienna: Alfred Hoelder, 1877.

Jimeno Jurio, José Maria, and Roldán Jimeno Aranguren, eds. *Archivo General de Navarra (1194–1234)*. San Sebastián: Sociedad de Estudios Vascos, 1998.

Johnson, R. C., ed. *The Crusade and Death of Richard I*. Oxford: Basil Blackwell, 1961.

Kay, Sarah, ed. and trans. *Raoul de Cambrai*. Oxford: Clarendon Press, 1992.

King James Bible.

Lacarra, José María, ed. *Estudios de Edad Media de la Corona de Aragón*. 10 volumes. Zaragoza: Consejo Superior de Investigaciones Cientificas, Escuela de Estudios Medievales, 1945–1975.

Landon, Lionel. *The Itinerary of King Richard I, with studies on certain matters of interest connected with his reign*. London: J. W. Ruddock & Sons, 1935.

Latouche, Robert. *Histoire du Comté du Maine pendant le Xe et le XIe siècle*. Paris: Honoré Champion, 1910.

Longnon, Auguste, ed. *Le livre des vassaux du comté de Champagne et de Brie (1172–1222)*. Paris: Franck, 1869.

Longnon, Auguste, ed. *Documents relatifs au comté de Champagne et de Brie, 1172–1361*. 4 volumes. Paris: Imprimerie Nationale, 1901–1914.

Lottin, René-Jean-François, ed. *Chartularium insignis ecclesiae Cenomanensis quod dicitur albus capitula*. Le Mans: Monnoyer, 1869.

Luard, Henry Richards, ed. *Matthæi Parisiensis, Monachi Sancti Albani, Chronica Majora*. 7 vols. London: Longman & Co. and Trübner & Co., 1872–1880.

Mannier, E., ed. *Ordre de Malte. Les commanderies du Grand-Prieuré de France, d'après les documents inédits consérvés aux Archives Nationales a Paris*. Paris: Aug. Aubry and Dumoulin, 1872.

Manrique, Ángel. *Cisterciensium seu verius Ecclesiasticorum annalium a condito Cistercio*. 4 volumes. Farnborough: Gregg International, 1970.

Marchegay, Paul, and Émile Mabille, eds. *Chroniques des Églises d'Anjou*. Paris: Jules Renouard, 1869.

Marichalar, Carlos, ed. *Colección Diplomática del Rey de Sancho el Fuerte de Navarra*. Pamplona: Aramburu, 1934. Accessed 17 July 2022. www.euskomedia.org/PDFAnlt/cmn/1934153222.pdf.

Martène, Edmond and Ursin Durand, eds. *Veterum Scriptorum et Monumentorum, Historicorum, Dogmaticorum, Moralium Amplissima Collectio.* 9 vols. Paris: 1724–1733. Accessed 18 July 2022. https://archive.org/veterum_scriptorum.

Martín Duque, Ángel J., ed. *Documentación medieval de Leire.* Pamplona: Diputación Foral de Navarra, Institución Príncipe de Viana, 1983.

Maxwell, H. C., ed. *Calendar of Patent Rolls, Henry III: Volume 1, 1216–1225.* London: Public Record Office, 1901. Accessed 28 December 2022 via *British History Online.* www.british-history.ac.uk/cal-pat-rolls/hen3/vol1/pp224-257.

Menéndez Pidal, Ramón, ed., and Diego Catalán. *Primera crónica general de España.* Madrid: Gredos, 1977.

Meyer, Paul, ed. *L'Histoire de Guillaume le Maréchal, comte de Striguil et de Pembroke, Régent d'Angleterre de 1216 a 1219. Poème Français.* 3 volumes. Paris: Librairie Renouard, 1891–1901.

Michel, Francisque, ed. and trans. *Histoire de la guerre de Navarre en 1276 et 1277, par Guillaume Anelier de Toulouse.* Paris: Imprimerie Impériale, 1856.

Migne, J-P., ed. *Innocentii III Romani Pontificus Opera Omnia.* 4 volumes. Montrouge: 1855.

Morel-Fatio, Alfred, ed. *Libro de los fechos et conquistas del principado de la Morea compilado por comandamiento de Don Fray Johan Ferrandez de Heredia maestro del Hospital de S. Johan de Jerusalem. Chronique de Morée aux XIIe et XIVe siècles, publiée & traduite pour la première fois pour la société de l'orient latin.* Geneva: Imprimerie Jules-Guillaume Fick, 1885.

Nicholson, Helen J., ed. and trans. *The Chronicle of the Third Crusade: The Itinerarium Peregrinorum et Gesta Regis Ricardi.* Abingdon: Routledge, 2016.

Nortier, Michel, and Charles Samaran, eds. *Recueil des Actes de Philippe Auguste, roi de France. Tome 4, Années du règne XXXVII à XLIV (1er nov. 1215–14 juillet 1223).* Paris: Imprimerie Nationale, 1976.

Orcástegui Gros, Carmen, and Angel J. Martin Duque, eds. *Garci Lópes de Roncesvalles, Crónica de Garci López de Roncevsalles. Estudio y Edición Critica.* Pamplona: Ediciones Universidad de Navarra, 1977.

Orcástegui Gros, Carmen, ed. *La Cronica de los Reyes de Navarra del Príncipe de Viana (Estudios, Fuentes y Edición Critica.* Pamplona: Diputación Foral de Navarra, Institución Príncipe de Viana, 1978.

Paden, Jr., William D., Tilde Sankovitch, and Patricia H. Stäblein, eds. *Bertran de Born. The poems of the troubadour Bertran de Born.* Berkeley: University of California Press, 1986.

Pferschy-Maleczek, Bettina, and Heinrich Appelt, eds. *Die Urkunden Heinrichs VI Die Urkunden Heinrichs VI. für deutsche, französische und italienische Empfänger. Monumenta Germanie Historica.* Online edition, 2020.

Piolin, Paul, ed. *Histoire de l'Eglise Du Mans.* 10 vols. Paris: Imprimerie Libraires au Mans, 1851–1871.

Piolin, Paul. 'Bérengère, reine d'Angleterre, dame du Mans, 1191–1230.' *Revue des questions historiques* 4 (1890): 174–183.

Pipe Rolls Richard I, 2ⁿᵈ to 10ᵗʰ Years. Edited by Doris Mary Stenton. Burlington: TannerRitchie Publishing, 2015–2016, reprinted.

Pipe Rolls John, 1st to 17ᵗʰ Years. Edited by Doris Mary Stenton, A. Mary Kirkus, Patricia M. Barnes, Sidney Smith, and J. C. Holt. Burlington: TannerRitchie Publishing, 2015–2016, reprinted.

Potthast, Augustus, ed. *Regesta Pontificum Romanorum inde ab anno post Christum natum MCXCVIII ad anno MCCCIV. Volume I.* Berlin: Rudolph Decker, 1874.

Raynaud, Gaston, ed. *Les Gestes des chiprois Recueil de Chroniques françaises écrites en orient aux XIIIe & XIVe siècles (Philippe de Navarre & Gérard de Monréal).* Geneva: Imprimerie Jules-Guillaume Fick, 1887.

Richards, D. S., trans. *The Chronicle of Ibn al-Athir for the Crusading Period from al-Kamil fi'l-Ta'rikh. Part 2. The Years 541–589/1146–1193: The Age of Nur al-Din and Saladin.* Farnham: Ashgate, 2010.

Riley, Henry Thomas, ed. and trans. *The Annals of Roger de Hoveden Comprising the History of England and of Other Countries of Europe from A.D. 732 to A.D. 1201.* 2 volumes. London: H. G. Bohn, 1853.

Robertson, James Craigie, ed. *Materials for the History of Thomas Becket, Archbishop of Canterbury (canonized by Pope Alexander III., A.D. 1173). Volume III.* London: Her Majesty's Stationery Office, 1965.

Romanet, Olivier de. *Géographie du Perche et chronologie de ses comtes suives de pieces justificatives formant le Cartulaire de cette province.* 3 volumes. Mortagne: L'Écho de l'Orne, 1890–1902.

Round, John Horace, ed. and trans. *Calendar of Documents preserved in France, Illustrative of the History of Great Britain and Ireland, I, 918–1206.* London: Her Majesty's Stationery Office, 1899.

Roux, Éric, ed., and trans. François Guizot. *Guibert de Nogent, abbé de Notre-Dame de Nogent sous Coucy. Histoire de Ma Vie 1053–1125.* Elemont Ferrand: Éditions Paleo, 2011.

Rymer, Thomas, ed. *Foedera, Conventiones, Literæ, Et Cujuscunque Generis Acta Publica inter Reges Angliæ et alios quosuis(?) imperatores, reges, pontifices, principes, vel communitates, ab ineunte sæculo duodecimo, viz ab anno 1101, ad nostra usque Tempora, Habita aut Tractatal ex autographis, infra secretiores archivorum regiorum thesaurarias, per multa sæcula reconditis, fideliter exscripta, Tomus I.* London: J. Tonson, 1727.

Sayers, Jane. *Original Papal Documents in the Lambeth Palace Library*. Bulletin of the Institute of Historical Research: 1967.

Shirley, Walter Waddington, ed. *Royal and other Historical Letters Illustrative of the Reign of Henry III. Volume I. 1216–1235*. London: Longman, Green, Longman, and Roberts, 1862.

Silvestre de Arlegui, Manuel, trans. and ed. *Anales del reino de Navarra, compuestos por el P. José Moret. Tomo Décimo*. Additions by Francisco de Alesón. Tolosa: Establecimiento tipográfico y Casa Editorial de Eusebio Lopez, 1912.

Sommerlechner, Andrea, ed. *Die Register Innocenz III. 13. Pontifikatsjahr, 1210/1211, Texte und Indices*. Wien: Austrian Academy of Sciences Press, 2015.

Sommerlechner, Andrea, ed. *Die Register Innocenz III. 14. Pontifikatsjahr, 1211/1212, Texte und Indices*. Wien: Austrian Academy of Sciences Press, 2018.

Sommerlechner, Andrea, ed. *Die Register Innocenz III. 15. Pontifikatsjahr, 1212/1213, Texte und Indices*. Wien: Austrian Academy of Sciences Press, 2022.

Stevenson, Joseph, ed. *Chronicon Ricardi Divisiensis de Rebus Gestis Ricardi Primi Regis Angliæ*. London: Sumptibus Societatis, 1838.

Strickland, Agnes. *Lives of the Queens of England, from the Norman Conquest. Volume I*. Fourth Edition. London: Henry Colburn, 1854.

Stapleton, Thomas, ed. *Magni Rotuli Scaccarii Normanniæ. Tomus I.* London: London Society of Antiquaries, 1840.

Stubbs, William, ed. *Gesta Regis Henrici Secundi Benedicti Abbatis. The Chronicle of the Reigns of Henry II. and Richard I. A.D. 1169–1192; known commonly under the name of Benedict of Peterborough*. 2 volumes. London: Longmans, Green, Reader, and Dyer, 1867.

Stubbs, William, ed. *Chronica magistri Rogeri de Houedene*. 4 volumes. London: Longmans, Green, Reader, and Dyer, 1868–1871.

Stubbs, William, ed. *The Historical Works of Master Ralph de Diceto, Dean of London*. 2 volumes. London: Longman & Co. and Trübner & Co., 1876.

Tautu, Aloysius L., ed. *Acta Honorii III (1216–1227) et Gregorii IX (1227–1241), e registris Vaticanis aliisque fontibus collegit*. Vatican: Typis polyglottis Vaticanis, 1950.

Teulet, Alexandre, ed. *Layettes du Trésor des Chartes*. 2 volumes. Paris: Henri Plon, 1863–1866.

Theiner, Augustino, ed. *Vetera Monumenta Slavorum Meridionalium. Historiam Illustrantia Maximam Partem Nondum Edita Ex Tabularis Vaticanis Deprompta Collecta ac serie chronologica disposita. Tomus Primus. Ab Innocentio PP. III. Usque Ad Paulum PP. III. 1198–1549*. Osnabrück: Otto Zeller, 1968.

Ubieto Arteta, Agustín, ed. *Pedro de Valencia: Crónica. Edición crítica e índices*. Zaragoza: Pedro Garcés de Cariñena, 1991.

Urricelqui, Merche Osés, ed. *Tomo I. Documentación Medieval de Estella (siglos XII-XVI)*. Pamplona: Fono de Publicaciones del Gobierno de Navarra, 2005.

Utrilla Utrilla, Juan F., ed. *El Fuero General de Navarra: estudio y edición de las redacciones protosistemáticas (Series A y B)*. Pamplona: Institución Príncipe de Viana, 1987.

Vaissete, Joseph. *Abregé de l'histoire générale de Languedoc. Tome III*. Paris: Jacques Vincent, 1749.

Vaquero, Eloísa Ramírez, Susana Herreros Lopetegui, Marcelino Beroiz Lazcano, Fermín Miranda García, and Véronique Lamazou-Duplan, eds. *El primer cartulario de los reyes de Navarra. El valor de lo escrito. Le premier cartulaire des rois de Navarre. La valeur de l'écrit. Tomo II*. Pamplona: Gobierno de Navarra, 2013.

Vaquero, Eloísa Ramírez, Susana Herreros Lopetegui, Roberto Ciganda Elizondo, and Fermín Miranda García, eds. *El Cartulario Magno del Archivo Real y General de Navarra. Tomo III*. Pamplona: Gobierno de Navarra, 2016.

Vincent, Nicholas, ed. *The letters and charters of Henry II, King of England, 1154–1189*. 6 volumes. Oxford: Oxford University Press, 2020.

Walsh, Peter G., and M. J. Kennedy, eds. and trans. *The History of English Affairs*. 2 volumes. Warminster and Oxford: Aris & Phillips, 1988–2007.

Webster, Paul, ed., and Janet Shirley, trans. *The History of the Dukes of Normandy and the Kings of England by the Anonymous of Béthune*. Abingdon: Routledge, 2021.

Wright, Thomas, ed. *The Chronicle of Pierre de Langtoft: in French verse, from the earliest period to the death of King Edward I*. London: Longmans, Green, Reader, and Dyer, 1866–1868.

Xieménius de Rada, Rodericus. *Rerum Hispanicarum Scriptores Aliquot, quorum nomina versa pagina indicabit*. 3 volumes. Frankfurt: Andreæ Wecheli, 1579–1581.

Yanguas y Miranda, José, ed. *Carlos, Príncipe de Viana. Crónica De Los Reyes De Navarra*. Pamplona: 1843.

Secondary Sources

Abenza, Verónica. 'In the Name of the Queen: Female patron portraits and inscriptions in 11th Century Navarre.' In *Zeichentragende Artefakte im sakralen Raum. Zwischen Präsenz und UnSichtbarkeit*, edited by

Wilfried E. Keil, Sarah Kiyanrad, Christoffer Theis, and Laura Willer, 285–307. Berlin: De Grutyer, 2018.

Amer, Sahar. 'Lesbian Sex and the Military: From the Medieval Arabic Tradition to French Literature.' In *Same Sex Love and Desire Among Women in the Middle Ages*, edited by Francesca Canadé Sautman and Pamela Sheingorn, 179–98. Basingstoke: Palgrave Macmillan, 2001.

Andrault-Schmitt, Claude. 'Fontevraud et Burgos: l'architecture reflète-t-elle une mémoire Plantagenêt?' In *Alfonso VIII y Leonor de Inglaterra: confluencias artísticas en el entorno de 1200*, edited by Marta Poza Yagüe and Diana Olivares Martínez, 203–33. Madrid: Ediciones Complutense, 2017.

Arizaleta, Amaia. 'Relatos cruzados: sobre algunas esquivas letras de princesas en el primer Doscientos.' In *Correspondencias entre mujeres en la Europea medieval*, edited by Jean-Pierre Jardin et al, online. Paris: e-Spania Books, 2020.

Armstrong-Partida, Michelle. 'Mothers and Daughters as Lords: The Countesses of Blois and Chartres.' *Medieval Prosopography* 26 (2005): 77–107.

Asbridge, Thomas. *The Crusades. The War for the Holy Land*. London: Pocket Books, 2010.

Aurell, Martin, and Yves Sassier, eds. *Autour de Philippe Auguste*. Paris: Classiques Garnier, 2017.

Aurell, Martin. '¿El arte como propaganda regia? Enrique II, Leonor de Aquitania y sus hijos (1154–1204).' In *Alfonso VIII y Leonor de Inglaterra: confluencias artísticas en el entorno de 1200*, edited by Marta Poza Yagüe and Diana Olivares Martínez, 19–69. Madrid: Ediciones Complutense, 2017.

Aurell, Martin, ed. *Gouverner l'empire Plantagenêt (1152–1224): autorité, symboles, idéologie: 7–9 octobre 2021, Abbaye royale de Fontevraud*. Nantes: 303, 2021.

Aurell, Martin, Ghislain Baury, Vincent Corriol, and Laurent Maillet, eds. *Les Plantagenêts et le Maine*. Rennes: Presses Universitaires de Rennes, 2022.

Aurell, Martin. 'Joan of England and al-ʿÂdil's Harem: The Impossible Marriage between Christians and Muslims (Eleventh–Twelfth Centuries).' *Anglo-Norman Studies* 43 (2021): 1–14.

Backerra, Charlotte. 'Personal Union, Composite Monarchy, and "Multiple Rule."' In *The Routledge History of Monarchy*, edited by Elena Woodacre, Lucinda H. S. Dean, Chris Jones, Russell E. Martin, and Zita Eva Rohr, 89–111. Abingdon: Routledge, 2019.

Bagerius, Henric, and Christine Ekholst. 'For Better or For Worse: Royal marital sexuality as political critique in late medieval Europe.' In *The Routledge History of Monarchy*, edited by Elena Woodacre, Lucinda

H. S. Dean, Chris Jones, Russell E. Martin, and Zita Eva Rohr, 636–54. Abingdon: Routledge, 2019.

Baldó Alcóz, Julia. 'Sancha o Baecia (1139–1179), esposa de Sancho VI el Sabio.' In *Reinas de Navarra*, edited by Julia Pavón, 299–333. Madrid: Sílex Ediciones, 2014.

Bárány, Attila. 'Medieval Queens and Queenship: A Retrospective on Income and Power.' *Annual of Medieval Studies at CEU* 19 (2013): 149–200.

Bard, Rachel. *Navarra, the Durable Kingdom*. Reno: University of Nevada Press, 1982.

Barrère, Jean. *La Piété-Dieu de L'Épau. Construction et Aménagement d'une Abbaye Cistercienne (1230–1365)*. PhD Thesis, Le Mans, 1968.

Barrigón, María. 'Textiles and Farewells: Revisiting the Grave Goods of King Alfonso VIII of Castile and Queen Eleanor Plantagenet.' *Textile History* 46.2 (2015): 235–57.

Barton, Richard E. *Lordship in the County of Maine, c. 890–1160*. Woodbridge: Boydell Press, 2004.

Barton, Richard. '*Enquête*, Exaction and Excommunication: Experiencing Power in Western France, c.1190–1245.' *Anglo-Norman Studies* 43 (2021): 177–96.

Barton, Simon. 'Marriages across frontiers: sexual mixing, power and identity in medieval Iberia.' *Journal of Medieval Iberian Studies* 3.1 (2011): 1–25.

Baury, Ghislain. *Les religieuses de Castille. Patronage aristocratique et ordre cistercien (XII–XIIIe siècles)*. Rennes: Presses Universitaires de Rennes, 2012.

Baury, Ghislain. 'Les moniales cisterciennes dans le Maine Médiéval.' *Annales de Bretagne et des Pays de l'Ouest* 120.3 (2013): 49–64.

Baury, Ghislain. Le sénéchal d'Anjou, les Plantagenêts et le Maine: le cas de Guillaume des Roches (1199–1222).' In *Les Plantagenêts et le Maine. Territoires, relais et représentations du pouvoir*, edited by Martin Aurell, Ghislain Baury, Vincent Corriol, and Laurent Maillet, 128–51. Rennes: Presses Universitaires de Rennes, 2022.

Baury, Ghislain, and Vincent Corriol. *Bérengère de Navarre (v. 1160–1230). Histoire et mémoire d'une reine d'Angleterre*. Rennes: Presses Universitaires de Rennes, 2022.

Bautier, Robert-Henri, ed. *La France de Philippe Auguste. Le Temps des Mutations. Actes du Colloque international organisé par le C.N.R.S. (Paris, 29 septembre – 4 octobre 1980)*. Paris: C.N.R.S., 1982.

Beem, Charles. '"Greatest in Her Offspring": Motherhood and the Empress Matilda.' In *Virtuous or Villainess? The Image of the Royal Mother from the Early Medieval to the Early Modern Era*, edited by Carey Fleiner and Elena Woodacre, 85–99. Basingstoke: Palgrave Macmillan, 2016.

Benjamin, Richard. 'Toulouse and the Plantagenets, 1156–96.' In *Medieval Warfare, 1000–1300*, edited by John France, 323–38. Abingdon: Routledge, 2006.

Benkov, Edith. 'The Erased Lesbian: Sodomy and the Legal Tradition in Medieval Europe.' In *Same Sex Love and Desire Among Women in the Middle Ages*, edited by Francesca Canadé Sautman and Pamela Sheingorn, 101–22. Basingstoke: Palgrave Macmillan, 2001.

Bennett, Judith M. 'Medievalism and Feminism.' *Speculum* 68.2 (1993): 309–31.

Beroiz Lazcano, Marcelino, ed. *Documentación medieval de Olite (siglos XII–XIV)*. Pamplona: Institución Príncipe de Viana, 2009.

Bianchini, Janna. 'The Infantazgo in the Reign of Alfonso VIII.' In *King Alfonso VIII of Castile: Government, Family, and War*, edited by Miguel Dolan Gómez, Kyle Lincoln, and Damian J. Smith, 59–79. New York: Fordham University Press, 2019.

Bianchini, Janna. *The Queen's Hand. Power and Authority in the Reign of Berenguela of Castile*. Philadelphia: University of Pennsylvania Press, 2012.

Bolton, Brenda, and Christine Meek, eds. *Aspects of Power and Authority in the Middle Ages*. Turnhout: Brepols, 2007.

Boussard, Jacques. 'Philippe Auguste et les Plantagenêts.' In *La France de Philippe Auguste. Le Temps des Mutations*, edited by Robert-Henri Bautier, 263–87. Paris: Éditions de CNRS, 1982.

Bouton, Étienne, and Michel Nissaut. *L'Épau, l'abbaye d'une reine*. Le Mans: Editions dela Reinette, 1999.

Boutoulle, Frédéric. 'Richard Coeur de Lion à Bayonne et dans le Labourd.' *Annales du Midi* 123.275 (2011): 325–51.

Bowie, Colette. *The Daughters of Henry II and Eleanor of Aquitaine*. Turnhout: Brepols, 2014.

Bratsch-Prince, Dawn. 'Pawn or Player?: Violant of Bar and the Game of Matrimonial Politics in the Crown of Aragon (1380–1396).' In *Marriage and Sexuality in Medieval and Early Modern Iberia*, edited by Eukene Lacarra Lanz, 59–89. Abingdon: Routledge, 2002.

Brown, Elizabeth A. R. 'Eleanor of Aquitaine: Parent, Queen, and Duchess.' In *Eleanor of Aquitaine: Patron and Politician*, edited by William W. Kibler, 9–35. Austin: University of Texas Press, 1975.

Brundage, James A. *Richard Lion Heart*. New York: Scribner, 1974.

Brundage, James A. 'The Politics of Sodomy: Rex V. Pons Hugh de Ampurias (1311).' In *Sex in the Middle Ages*, edited by Joyce E. Salisbury, 239–46. London: Garland Publishing, 1991.

Bur, Michel. 'Rôle et place de la Champagne dans le royaume de France au temps de Philippe Auguste.' In *La France de Philippe Auguste. Le Temps du Mutations. Actes du Colloque international organisé par le C.N.R.S. (Paris, 29 novembre – 4 octobre 1980)*, edited by Robert-Henri Bautier, 237–54. Paris: C.N.R.S., 1982.

Bur, Michel. 'Neveux ou cousins? Capétiens et Thibaudiens autour de 1198.' In *Art et architecture à Melun au Moyen Age. Actes du colloque d'histoire et de l'art et d'archéologie tenu à Melun les 28 et 29 novembre 1998*, edited by Yves Gallet, 29–40. Paris: Picard, 2000.

Burgo, Jamie del. *Historia de Navarra: desde la prehistoria hasta su integración en la Monarquía Española (S. XVI)*. Madrid: Ediciones Académicas, 2012.

Burgwinkle, William E. *Sodomy, Masculinity, and Law in Medieval Literature: France and England, 1050–1230*. Cambridge: Cambridge University Press, 2004.

Cadden, Joan. *Meanings of sex difference in the Middle Ages*. Cambridge: Cambridge University Press, 1993.

Campo Jesús, Luis del. *Berenguela, princesa de Navarra, reina de Inglaterra*. Pamplona: 1992.

Carpenter, David A. *The Minority of Henry III*. London: Methuen, 1990.

Carpenter, David. *Henry III. The Rise to Power and Personal Rule. 1207–1258*. London: Yale University Press, 2020.

Carpenter, David. *Henry III. Reform, Rebellion, Civil War, Settlement. 1258–1272*. London: Yale University Press, 2023.

Carrasco-Perez, Juan. 'L'infante Berenguela (1170?–1230) et la Navarre de son temps.' *La Province du Maine* 17 (1991): 19–22.

Cavallo, Sandra, and Lyndan Warner, eds. *Widowhood in medieval and early modern Europe*. Harlow: Longman, 1999.

Cerda, Jose Manuel. 'La dot gasconne d'Aliénor D'Angleterre: enter royaume de Castille, royaume de France et royaume d'Angleterre.' *Cahiers de civilisation médiévale* 54 (2011): 225–42.

Chalmel, J.-L. *Histoire de Touraine, depuis la conquête des Gaules par les Romans, jusqu'a l'année 1790; suive du dictionnaire biographique de tous les hommes célèbres nés dans cette province. Tome III*. Paris and Tours: H. Fournier Jᵉ Libraire, and A. Mame Imprimerie-Libraire; Moisy Libraire, 1828.

Chardon, Henri. *Histoire de la reine Bérengère, femme de Richard Cœur de-Lion et dame douairière du Mans, d'après des documents inédits sur son séjour en France*. Le Mans: Monnoyer, 1866.

Church, Stephen. *King John. England, Magna Carta and the Making of a Tyrant*. London: Pan Books, 2016.

Church, Stephen D. 'The "Angevin Empire" (1150–1204): A Twelfth-Century Union.' In *Unions and Divisions: New Forms of Rule in Medieval and Renaissance Europe*, edited by P. Srodecki, N. Kersken, and R. Petrauskas, 68–82. Abingdon: Routledge, 2022.

Clanchy, Michael. *England and Its Rulers. 1066–1307.* Fourth edition. Oxford: John Wiley & Sons, 2014.

Cloulas, Ivan. 'Le douaire de Bérengère de Navarre, veuve de Richard Cœur de Lion, et sa retraite au Mans.' In *La Cour Plantagenêt (1154–1204). Actes du colloque tenu à Thouars du 30 avril au 2 mai 1999*, edited by Martin Aurell, 89–94. Poitiers: Université de Poitiers, Centre d'Études Supérieures de Civilisation Médiévale, 2004.

Collins, Roger. *The Basques.* Oxford: Basil Blackwell, 1986.

Collins, Roger. 'Queens-Dowager and Queens-Regent in Tenth Century León and Navarre.' In *Medieval Queenship*, edited by John Carmi Parsons, 79–92. Stroud: Sutton Publishing, 1998.

Colloquio italo-britannico sul tema Riccardo Cuor di Leone nella storia e nella leggenda: Roma, 11 aprile 1980. Rome: Accademia nazionale dei Lincei, 1981.

Conde-Luque, Mariano González-Arnao. 'Berenguela de Navarra y Ricardo Corazón de León.' *History 16* 111 (1985): 67–75.

Congresso el Fuero de San Sebastián y su época. San Sebastián: Sociedad de Estudios Vascos, 1982.

Cosandey, Fanny. 'Puissance maternelle et pouvoir politique. La régence des reines mères.' *Clio. Femmes, Genre, Histoire* 21 (2005): 69–90.

Dectot, Xavier. 'Les tombeaux des comtes de Champagne (1151–1284). Un manifeste politique.' *Bulletin Monumental* 162.1 (2004): 3–62.

Dectot, Xavier. *Les tombeaux des familles royales de la péninsule ibérique au Moyen Age.* Turnhout: Brepols, 2009.

Dinshaw, Carolyn. 'Touching On the Past.' In *The Boswell Thesis. Essays on Christianity, Social Tolerance, and Homosexuality*, edited by Mathew Kuefler, 57–73. London: The University of Chicago Press, 2006.

Doran, John, and Damian J. Smith, eds. *Pope Celestine III (1191–1198). Diplomat and Pastor.* Farnham: Ashgate, 2008.

Ducom, Pauline, and Bénédicte Fillion-Brauget, 'Le Mans. Abbaye de l'Épau: le tombeau à gisant de la reine Bérengère de Navarre.' *Bulletin Monumental société française d'archéologie* 181.1 (2023): 77–82.

Dunbabin, Jean. *France in the Making 843–1180.* Second Edition. Oxford: Oxford University Press, 2000.

Earenfight, Theresa. 'Without the Persona of the Prince: Kings, Queens and the Idea of Monarchy in Late Medieval Europe.' *Gender & History* 19 (2007): 1–21.

Earenfight, Theresa. 'Highly Visible, Often Obscured: The Difficulty of Seeing Queens and Noble Women.' *Medieval Feminist Forum: A Journal of Gender and Sexuality* 44.1 (2008): 86–90.

Earenfight, Theresa. 'A Lifetime of Power: Beyond Binaries of Gender.' In *Medieval Elite Women and the Exercise of Power, 100–1400. Moving Beyond the Exceptionalist Debate*, edited by Heather J. Tanner, 271–93. Cham: Palgrave Macmillan, 2019.

Echard, Laurence. *The History of England. From the First Entrance of Julius Caesar and the Romans to the Conclusion of the Reign of King James the Second and the Establishment of King William and Queen Mary on Upon the Throne, in the year 1688.* Third Edition. London: Jacob Tonson, 1720.

Edbury, Peter W. *The Kingdom of Cyprus and the Crusades, 1191–1374.* Cambridge: Cambridge University Press, 1991.

Edbury, Peter W. 'Celestine III, the Crusade and the Latin East.' In *Pope Celestine III (1191–1198). Diplomat and Pastor*, edited by John Doran and Damian J. Smith, 129–43. Farnham: Ashgate, 2008.

Elizari Huarte, Juan Francisco. *Sancho VI El Sabio.* Iruna: Editorial Mintzoa, 1991.

Elliott, John Huxtable. 'A Europe of Composite Monarchies.' *Past & Present* 137 (1992): 48–71.

Erlande-Brandenburg, Alain. *Le Cimetière des rois à Fontevrault.* Paris: 1964.

Erlande-Brandenburg, Alain. *Le Roi est Mort, étude sur les funérailles, sépultures et les tombeaux des rois de France jusqu'à la fin du XIIIe siècle.* Paris: Droz, Genève, and Arts et Métiers Graphiques, 1975.

Evans, Michael R. *Inventing Eleanor. The Post-Medieval Image of Eleanor of Aquitaine.* London: Bloomsbury, 2014.

Everard, Judith A. *Brittany and the Angevins: Province and Empire, 1158–1203.* Cambridge: Cambridge University Press, 2000.

Evergates, Theodore. 'Aristocratic Women in the County of Champagne.' In *Aristocratic Women in Medieval France*, edited by Theodore Evergates, 74–110. Philadelphia: University of Pennsylvania Press, 1999.

Evergates, Theodore. 'Countess Blanche, Philip Augustus, and the War of Succession in Champagne, 1201–1222.' In *Political Ritual and Practice in Capetian France*, edited by M. Cecilia Gaposchkin and Jay Rubenstein, 77–104. Turnhout: Brepols, 2021.

Fillion-Braguet, Bénédicte. '"L'utilisation" de la sculpture dans le domaine Plantagenêt et la représentation des figures de pouvoir: mythe ou réalité?' In *Gouverner l'empire Plantagenêt (1152–1224): autorité, symboles, idéologie: 7–9 octobre 2021, Abbaye royale de Fontevraud*, edited by Martin Aurell, 258–73. Nantes: 303, 2021.

Flambard Héricher, Anne-Marie, and Véronique Gazeau, eds. *1204, la Normandie entre Plantagenêts et Capétiens.* Caen: CRAHM, 2007.

Foreville, Raymonde. *Le Pape Innocent III et la France.* Stuttgart: Anton Hiersemann, 1992.

Fortún Pérez de Ciriza, Luis Javier. 'San Sebastián en el dominio del Monasterio de Leire (Siglo IX – 1235).' In *Congresso el Fuero de San Sebastián y su época*, 451–68. San Sebastián: Sociedad de Estudios Vascos, 1982.

Fortún Pérez de Ciriza, Luis Javier. *Sancho VII El Fuerte (1194–1234)*. Iruna: Editorial Mintzoa, 1986.

Fortún Pérez de Ciriza, Luis Javier. *Leire, un señorio monástico en Navarra (siglos IX–XIX)*. Pamplona: Gobierno de Navarra, 1993.

Fößel, Amalie. 'The Queen's Wealth in the Middle Ages.' *Maiestas* 13 (2005): 23–45.

France, John, ed. *Medieval Warfare 1000–1300*. Abingdon: Routledge, 2006.

Gallet, Yves, ed. *Art et architecture à Melun au Moyen Age: actes du Colloque d'histoire de l'art et d'archéologie tenu à Melun les 28 et 29 novembre 1998*. Paris: Picard, 2000.

Gaposchkin, M. Cecilia, and Jay Rubenstein, eds. *Political Ritual and Practice in Capetian France. Studies in Honour of Elizabeth A. R. Brown*. Turnhout: Brepols, 2021.

Gaude-Ferragu, Murielle. *D'or et de cendres. La mort et les funérailles des princes dans le royaume de France au bas Moyen Age*. Paris: Presses Universitaires du Septentrion, 2005.

Gauthier, Marie-Madeleine. *Émaux Méridionaux. Catalogue international de l'œuvre de Limoges*. 2 volumes. Paris: Éditions du centre national de la recherche scientifique, 1987.

Geaman, Kristen. 'Childless Queens and Child-like Kings: Negotiating Royal Infertility in England, 1382–1471.' PhD Thesis, University of Southern California, 2013.

Geaman, Kristen. 'Queen's Gold and Intercession: The Case of Eleanor of Aquitaine.' *Medieval Feminist Forum. A Journal of Gender and Sexuality* 46 (2010): 10–33.

Geaman, Kristen L. and Theresa Earenfight. 'Neither Heir Nor Spare. Childless queens and the practice of monarchy in pre-modern Europe.' In *The Routledge History of Monarchy*, edited by Elena Woodacre, Lucinda H. S. Dean, Chris Jones, Russell E. Martin, and Zita Eva Rohr, 518–33. Abingdon: Routledge, 2019.

Gerges, Fawaz A. *Making the Arab World: Nasser, Qutb, and the Clash That Shaped the Middle East*. Princeton: Princeton University Press, 2018.

Gillingham, John. 'Richard I and Berengaria of Navarre.' *Historical Research* 53 (1980): 157–73.

Gillingham, John. *Richard the Lionheart*. Second Edition. London: Weidenfeld and Nicholson, 1989.

Gillingham, John. *Richard Coeur de Lion. Kingship, Chivalry and War in the Twelfth Century*. London: The Hambledon Press, 1994.

Gillingham, John. *Richard I*. London: Yale University Press, 1999.

Gillingham, John. 'Richard I and the Science of War in the Middle Ages.' In *Medieval Warfare 1000–1300*, edited by John France, 299–312. Abingdon: Routledge, 2006.

Gomez, Miguel, Damian J. Smith, and Kyle C. Lincoln, eds. *King Alfonso VIII of Castile: government, family, and war*. New York: Fordham University Press, 2019.

González, Julio, ed. *El reino de Castilla en la época de Alfonso VIII*. 3 volumes. Madrid: Escuela de Estudios Medievales, 1960.

Gosse-Kischinewski, Annick. 'La fondation de l'abbaye de Bonport: de la légende à la réalité politique.' In *1204, la Normandie entre Plantagenêts et Capétiens*, edited by Anne-Marie Flambard Héricher and Véronique Gazeau, 61–74. Caen: CRAHM, 2007.

Grant, Lindy. *Blanche of Castile*. London: Yale University Press, 2016.

Gray, Fabia Ann. 'Formal and informal contacts between the House of Navarre and the English during the fourteenth-century phase of the Hundred Years War.' PhD Thesis, University of East Anglia, 2005.

Guerra Medici, Maria Teresa. 'La régence de la mère dans le droit médiéval.' *Parliaments, Estates and Representation* 17.1 (1997): 1–11.

Hallam, Elizabeth M. 'Bérengère de Navarre.' *La Province du Maine 93* (1991): 225–37.

Harvey, John H. *The Plantagenets. 1154–1485*. London: B. T. Batsford, 1948.

Higounet, Charles. 'Berenguela von Navarra, Königin von England (+1230).' In *Lexikon des Mittelalters*. Turnhout: Brepols, 1980–present. Online resource.

Hirel, Sophie. 'La reine veuve et le Pape. Présentation et étude des lettres de Marguerite de Prades à Benoît XIII (1412–1416).' In *Histoires, femmes, pouvoirs. Péninsule Ibérique (IXe–XVe siècle). Mélanges offerts au Professeur Georges Martin*, edited by Jean-Pierre Jardin, Patricia Rochwert-Zuili, and Hélène Thieulin-Pardo, 459–76. Paris: Classiques Garnier, 2018.

Hivergneaux, Marie. 'Queen Eleanor and Aquitaine, 1137–1189.' In *Eleanor of Aquitaine: Lord and Lady*, edited by Bonnie Wheeler and John Carmi Parsons, 55–76. Basingstoke: Palgrave Macmillan, 2003.

Hivergneaux, Marie. 'Aliénor d'Aquitaine: le pouvoir d'une femme à la lumière de ses chartes (1152–1204).' In *La Cour Plantagenêt (1154–1204). Actes du colloque tenu à Thouars du 30 avril au 2 mai 1999*, edited by Martin Aurell, 63–87. Poitiers: Université de Poitiers, Centre d'Études Supérieures de Civilisation Médiévale, 2004.

Huneycutt, Lois L. '*Alianora Regina Anglorum*: Eleanor of Aquitaine and Her Anglo-Norman Predecessors as Queens of England.' In *Eleanor of Aquitaine: Lord and Lady*, edited by Bonnie Wheeler and John Carmi Parsons, 115–132. Basingstoke: Palgrave Macmillan, 2003.

Hutcheson, Gregory S. 'Leonor López de Córdoba and the Configuration of Female-Female Desire.' In *Same Sex Love and Desire Among Women in the Middle Ages*, edited by Francesca Canadé Sautman and Pamela Sheingorn, 251–76. Basingstoke: Palgrave Macmillan, 2001.

Jahner, Jennifer, Emily Steiner, and Elizabeth M. Tyler, eds. *Medieval historical writing: Britain and Ireland, 500–1500*. Cambridge: Cambridge University Press, 2019.

Jardin, Jean-Pierre, Patricia Rochwert-Zuili, and Hélène Thieulin-Pardo, eds. *Histoires, femmes, pouvoirs. Péninsule Ibérique (IXᵉ–XVᵉ siècle). Mélanges offerts au Professeur Georges Martin*. Paris: Classiques Garnier, 2018.

Jobson, Adrian, ed. *English Government in the Thirteenth Century*. Woodbridge: The Boydell Press, 2004.

Jobson, Adrian. 'Introduction.' In *English Government in the Thirteenth Century*, edited by Adrian Jobson, 1–16. Woodbridge: Boydell Press, 2004.

Johnstone, Hilda. 'The Queen's Household.' In *Chapters in the Administrative History of medieval England*, Volume 5, edited by Thomas Frederick Tout, 262–67. Manchester: Manchester University Press, 1930.

Jones, Michael, and Malcolm Vale, eds. *England and Her Neighbours, 1066–1453. Essays in Honour of Pierre Chaplais*. London: The Hambledon Press, 1989.

Karras, Ruth Mazo. 'Knighthood, Compulsory Heterosexuality, and Sodomy.' In *The Boswell Thesis. Essays on Christianity, Social Tolerance, and Homosexuality*, edited by Mathew Kuefler, 273–86. London: University of Chicago Press, 2006.

Karras, Ruth Mazo. *Sexuality in Medieval Europe. Doing Unto Others*. Second Edition. Abingdon: Routledge, 2012.

Keenan-Kedar, Nurith. 'The Enigmatic Sepulchral Monument of Berengaria (ca. 1170–1230), Queen of England (1191–1199).' *Assaph - Studies in Art History* 12 (2007): 49–62.

Klinka, Emmanuelle. 'El entramado cultural de la carta de la reina Berenguela a Gregorio IX.' In *Saberes, cultura y mecenazgo en la correspondencia de las mujeres Medievales*, edited by Ángela Muñoz Fernández and Hélène Thieulin-Pardo, online. Paris: e-Spania Books, 2021. Accessed 23 January 2023. http://books.openedition.org/esb/2987.

Kuefler, Mathew. 'The Boswell Thesis.' In *The Boswell Thesis. Essays on Christianity, Social Tolerance, and Homosexuality*, edited by Mathew Kuefler, 1–31. London: The University of Chicago Press, 2006.

Kuefler, Mathew. 'Male Friendship and the Suspicion of Sodomy in Twelfth-Century France.' In *The Boswell Thesis. Essays on Christianity, Social Tolerance, and Homosexuality*, edited by Mathew Kuefler, 179–212. London: The University of Chicago Press, 2006.

Lacarra, Jose Maria. *Historia Política del Reino de Navarra, desde sus orígenes hasta su incorporación a Castilla. Volumen Segundo*. Pamplona: Editorial Aranzadi, 1972.

Lacarra, José Maria. *Historia del reino de Navarra en la Edad Media*. Navarra: Caja de Ahorros de Navarra, 1975.

Lacarra Lanz, Eukene, ed. *Marriage and Sexuality in Medieval and Early Modern Iberia*. Abingdon: Routledge, 2002.

Lachaud, Frédérique, and Michael Penman, eds. *Absentee Authority across Medieval Europe*. Woodbridge: The Boydell Press, 2017.

Lachaud, Frédérique, and Michael Penman. 'Introduction.' In *Absentee Authority across Medieval Europe*, edited by Frédérique Lachaud and Michael Penman, 1–20. Woodbridge: The Boydell Press, 2017.

Lauranson-Rosaz, Christian. '*Douaire* et sponsalicium durant le haut Moyen Age.' In *Veuves et Veuvage dans le Haut Moyen Age*, edited by Michel Parisse, 99–105. Paris: Picard, 1993.

Le Goff, Jacques. *Saint Louis*. Paris: Éditions Gaillmard, 1996.

Le Jan-Hennebicque, Regine. 'Aux origines du Douaire médiéval (Vi^c–Xe siècles.' In *Veuves et Veuvage dans le Haut Moyen Age*, edited by Michel Parisse, 107–21. Paris: Picard, 1993.

Lemesle, Bruno. *La société aristocratique dans le Haut-Maine (XIe–XIIe siècles)*. Rennes: Presses Universitaires de Rennes, 1999.

Levacher, Gérard. *La Reine oubliée. Bérengère de Navarre*. France: Thélès, 2005.

LoPrete, Kimberly A. 'Adela of Blois as Mother and Countess.' In *Medieval Mothering*, edited by John Carmi Parsons and Bonnie Wheeler, 313–34. London: Garland Publishing, 1996.

LoPrete, Kimberley A. 'The gender of lordly women: the case of Adela of Blois.' In *Pawns or Players?*, edited by Christine Meek and Catherine Lawless, 90–110. Dublin: Four Courts Press, 2003.

Maier, Christoph T. 'The roles of women in the crusade movement: a survey.' *Journal of Medieval History* 30. 1 (2004): 61–82.

Mayer, Hans Eberhard. 'The Succession to Baldwin II of Jerusalem: English Impact on the East.' *Dumbarton Oaks Papers* 39 (1985): 139–47.

Maillet, Laurent. 'Les missions d'Adam de Perseigne, émissaire de Rome et de Cîteaux (1190–1221).' *Annales de Bretagne et des Pays de l'Ouest* 120.3 (2013): 99–116.

Martin, Fernandez de Navarrete, ed. *Colección de documentos inéditos para la historia de España*. 112 volumes. Madrid: 1842–present.

Martin, Therese. *Queen as King: Politics and Architectural Propaganda in Twelfth-Century Spain*. Leiden: Brill, 2006.

Martin, Therese. 'Hacia una clarificación del infantazgo en tiempos de la reina Urraca y su hija la infanta Sancha (ca. 1107–1159).' *e-Spania* 5 (2008). Accessed 21 September 2022. https://journals.openedition.org/e-spania/12163.

Martin, Therese. 'Sources of Power for Queens and Infantas: The Infantazgo in the Central Middle Ages.' *Anuario de Estudios Medievales* 46.1 (2016): 97–136.

Martindale, Jane. 'Eleanor of Aquitaine: The Last Years.' In *King John: New Interpretations*, edited by Stephen D. Church, 136–64. Woodbridge: Boydell Press, 1999.

Matz, Jean-Michel, and François Comte. *Diocèse d'Angers*. Turnhout: Brepols, 2003.

Matz, Jean-Michel. *Diocèse du Mans*. Turnhout: Brepols, 2018.

Mcdougall, Sara. 'Women and Gender in Canon Law.' In *The Oxford Handbook of Women & Gender in Medieval Europe*, edited by Judith M. Bennett and Ruth Mazo Karras, 163–78. Oxford: Oxford University Press, 2013.

Meek, Christine, and Catherine Lawless, eds. *Pawns or Players? Studies on Medieval and Early Modern Women*. Dublin: Four Courts Press, 2003.

Menéndez Pidal, Ramón, and José María Jover Zamora. *Historia de España*. Madrid: Espasa-Calpe, 1935, reprint 2005.

Mills, Robert. *Seeing Sodomy in the Middle Ages*. Chicago: University of Chicago Press, 2015.

Mitchell, Mairin. *Berengaria. Enigmatic Queen of England*. Burwash: A. Wright, 1986.

Murray, Jacqueline, ed. *Conflicted Identities and Multiple Masculinities. Men in the Medieval West*. New York and London: Garland, 1999.

Nakashian, Craig M. *Warrior Churchmen of Medieval England 1000–1250. Theory and Reality*. Woodbridge: The Boydell Press, 2016.

Neocleous, Savvas. 'Imaging Isaak Komnenos of Cyprus (1184–1191) and the Cypriots: Evidence from the Latin historiography of the Third Crusade.' *Byzantion* 83 (2013): 297–337.

Niaussat, Michel. *The Royal Abbey of L'Épau*. Le Mans: Éditions Libra Diffusio, 2018.

Nicolaou-Konnari, Angel. 'The Conquest of Cyprus by Richard the Lionheart and its Aftermath: A Study of the Sources and Legend, Politics and Attitudes in the year 1191–1192.' *Επετηρίδα Κέντρου Επιστημονικών Ερευνών*, 26 (2000): 25–123.

Nicholson, Helen J. 'Women on the Third Crusade.' *Journal of Medieval History* 23.4 (1997): 335–49.

Nolan, Kathleen. 'Symbolic Geography in the Tomb and Seal of Berengaria of Navarre, Queen of England.' In *Moving Women, Moving Objects (400–1500)*, edited by Tracy Chapman-Hamilton and Mariah Proctor-Tiffany, 59–85. Leiden: Brill, 2019.

Norrie, Aidan, Carolyn Harris, J. L. Laynesmith, Danna Messer, and Elena Woodacre, eds. *English Consorts: Power, Influence, Dynasty*. 4 volumes. Cham: Palgrave Macmillan, 2022–2023.

Norris, Jennifer L. '"Según parecía por las Crónicas antiguas": Representing Ruling Queens in Medieval Castilian Historiography.' PhD Thesis, Lincoln College, Oxford, 2017.

North, Janice, Karl C. Alvestad, and Elena Woodacre, eds. *Premodern Rulers and Postmodern Viewers. Gender, Sex, and Power in Popular Culture*. Cham: Palgrave Macmillan, 2018.

Olsen, G. W. *Of Sodomites, Effeminates, Hermaphrodites, and Androgynes: Sodomy in the Age of Peter Damian*. Toronto: Pontifical Institute of Mediaeval Studies, 2011.

Parisse, Michel, ed. *Veuves et Veuvage dans le Haut Moyen Age*. Paris: Picard, 1993.

Parsons, John Carmi. 'Mothers, Daughters, Marriage, Power: Some Plantagenet Evidence, 1150–1500.' In *Medieval Queenship*, edited by John Carmi Parsons, 63–78. Stroud: Sutton Publishing, 1993.

Parsons, John Carmi, and Bonnie Wheeler, eds. *Medieval Mothering*. London: Garland Publishing, 1996.

Pavón, Julia, ed. *Reinas de Navarra*. Madrid: Sílex Ediciones, 2014.

Pélissié du Rausas, Amicie. 'Le Quercy Plantagenêt a-t-il existé? L'enquête sur la dot de Jeanne d'Angleterre (1196–1286).' In *Gouverner l'empire Plantagenêt (1152–1224): autorité, symboles, idéologie: 7–9 octobre 2021, Abbaye royale de Fontevraud*, edited by Martin Aurell, 190–205. Nantes: 303, 2021.

Pick, Lucy. *Her Father's Daughter. Gender, Power, and Religion in the Early Spanish Kingdoms*. Ithaca: Cornell University Press, 2017.

Piolin, Paul. 'Bérengère, reine d'Angleterre, dame du Mans. 1191–1230.' *Revue des Questions Historiques* 4 (1890): 174–83.

Powicke, Maurice. *The Loss of Normandy, 1189–1204. Studies in the History of the Angevin Empire*. Second Edition. Manchester: Manchester University Press, 1960.

Poza Yagüe, Marta, and Diana Olivares Martínez, eds. *Alfonso VIII y Leonor de Inglaterra: confluencias artísticas en el entorno de 1200*. Madrid: Ediciones Complutense, 2017.

Quaghebeur, Joëlle. *La Cornouaille du XIème au XIIème siècles: mémoire, pouvoirs, noblesse*. Rennes Quimper: Presses universitaires de Rennes, Société archéologique du Finistère, 2002.

Ramírez Vaquero, Eloísa. 'La ciudad y el Rey: Renovación de la red urbana de Navarra al final de la Edad Media.' *Anuario de Estudios Medievales* 48.1 (2018): 49–80.

Ramírez Vaquero, Eloísa. 'La reina ha muerto: Memoria y representación en la Navarra medieval.' In *Espacios de memoria y representación: Reinas, infantas y damas de la corte ante la muerte en las monarquías ibéricas Medievales*, edited by Ángela Muñoz and Sonia Morales, forthcoming.

Reilly, Bernard F. *The Kingdom of León-Castilla under Queen Urraca 1109–1126*. Philadelphia: Princeton University Press, 1982.

Reilly, Bernard F. *The Kingdom of León-Castilla under King Alfonso VII 1126–1157*. Philadelphia: University of Pennsylvania Press, 1998.

Richard, Alfred. *Histoire des comtes de Poitou, 778–1204.* 6 volumes. Pau: Princi Negue, 1903, 2005.

Rohr, Zita Eva, and Lisa Benz, eds., *Queenship and the Women of Westeros: Female Agency and Advice in* Game of Thrones *and* A Song of Ice and Fire. Cham: Palgrave Macmillan, 2020.

Salisbury, Joyce E., ed. *Sex in the Middle Ages. A Book of Essays.* London: Garland Publishing, 1991.

Salvador Martínez, H. *Berenguela the Great and Her Times (1180–1246).* Translated by Odile Cisneros. Leiden: Brill, 2021.

Sánchez-Albornoz, Claudio. *Vascos y navarros en su primera historia.* Madrid: Ediciones del Centro, 1974.

Sánchez-Albornoz, Claudio. *Orígenes y destino de Navarra; Trayectoria histórica de Vasconia: otros escritos.* Barcelona: Planeta, 1984.

Sautman, Francesca Canadé, and Pamela Sheingorn, eds. *Same Sex Love and Desire Among Women in the Middle Ages.* Basingstoke: Palgrave Macmillan, 2001.

Sautman, Francesca Canadé, and Pamela Sheingorn. 'Introduction: Charting the Field.' In *Same Sex Love and Desire Among Women in the Middle Ages*, edited by Francesca Canadé Sautman and Pamela Sheingorn, 1–48. Basingstoke: Palgrave Macmillan, 2001.

Sayers, Jane E. 'English Charters from the Third Crusade.' In *Law and Records in Medieval England. Studies on the Medieval Papacy, Monasteries and Records*, edited by Jane E. Sayers, 195–213. London: Variorum, 1988.

Shadis, Miriam. 'Berenguela of Castile's political motherhood: the management of sexuality, marriage, and succession.' In *Medieval Mothering*, edited by John Carmi Parsons and Bonnie Wheeler, 335–58. London: Garland Publishing, 1996.

Shadis, Miriam. *Berenguela of Castile (1180–1246) and Political Women in the High Middle Ages.* Basingstoke: Palgrave Macmillan, 2010.

Shadis, Miriam. 'The First Queens of Portugal and the Building of the Realm.' In *Reassessing the Roles of Women as 'Makers' of Medieval Art and Architecture. Volume Two*, edited by Therese Martin, 671–702. Leiden: Brill, 2012.

Shadis, Miriam. '"Happier in Daughters than in Sons": The Children of Alfonso VIII of Castile and Leonor Plantagenet.' In *King Alfonso VIII of Castile. Government, Family, and War*, edited by Miguel Gómez, Damian Smith, and Kyle C. Lincoln, 80–101. New York: Fordham University Press, 2019.

Sjursen, Katrin E. 'Weathering Thirteenth-Century Warfare: The Case of Blanche of Navarre.' *Haskins Society Journal* 25 (2014), 205–22.

Spencer, Stephen J. '"Like a Raging Lion": Richard the Lionheart's Anger during the Third Crusade in Medieval and Modern Historiography.' *The English Historical Review* 132.556 (2017): 495–532.

Spencer, Stephen J. *Emotions in a crusading context, 1095–1291*. Oxford: Oxford University Press, 2019.

Stafford, Pauline. *Queen Emma & Queen Edith, Queenship and Women's Power in Eleventh-Century England*. Oxford: Blackwell Publishers, 1997.

Stock, Lorraine K. 'Now Starring in the Third Crusade: Depictions of Richard I and Saladin in Films and Television Series.' In *Hollywood in the Holy Land: Essays on Film Depictions of the Crusades and Christian-Muslim Clashes*, edited by Nickolas Haydock and Edward L. Risden, 93–122. Jefferson, NC: McFarland, 2009.

Storey, Gabrielle. 'Berengaria of Navarre and Joanna of Sicily as crusading queens: Manipulation, reputation, and agency.' In *Forgotten Queens in Medieval and Early Modern Europe, Political Agency, Myth-making, and Patronage*, edited by Estelle Paranque and Valerie Schutte, 41–59. Abingdon: Routledge, 2018.

Storey, Gabrielle. 'Co-Operation, Co-Rulership and Competition: Queenship in the Angevin Domains, 1135–1230.' PhD Thesis, University of Winchester, 2020.

Storey, Gabrielle, ed. *Memorialising Premodern Monarchs. Medias of Commemoration and Remembrance*. Cham: Palgrave Macmillan, 2020.

Storey, Gabrielle. 'Questioning Terminologies: Homosocial and "Homosexual" Bonds in the Royal Bedchamber and Kingship in Medieval England and France.' *Royal Studies Journal* 9.1 (2022): 33–45.

Stothard, Charles Alfred. *The Monumental Effigies of Great Britain, selected from our cathedrals and churches, for the purpose of bringing together, and preserving correct representations of the best historical illustrations extant, from the Norman Conquest to the reign of Henry the Eighth*. London: J. McCreery, 1817.

Tanner, Heather J. 'Queenship: Office, Custom, or Ad Hoc? The Case of Queen Matilda III of England (1135–1152).' In *Eleanor of Aquitaine: Lord and Lady*, edited by Bonnie Wheeler and John Carmi Parsons, 133–58. Basingstoke: Palgrave Macmillan, 2003.

Tanner, Heather J. *Families, Friends and Allies. Boulogne and Politics in Northern France and England, c. 879–1160*. Leiden: Brill, 2004.

Tanner, Heather J., ed. *Medieval Elite Women and the Exercise of Power, 1100–1400. Moving Beyond the Exceptionalist Debate*. Cham: Palgrave Macmillan, 2020.

Thompson, Kathleen. *Power and Border Lordship in Medieval France: The County of the Perche, 1000–1226*. Woodbridge: Boydell Press, 2002.

Tingle, Louise. '*Aurum reginae*: Queen's Gold in Late Fourteenth-Century England.' *Royal Studies Journal* 7.1 (2020): 77–90

Tout, Thomas Frederick. *Chapters in the Administrative History of medieval England*. 6 volumes. Manchester: Manchester University Press, 1920–1933.

Triger, Robert. 'La maison dite de la Reine Bérengère au Mans.' *Bulletin Monumental* 58 (1892): 4–26.

Triger, Robert. 'Le Tombeau de la Reine Bérengère a la Cathedrale du Mans.' *Revue Historique et Archéologique du Maine* 75 (1920–1921): 83–94.

Trindade, Ann. *Berengaria. In Search of Richard the Lionheart's Queen.* Dublin: Four Courts Press, 1999.

Trindade, Ann. *Berenguela de Navarra. Reina de Inglaterra. Buscando a la consorte de Ricardo Corazón de León.* Translated by Manuel Sagastibelza. Second edition. Pamplona: Editorial Mintzoa S. L., 2022.

Turner, Ralph V. 'Eleanor of Aquitaine in the Governments of Her Sons Richard and John.' In *Eleanor of Aquitaine: Lord and Lady*, edited by Bonnie Wheeler and John Carmi Parsons, 77–95. Basingstoke: Palgrave Macmillan, 2003.

Turner, Ralph V. *Eleanor of Aquitaine.* London: Yale University Press, 2009.

Tyler, Elizabeth M. *England in Europe: English Royal Women and Literary Patronage, c.1000–c.1150.* Toronto: University of Toronto Press, 2017.

Ubieto Arteta, Agustín. 'Asistió Sancho el Fuerte de Navarra a la tercera cruzada?' *Príncipe de Viana* 31 (1970): 171–9.

Ubieto Arteta, Agustín. 'Aportación al estudio de la "tenencia" medieval: la mujer "tenente."' In *Estudios de Edad Media de la Corona de Aragon. Volume X*, edited by José María Lacarra, 47–61. Zaragoza: Consejo Superior de Investigaciones Científicas, Escuela de Estudios Medievales, 1975.

Ubieto Arteta, Antonio. *Obituario de la Catedral de Pamplona.* Pamplona: Diputación Foral de Navarra, Institución 'Príncipe de Viana,' 1954.

Urzainqui, Tomás, and Juan Maria Olaizola. *La Navarra marítima.* Pamplona: Pamiela, 1998.

Van Houts, Elisabeth. 'Queens in the Anglo-Norman/Angevin realm 1066–1216.' In *Mächtige Frauen? Königinnen und Fürstinnen im europäischen Mittelalter*, edited by Claudia Zey, 199–224. Ostfildern: Jan Thorbecke Verlag, 2015.

Van Houts, Elisabeth. *Married Life in the Middle Ages, 900–1300.* Oxford: Oxford University Press, 2019.

Vann, Theresa M. '"Our father has won a great victory": the authorship of Berenguela's account of the battle of Las Navas de Tolosa, 1212.' *Journal of Medieval Iberian Studies* 3.1 (2011): 79–92.

Verdon, Jean. 'Les veuves des rois de France aux Xe et XIe siècles.' In *Veuves et Veuvage dans le Haut Moyen Age*, edited by Michel Parisse, 187–99. Paris: Picard, 1993.

Vergnolle, Éliane. 'Le gisant de Blanche de Navarre, comtesse de Champagne.' *Bulletin Monumental* 143.1 (1985): 73.

Vincent, Nicholas. *Peter des Roches: An Alien in English Politics, 1205–1238.* Cambridge: Cambridge University Press, 1996.

Vincent, Nicholas. 'Isabella of Angoulême: John's Jezebel.' In *King John: New Interpretations*, edited by Stephen D. Church, 165–219. Woodbridge: The Boydell Press, 1999.

Vincent, Nicholas. 'Why 1199? Bureaucracies and Enrolment under John and his Contemporaries.' In *English Government in the Thirteenth Century*, edited by Adrian Jobson, 17–48. Woodbridge: The Boydell Press, 2004.

Vincent, Nicholas. 'A Forgotten War?: England and Navarre, 1243–4.' In *Thirteenth Century England XI. Proceedings of the Gregynog Conference, 2005*, edited by Björn Weiler, Janet Burton, Phillipp Schofield, and Karen Stöber, 109–46. Woodbridge: Boydell & Brewer, 2007.

Vincent, Nicholas. 'Jean sans Terre et les origines de la Gascogne anglaise: droits et pouvoirs dans les arcanes des sources.' *Annales du Midi* 123 (2011): 533–66.

Vones-Liebenstein, Ursula. 'Une femme gardienne du royaume? Régentes en temps de guerre (France-Castille, XIIIᵉ siècle).' In *La guerre, la violence et les gens au Moyen Âge. Vol. II. Guerre et Gens*, edited by Philippe Contamine and Olivier Guyotjennin, 9–22. Paris: Éditions du CTTS, 1996.

Waag, Anaïs. 'Rethinking Battle Commemoration: Female Letters and the Myth of the Battle of Las Navas de Tolosa (1212).' *Journal of Medieval History* 45.4 (2019): 457–80.

Waag, Anaïs. 'Female Royal Rulership in Theory and Practice: Queens Regnant, 1190–1328.' Leverhulme Postdoctoral Fellowship, University of Lincoln, 2020–2023.

Waag, Anaïs. 'Rulership, Authority, and Power in the Middle Ages: The Proprietary Queen as Head of Dynasty.' *Anglo-Norman Studies* 44 (2022): 71–104.

Walker, Rose. 'Leonor of England, Plantagenet queen of King Alfonso VIII of Castile, and her foundation of the Cistercian abbey of Las Huelgas. In imitation of Fontevraud?' *Journal of Medieval History* 31.4 (2005): 346–68.

Ward, Emily J. 'Child Kingship in England, Scotland, France, and Germany, c. 1050–c. 1250.' PhD Thesis, University of Cambridge, 2017.

Weiler, Bjorn. 'Historical Writing in Medieval Britain: The Case of Matthew Paris.' In *Medieval historical writing: Britain and Ireland, 500–1500*, edited by Jennifer Jahner, Emily Steiner, and Elizabeth M. Tyler, 319–38. Cambridge: Cambridge University Press, 2019

Woodacre, Elena. *The Queens Regnant of Navarre: Succession, Politics, and Partnership, 1274–1512.* Basingstoke: Palgrave Macmillan, 2012.

Woodacre, Elena. 'Questionable Authority: Female Sovereigns and their Consorts in Medieval and Renaissance Chronicles.' In *Authority and*

Gender in Medieval and Renaissance Chronicles, edited by Juliana Dresvina and Nicholas Sparks, 376–407. Newcastle upon Tyne: Cambridge Scholars Publishing, 2012.

Woodacre, Elena, and Carey Fleiner, eds. *Royal Mothers and their Ruling Children, Wielding Political Authority from Antiquity to the Early Modern Era*. Basingstoke: Palgrave Macmillan, 2015.

Woodacre, Elena. *Queens and Queenship*. Leeds: Arc Humanities Press, 2021.

Wright, Katia. 'The Queen's Lands: Examining the role of queens as female lords in fourteenth century England.' PhD Thesis, University of Winchester, 2022.

Wright, Katia. 'A Dower for Life: Understanding the Dowers of England's Medieval Queens.' In *Later Plantagenets and Wars of the Roses Consorts. Power, Influence, and Dynasty*, edited by Aidan Norrie, Carolyn Harris, J. L. Laynesmith, Danna R. Messer, and Elena Woodacre, 145–64. Cham: Palgrave Macmillan, 2023.

Online Sources

Cawley, Charles. 'Foundation for Medieval Genealogy, Kings of Navarre.' Accessed 14 May 2023. http://fmg.ac/Projects/MedLands/NAVARRE.htm#_ftn396.

The National Archives. Accessed 17 July 2022. www.nationalarchives.gov.uk/help-with-your-research/research-guides/royal-grants-letters-patent-charters-from-1199/.

The National Archives. Accessed 17 July 2022. www.nationalarchives.gov.uk/help-with-your-research/research-guides/medieval-financial-records-pipe-rolls-1130-1300/.

Novels, Films, and Other Media

Bard, Rachel. *Queen Without A Country*. London: Minerva Press, 2000.

Bramall, Richard, dir. *The Talisman*. London: British Broadcasting Corporation, 1980–1981.

Butler, David, dir. *King Richard and the Crusaders*. USA: Warner Bros, 1954.

Campbell Barnes, Margaret. *The Passionate Brood*. Philadelphia: Macrae-Smith, 1945.

Chadwick, Elizabeth. *The Autumn Throne*. London: Sphere, 2016.

Chahine, Youssef, dir. *Al Nasser Salah Ad-Din*. Egypt: Lotus Films, General Egyptian Corporation for Cinema Production, 1963.

Cooke, Alan, Jane Howell, and Ronald Wilson, dirs. *The Devil's Crown*. London: British Broadcasting Corporation, 1978.

DeMille, Cecil B., dir. *The Crusades*. New York: Paramount Pictures, 1935.

Exhibition. *Bérengère, à la rencontre d'une Reine*. L'Abbaye de L'Épau, 19/11/2022–13/03/2023.

Gerasimov, Evgeniy, dir. *Richard Lvinoe Serdtse*. Russia: Amidas, Ganemfilm, Kinostudiya Imeni M. Gorkofo, Okean, and Trest, 1992.

Gerasimov, Evgeniy, dir. *Rytsar Kennet*. Russia: Okean, Rosomkino, and Gorky Film Studios, 1993.

Haycraft, Molly Costain. *My Lord Brother the Lionheart*. Philadelphia: J. B. Lippincott, 1968.

Henty, G. A. *Winning His Spurs*. London: Sampson Low, 1882.

Henty, G. A. *The Boy Knight. A Tale of the Crusades*. 1882, reprint 2004. Accessed 23 January 2023. www.gutenberg.org/cache/epub/13354/pg13354-images.html.

Holland, Cecelia. *The Queen's Witch*. New York: Berkley Books, 2011.

Il Talismano. Società Italiana Cines, 1911.

Kaufman, Pamela. *Shield of Three Lions*. New York: Crown, 1983.

Kaufman, Pamela. *Banners of Gold*. New York: Crown, 1986.

Lofts, Norah. *The Lute Player*. London: Michael Joseph, 1951.

Macgregor, John. *Propinquity*. Adelaide: Wakefield Press, 1986.

Michaels, Fern. *Valentina*. New York: Ballantine Books, 1978.

Mira García, Concepción. *Berenguela: Corazón de León*. Pamplona: Eunate, D.L. 2021.

Morris, Ernest, dir. *Richard the Lionheart*. London: British Broadcasting Corporation, 1962–1963.

Penman, Sharon Kay. *Lionheart*. London: Pan, 2012.

Penman, Sharon Kay. *A King's Ransom*. New York: Penguin Putnam, 2014.

Peters, Maureen. *Willow Maid*. London: Robert Hale Press, 1974.

Plaidy, Jean. *The Heart Of The Lion*: London: Robert Hale Press, 1977.

Rocco, Bruno, Olivier Renault, Bénédicte Fillion-Braguet, Ghislain Baury, and Vincent Corriol. *Bérengère de Navarre, du trône de l'Angleterre à l'abbaye de l'Épau*. Nantes: Petit à Petit, 2022.

Sauers, Victoria. *Lionhearted Queen: Berengaria of Navarre*. Philadelphia: Blue Bear Press, 2000.

Scott, Ridley, dir. *Kingdom of Heaven*. London: Scott Free Productions, Inside Track, and Studio Babelsberg, 2005.

Scott, Walter. *The Talisman*. 1825, reprint 1998. Accessed 23 January 2023. https://gutenberg.org/cache/epub/1377/pg1377-images.html.

Whyte, Jack. *Standard of Honour*. London: HarperCollins, 2007.

Withey, Chester, dir. *Richard the Lion-Hearted*. United States of America: Associated Authors, 1923.

INDEX

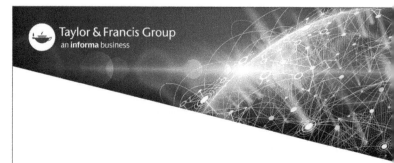

Milton Keynes UK
Ingram Content Group UK Ltd.
UKHW020713230524
443074UK00010B/124